Reclaiming Your Self

THE CODEPENDENT'S RECOVERY PLAN

D1315135

Reclaiming Your Self

THE CODEPENDENT'S RECOVERY PLAN

Brian DesRoches

A Dell Trade Paperback

A DELL TRADE PAPERBACK
Published by
Dell Publishing
a division of
Bantam Doubleday Dell Publishing Group, Inc.
666 Fifth Avenue
New York, New York 10103

ISBN: 0-440-50261-6

Printed in the United States of America
Published simultaneously in Canada

April 1990

10 9 8 7 6 5 4 3

RRH

Dedicated to

my father, Henry,

and

my mother, Mary

Contents

P A R T F O U R
Experiencing the Inner Self

A P P E N D I X

Acknowledgments

Many people have contributed to creating this book, both directly and indirectly. First of all, I want to acknowledge my wife, Patti. Her support, enthusiasm, and belief in this book were great sources of inspiration to me.

The writing expertise of Waverly Fitzgerald and her commitment to the message of this book have also been essential ingredients in the process of growth that brought an idea and a few rough chapters into fruition as a book.

This book would not have been possible without the contributions of the many people, friends and clients, who have blessed me by including me in their own recovery process. The stories and personal experiences contained in this book derive from their struggles to change, grow, and feel good about themselves. I am deeply grateful to all of you who allowed me to walk alongside of you during the journey of recovery and to share that process with others through this book.

I want to acknowledge the encouragement of my agent, Candace Fuhrman. I am glad I have her in my corner, pulling for and supporting me.

This book has become much more than I originally thought possible because Jody Rein, my editor at Dell, asked some good questions about recovery. Her vision of what this book could be was inspiring and insightful.

Finally, I want to acknowledge the many people I have known since I started my own recovery. They have all been part of my journey and thus part of the creation of this book.

Author's Note

All case histories and examples involving the personal lives of people have been taken from real-life experiences and situations. In some cases stories from different individuals have been merged in the interests of providing more information and ensuring confidentiality. In addition details, names, and circumstances have been changed to protect the confidentiality of the individuals involved. Any resemblance to a known person or situation is coincidental.

Reclaiming Your Self

THE CODEPENDENT'S RECOVERY PLAN

Introduction

THIS BOOK IS ABOUT RE-claiming your self. To reclaim something is to restate your claim to that which was originally yours but was somehow given away or taken from you. Few of us would intentionally give away a precious keepsake unless we were threatened. If a thief demands that you give him your watch or ring, your choices are few. Either you cooperate or you risk getting hurt. But even if you give your valuables up, you don't give away your right to them—you can reclaim them.

So it is with reclaiming your self. As a child, you had to deny your feelings and thoughts to participate and feel safe in your family. In essence, you had to give away your self and your experiences of life. You have probably continued to do this as an adult without even knowing it.

What you had to give away as a child you can reclaim as an adult. You have a right to be yourself and to express your thoughts and feelings.

Reclaiming your self also means healing the emotional wounds and psychological distortions that result from not being yourself. Ultimately, it is about experiencing the self-worth and self-esteem that are your birthright.

I first realized I had to write this book in 1984, while I was the executive director of a chemical dependency treatment center. Along with the regular treatment program, each resident was asked to invite his or her family to participate in an intensive week-long session wherein the family members had an opportunity to begin recovering themselves. Like the individual in treatment, family members had also developed unhealthy patterns of living and were suffering. Each family week closed with the playing of the song "It's My Turn" by Carole Bayer Sager. Two lines of the song stood out: "I've given up the truth to those I've tried to please" and "For years I've seen my life through someone else's eyes, and now it's my turn to try and find my way." When that song played, the faces of the family members present revealed the anguish and pain that they had suffered from having suppressed their own feelings. That song touched into the hidden reality of their emotional pain. But their faces and their tears also revealed another feeling—hope.

When I play this song at my workshops, I also see anguish mixed with hope on the faces of people who were not raised in chemically dependent families. I believe that's when they realize how much they have denied themselves and their feelings as adults just as they did in their families as children.

I also believe the strongest of these feelings comes from deep within, from knowing that one's inner self has also been denied and given away. Heeding the feelings of the inner self, no matter how faint, is the beginning of reclaiming your self. This is what the family members and people attending my workshops were experiencing. I also know that experience, for the words of that song had an impact on me. Even today I play the song often to reinforce my commitment to being myself. I, too, had given up the truth of my feelings to please and take care of others and avoid making them upset. I had been trying to change these patterns in my life and had made a few strides. What I really wanted was to find a way to reclaim my ability to be authentically me. What emerged during 1984 was a decision to write a book that would empower me and others in reclaiming our inner selves and experiencing and expressing our feelings. By Christmas 1986 I was ready to make my decision a concrete reality. I prayed to my higher power for help. Rather than just explore problems, I wanted to focus on practical ways for people to develop their own solutions. I also believed strongly that this process of developing solutions had to involve the mind, the body, and the spirit.

So many books talk about the inner self that it is almost a cliché; it's lost its meaning. So rather than write a book talking about this inner self, I believe I've written one that supports you in reclaiming, experiencing, and expressing your inner self. This book provides resources, tools, and techniques and a descriptive overview of the process of recovery, enabling you to create your own solutions to the challenges that you will face in recovery. Along the way you will discover the gifts that have been buried within your emotional pain. This paradox is a great mystery to me. You will experience these gifts, just as I have, on your own journey of reclaiming your self. For me, being able to write this book has been a gift and is what this book is all about.

As I write this introduction, I feel grateful and satisfied knowing that through the grace and help of my higher power, I have written a book that goes a long way toward fulfilling my prayer in supporting you and me in experiencing and expressing our inner selves.

There were several factors that influenced the development and evolution of this book: my educational and professional background; my growth and work as a psychotherapist; and my personal experiences. These factors are not mutually exclusive, and each one influences the others. In this introduction I will briefly discuss the first two factors. As you read the book you will learn more about me personally.

My professional background reflects an evolution from health care administration and management consulting to my work as a counselor and psychotherapist. Although I felt pulled to the field of counseling in the mid-1970s, it wasn't until the 1980s that my interest in becoming a therapist began to take expression.

In 1973 I obtained a master's degree in health care administration. This was followed by a master's degree in counseling in 1977 and a master's degree in business administration in 1981. In 1987 I began studies for a doctorate in pastoral counseling and psychology. In this program I am combining a specific focus on marriage and family therapy with two other areas of interest: spirituality and the psychobiology of the mind-body connection.

In my own quest to maintain my recovery process and to enhance my psychotherapeutic skills, I have also taken extensive courses and training in a variety of mental health and addiction recovery therapies.

This book reflects my own bias about the psychotherapeutic process. I strongly believe that any process of healing and recovery—whether from a physical, mental, or spiritual disorder—must involve the mind, body, and spirit. This holistic orientation marks the approach I take in my work with people. I also take a systems approach to therapy. A systems approach takes into consideration the influence of a person's relationships on the process of growth and change. This holistic systemic orientation forms the foundation of the work that I do with individuals, couples and families, and groups.

I believe that each of us is striving to express and experience love. Unfortunately, few of us learn how to do this very well as children. Still, the force of love pushes up within us to be expressed and experienced. As a result, when we are adults we are often faced with having to transform the barriers that get in the way of love. These barriers include our beliefs and defenses and the roles we play. Transforming these barriers and healing the self-alienation they create involves a process of change and growth that, I believe, is the essence of reclaiming your self. This process of transformation is what lies ahead for you in this book.

"It can so happen that a man who has missed the way towards the realization of his essential self may so suffer as a result that he is brought closer to spiritual birth than someone who has been denied this special kind of anguish. That man who feels himself in utter darkness in the world which . . . thrusts him into fear, despair and loneliness may be uniquely ready to hear the call of his essential being—ready to respond to the summons that, breaking through his ego shell, brings him to awareness of his inner core."

KARLFRIED GRAF VON DURCKHEIM
The Way of Transformation

PART ONE

· · · · · · · ·

Understanding Your Choice to Reclaim Your Self

of this until something happens in your life that leaves you with an uncomfortable feeling that you can't explain and from which you may want to run.

I had a gnawing feeling inside for years before I was ready to admit to myself and others that it was there. After all, I could point to my successes, my possessions, and my popularity as signs that I was okay. Yet none of these really took away this feeling. When events occurred that forced me to slow down enough to look inside, it seemed as if nothing was there. I had lost touch with myself, and it was painful. Even more painful was the realization that I didn't know what I would feel if I felt like myself.

I experienced what thousands of you are also discovering. Starting in our earliest experiences in childhood and continuing into our adult relationships, we have learned, developed, and used patterns of relating that cause us to avoid and deny our feelings. In the process we missed the way to becoming our real selves. When this happens, it's hard to figure out what's wrong.

Perhaps your life seems constricted or dull. You sense that there should be something more, some zest or vitality, but you don't know where to find it. Or you maintain a hectic schedule and achieve at a high level, but you're never satisfied. You feel empty and lonely inside, but you try to avoid these feelings by scheduling still more things to do or by getting involved in some drama that's occurring in a friend's life. Perhaps you feel a vague sense of restlessness or uneasiness, which you try to ignore. You may have had the same experience I had of facing an inner void. All of these are signs of the self-alienation that sets in when you avoid feeling your feelings.

When Not Feeling Hurts More than Feeling

There are good reasons for not wanting to feel. Certain feelings hurt. It's human to avoid something that is painful. However, avoiding feelings leads to more damaging emotional pain.

As you will see in the next three chapters, very few of us learn how to handle our feelings in constructive and healthy ways. Instead, in our attempts to repress painful feelings we end up causing ourselves more pain.

Some people drink alcohol, smoke cigarettes, or use other drugs to help muffle their feelings and thus run the risk of becoming addicted to one of these substances. Other people stay constantly busy or worry all the time or fantasize about how things are going to get better—these processes distract them from their feelings; but suppressed feelings still take their toll. One of the consequences of avoiding feelings is having difficulty with relationships. Another consequence is stress-related illnesses: headaches, stomachaches, frequent bouts of flu, chronic fatigue, even, recent research has established, cancer.

When you don't want to feel, you develop ways to defend and protect yourself in situations that provoke feelings. Several defenses are commonly used to distance feelings; for example, you may focus on meeting the needs of others or try to control other people's behavior. In this book you'll learn more about these and other defenses and how ultimately destructive they are. Because not feeling keeps you at a distance from what is happening to you, you may be unaware of the hurt you have inflicted on yourself.

Losing Touch with Yourself

I believe that the worst thing that happens to you when you avoid your feelings is that you lose touch with yourself. You have a restlessness, a discomfort deep inside, a special kind of anguish that develops when you have lost the way to you.

A spiritual distress sets in. You lose the ability to acknowledge and express your own uniqueness. You lose touch with your values, needs, abilities, and choices.

Many people describe themselves as being on automatic pilot. They feel very little emotional pain and also very little joy or happiness. My client, Bill, is a good example of this.

Bill is 35 years old and a successful sales manager. He's financially secure and well respected. He has a busy social life, enjoys a number of recreational and athletic activities, and takes vacations in exotic countries. Most people would find it hard to believe that Bill feels empty and hopeless. Yet during our first session together those were the two words he used over and over again to describe his life.

Bill is used to presenting a polished and confident image. Yet I could see glimpses of his emotional pain in the tension of his jaw and the guarded look in his eyes. His voice was pleading as he asked me: "What can I do to change? I don't even know where to start. I've completely hidden myself from people. No one knows who I am or what I'm like. I get lots of strokes and recognition. But for what? They like the person they think I am, not the real me. And you know what's the worst?" A look of terror flickered in Bill's eyes. "I don't even know the real me. I have no idea who I am."

Many of us cope with these feelings by trying to keep things the same. We try to get other people to behave in the ways that we are used to. We work at keeping them happy so they won't start treating us differently. We spend lots of time worrying about other people and how they are feeling and forget to pay attention to ourselves. As long as you avoid the feelings that accompany change, you won't grow as a person.

Paradoxically, our reluctance to change is as natural as change itself. Any attempts to change yourself must take this paradox into consideration and work with this understanding. This book is written with this paradox in mind. It is intended to guide you through the change process. You can change and grow. The rewards of this process will take you to new expressions and experiences of yourself. This process does take work. Part Three of this book helps you with this work. It not only focuses on instructing you in skill building, it provides an overview of what you can expect and help in understanding the process. You will experience the promise that change and growth offer as you work through the problems that avoiding change and growth have created.

It's Called Codependence

There's a word that is used to define the behavior patterns I've been describing. It's called *codependence*.

Codependence blocks the process of personal change and growth and hinders the development of healthy relationships and self-esteem. The roots of the term and the dynamics of codependence will be explored in detail in the first two sections of this book. After you read these sections, you will grasp the meaning and understand the source of the special kind of anguish that codependence creates. And understanding the *problem* will reveal to you the *promise* and enable you to begin changing. You will begin to find your true self.

Recovery: A Journey to Selfhood

There is a way to realize, experience, and express your inner core. That journey to selfhood is called *recovery*. Recovery from codependence involves a lot of hard work and a commitment to yourself and your experiences. This book is intended to assist you, support you, and invite you on your own journey of recovery.

This book is divided into four sections. Part One provides an overview of codependence. You'll learn about the characteristics of codependence in Chapter 2 and how it develops in Chapter 3. Chapter 4 illustrates the vicious cycle of codependence and introduces the process of recovery. In particular you will find in Chapter 4 a description of the cycle of codependence that illustrates its self-perpetuating nature. If you've ever wondered why you keep repeating unhealthy patterns of behavior, this chapter will give you a way of understanding what is going on.

Codependence affects you physically, mentally, and spiritually. Most books on codependence make reference to this fact. However, I don't believe they go deep enough in presenting this critical information to you. In my opinion, it is essential that you know the impact of codependence on these three dimensions of your being in order to prepare yourself for the process of recovery. That's why I've written Part Two. It explains in detail how codependence affects you physically, mentally, and spiritually. Research into the stress response and from the emerging field of psychoneuroimmunology clearly shows the biochemical connection between your physical health and how you deal with your feelings. Your ability to be a healthy person and to experience and express your thoughts and feelings is related to physical, mental, and spiritual well-being. After reading Part Two you will understand how the mind-body connection and your spiritual well-being are related. This information provides the foundation for the recovery program laid out in Part Three.

Part Three sets forth a comprehensive, in-depth program of recovery. Recovery from codependence involves finding your own truth and trusting your inner guidance. Part Three gives you tools to develop your own sense of self, the wisest guide you have. This book was created to take you on an inward journey. All travelers on this journey need information about the road and the destination. Although the journey is different for each individual, there are certain common experiences for which you can be prepared. Chapter 8 graphically illustrates the inward journey of recovery and the four stages you will experience. Chapters 9 through 12 cover each of the four stages of recovery. Each chapter provides tools, resources, and exercises that you will need to maintain your recovery when the going gets tough.

Part Four reveals the nature of the gift you will receive as you recover your sense of self.

How to Use This Book

There's a lot of information in this book. You will find many issues that have not been explored in depth in other self-help books and books on codependence. This may be your first book on codependence, or you may have already read much on the subject. Regardless of your background, I encourage you to read Parts One and Two before jumping ahead to the sections on recovery, even though some of the early ground may seem familiar. Both identification and understanding are essential to recovery. When the going gets tough and you start feeling stuck or afraid, it helps to know what's happening and why. So give yourself time to absorb and assimilate the preliminary information in preparation for the work ahead. With this foundation of understanding you will have the awareness you need to move into Parts Three and Four on recovery.

This book is intended to be your companion and friend. The tools and resources have been tested by many people. They work. There are no "musts" or "shoulds" in this book—just suggestions and recommendations. Follow your own process and do what you feel drawn to do. Try out various exercises and tools to see how they work. Some might feel more appropriate for you than others. That's okay. That's just one more thing you'll learn about yourself.

As you will see as you read through this book, I use illustrations to clarify and explain difficult concepts. These illustrations are designed to give you another way of understanding these concepts. They can also be useful in another way. Some of my clients have copied some of the charts that describe the process of recovery. They carry them around with them and check them occasionally the way you check a road map, to remind themselves of the journey they are making every day of their lives.

Although the issues you face during recovery may seem unique to you, they really aren't. Everybody in recovery faces similar issues. But your *path* is unique.

I believe the journey of recovery is the most creative and courageous act a person can undertake. Congratulations and welcome to the process that will bring you to the realization of your inner self.

2

·······

What Is Codependence?

''**T**HAT'S ME!''

I've heard this comment countless times, spoken by clients and workshop participants when they first learn the characteristics of codependence. I can recall when I said it myself.

I struggled for years with a pervasive sense of inner emptiness. This feeling of emptiness was profound in my early twenties, when I felt isolated and lonely despite my success in a computer business. I filled up the void, as many codependents do, with compulsive behavior, switching careers and focusing my attention on forging my position in the world. I also got married. Seven years later, my marriage ended in divorce and the feeling of emptiness came back, this time more acutely and accompanied by feelings of fear and anxiety.

When my marriage dissolved, I went into counseling and continued my career and recreational activities at a frantic pace. I was busy all the time, I was involved in a series of relationships, I abused alcohol and experimented with drugs—anything to dull the pain, especially the pain of being alone.

In an attempt to understand myself better, I attended many personal growth seminars and classes on assertiveness, self-esteem, intimacy, and communication. I also studied bioenergetics, psychosynthesis, and Gestalt therapy. I pounded pillows at anger workshops and cried at grief workshops, yet nothing really changed. I learned a great deal from these experiences, but nothing fully explained my behavior or my feelings.

My career interests shifted again—whenever I achieved success in one field, I switched directions and looked for a new arena in which to succeed so that others would see me as successful—and I thrived as a management consultant. My neighbors probably thought I had everything—an interesting and high-paying job, a waterfront condominium, a sailboat, and a Volvo—but these external signs of success only made me more anxious and uncomfortable. I felt like a fraud, and the feeling was getting worse.

In 1982 I read *Peoplemaking* by Virginia Satir, which helped me look at my family with a new perspective. Then, in early 1983, I read Sharon Wegscheider-Cruse's book, *Another Chance*, about adult children of alcoholics.

"That's me!" I said as I read the description of adult children of alcoholics. The book describes typical roles adopted by children in alcoholic families, and I recognized myself as the hero, the compulsive overachiever whose accomplishments the family can point to with pride as evidence of their normality. At that time the behavior now called codependent—which we know develops in children raised in all dysfunctional families—had only been identified in Adult Children of Alcoholics and was known as the ACOA syndrome.

That book made a big difference in my life. I realized I was not alone; other people were struggling with the same problems and feelings I was. And I felt relieved—at last I had the explanation I was looking for, something I could hold on to. But mostly I felt hopeful. Once I understood the source of my pain, I could make the choice to change.

Identification is the first and most important step toward recovery. Although there is some pain involved in identifying yourself as a codependent, the usual response is an overwhelming sense of relief and hope. Once you acknowledge that you are codependent, you can look at your own behavior and beliefs more clearly, you can look at your past with greater understanding and compassion, and you can look forward—perhaps for the first time—to a bright future.

The Characteristics of Codependence

Read through the following list of the characteristics of codependence and see if any of them describe you. Please remember that this list is offered as a guideline for your own self-assessment. It is not a complete list, nor is it a definitive one. But if you are codependent, you'll probably recognize yourself immediately.

- You focus your attention on pleasing others.
- When your personal interests and needs conflict with those of others, you give up your own interests and needs.
- You base your responses to others on your fear of their rejection or anger.
- You spend a lot of time trying to get other people to do things your way.
- When your values are challenged, put down, or violated by other people, you don't defend them.
- You base your self-image on what other people say and think about you.
- Afraid of facing reality, you often fantasize about how things will be different when "something" happens or someone important to you changes.
- You are out of touch with your feelings; sometimes you're not sure what you're feeling, and other times you can't identify any feelings at all.
- You are addicted to the sensations associated with drugs, alcohol, food, sex, work, adrenaline rushes, emotional highs, intense intellectual activity, or intense emotional relationships.
- You need a high degree of control over people, circumstances, and events.
- You have trouble developing or maintaining intimate relationships.
- You have low self-esteem.
- You have unrealistic expectations of yourself and others.
- You often take responsibility for others, particularly for their feelings.
- You have a history of minor chronic ailments, frequent injuries, or serious physical illnesses.
- You find yourself thinking obsessively about people, situations, or events.
- You have difficulty making decisions.
- You live under a high degree of stress, but you deny it and delude yourself into thinking that it isn't affecting you.

Remember, this is only a partial list. The study of codependence is just beginning. As we learn more about codependence, we may be able to identify the characteristics of codependence more precisely.

In the rest of this chapter I will review those characteristics in greater depth. As you read through the descriptions, think about your own experiences. At the end of the chapter you will find a questionnaire you can use to assess your degree of codependence. The path of recovery begins with a small step of honest self-assessment.

People Pleasing

If you grew up believing that the goodwill of others was necessary for your survival, you are probably codependent. You focused a lot of attention on doing the right thing to please others and make them happy with you, particularly significant others such as Mom, Dad, grandparents, teachers, or other people upon whom you were emotionally dependent. Their approval was so important that you may have felt like you would die if you didn't get it. Perhaps your parents were emotionally inconsistent or neglectful and you felt that they might abandon you. Or perhaps your parents actually beat you or abused you. Keeping them calm and happy was crucial.

As an adult, people pleasing pervades every area of your life. You focus on pleasing others in your intimate relationships, in your friendships, at work, in groups and organizations. You often say yes when you want to say no. You say it doesn't matter when it really does.

At one time in the late seventies and early eighties, when I was climbing the corporate ladder, I realized that I had gotten the reputation of being "a nice guy." Although I was liked, I wasn't respected. I was perceived as wishy-washy, not for real. Nobody had to tell me this, and no one did. I knew by seeing how others responded to me and also by how I felt. During this time I found a bumper sticker that said "No More Mr. Nice Guy" and pasted it into my briefcase to remind me that I didn't need to please others. If you are a people pleaser, you know it isn't that easy to stop. A lot of me was invested in that role.

In her book, *Choice-Making*, Sharon Wegscheider-Cruse describes "tunnel vision" as one of the characteristics of codependence. By this she meant an inability to relate to more than one person at a time. Waverly, my writing partner and editor, identified strongly with this behavior. She found it extremely difficult to be with both her boyfriend and her daughter at the same time, so she compartmentalized her life, giving her daughter her full attention in the evening and seeing her boyfriend late at night. On the rare occasions when she spent time with both of them, she felt she was being torn in two. As she explored her codependence, she realized her distress stemmed from the fact that she couldn't please both of them at the same time. The idea that their company might please *her* was a shocking revelation.

Ignoring Your Own Interests and Needs

If you believe your survival depends on controlling the behavior of others, you must give up your own interests and needs. Growing up in a dysfunctional family, you spent most of your time monitoring the needs of others. Basically you got used to ignoring yourself.

As an adult you continue in this pattern. You find it difficult to ask for what you need; you may not even be aware of your needs. You're uncomfortable expressing your opinion. You feel it's too risky to speak up for your beliefs. You tolerate behavior and statements that you find offensive without protest, then feel sheepish and embarrassed because you didn't speak up or do something. I can think of countless times when I've said to myself, "I wish I had said something," after remaining silent while someone expressed an opinion that was ethically repugnant to me.

This is one of the paradoxes of codependence. You feel empty or sad and don't want to feel these feelings, so you focus on pleasing others and ignoring your own needs and interests, which only makes you feel more empty, unfulfilled, and unhappy. The classic question of the codependent, one I hear from every client and one that I'm still exploring myself, is "Who am I?" This question is often asked with anguish. It's frightening to look inside for your self and find nothing, a void. Frequently my clients say they're afraid to give up their codependent behaviors because they're afraid that's all they are. "What if there's nothing there?" they ask. It's a reasonable question to ask if you've spent your entire life trying to blot out every trace of interests and needs, your true self.

Fear of Rejection and Anger

If you grew up in a dysfunctional family, you developed survival techniques for coping with the ever-present conflict, anger, or tension. While every family has arguments, the arguments in a dysfunctional family feel life-threatening and are seldom resolved. You learned to assess the risk of rejection or anger in all your interactions so you could arm yourself with appropriate defenses. As an adult you continue to use these methods for dealing with people.

You may not even be aware that you're doing this; the whole process is so instinctive and happens at such lightning speed. In every situation you are constantly assessing the possibility for rejection or conflict and choosing behavior that will minimize those risks. This usually means being dishonest with yourself or doing something you dislike or that is against your values. There are hundreds of ways to do this: suppressing your honest reactions, agreeing to take on a task you dislike, not speaking up when you see something you consider wrong happening. You try always to respond safely. Rather than experience conflict in your intimate relationships, you swallow your anger and your disappointment. You'd "rather not talk about it." You're so concerned with rejection that you choose not to ask for what you want rather than face possible rejection.

Do you often ask other people what they want to do or what they think before giving your opinion? Then base your response on their response? This way you can avoid stating your opinion and minimize the risk that it will be rejected or will provoke anger. As a bonus you have an opportunity to make sure the other person's needs are met. This is a subtle way of maintaining control and making sure you never have to experience anger and rejection.

Marian Henley's cartoon character Maxine illustrates this point in a humorous way.

MAXINE   **by Marian Henley**

Taking Responsibility for Others

Codependents carry a huge burden of guilt and shame from the past, because they believe on a very deep level that what happened in their dysfunctional families was their fault. Some of us were told directly by our parents that they would have been better off without us. Others of us only intuited this, perhaps reading the undercurrent of frustration and bitterness left by our parents' unactualized ambitions or unresolved tensions. Somehow, somewhere we started believing that if we could only be good enough, quiet enough, successful enough, we could fix all the problems.

It's a big burden, this assumption of responsibility for the welfare of others. It gives us a tremendous sense of power and a corresponding amount of guilt and fear. It's an attitude that is supported by a society that values being nice to people—and concealing our true opinions: "If you don't have anything nice to say, don't say anything at all." If you assumed this responsibility as a child, you constantly assess how others will respond. You couch your words diplomatically so as not to hurt others. You often take responsibility for the environment, for situations, and for other people's feelings, which are not really your responsibility.

Do you get embarrassed when your friend or lover acts foolishly? Do you try to distract others from noticing the person's behavior? Do you feel much more critical about the behavior of your child when you're in public than when you're home alone? Do you proffer excuses—"He's tired right now"; "She had a bad day"—for other people's behavior?

If you are codependent, you may have an unclear sense of the boundaries between you and others. You feel as if you are responsible for your lover's behavior. You probably feel uncomfortable when those close to you are sad or angry because you see it as your responsibility to make them happy. So you spend a lot of time assessing the behavior of others and fine-tuning your sensitivity. Pretty soon you are unable to distinguish where another person's feelings start and yours stop.

This is one of many reasons that codependents have problems with intimate relationships. Because of this haziness of boundaries, codependents often feel overwhelmed when someone gets close to them. If you have little sense of yourself—since you've been suppressing your own feelings—and you're sensitive to the feelings of others, you can easily feel engulfed.

This assumption of responsibility also paves the way for emotionally abusive relationships. If other people's feelings are your responsibility, then it's your fault whenever your spouse or partner or child is unhappy. If you figure out the correct response and change your behavior, you can make your loved one happy. I often work with clients who are unhappy in a relationship but can't leave because "If I told him how I really feel, it would hurt him so much," or "I can't tell her how I feel because she'll get angry." They will stay in a disintegrating relationship, despite the pain they suffer, because their own happiness is less important than the elusive goal of making someone else happy and because, if the relationship isn't working, it must be their fault.

Basing Your Self-Image on What Others Say

Codependents pay more attention to what other people say and think about them than to what they say and think about themselves. If you are codependent, you focus on obtaining the approval and recognition of others and create a self-image to achieve this end.

When you were a child, you spent a lot of time observing and interpreting the behavior of the people around you. You were looking for clues about how they perceived you, information you could use to guide your actions and your words so that you would never do anything wrong. Of course what other people say and think is more important than what you say and think. You've given away your powers of self-assessment, self-acknowledgment, self-approval.

This abnegation of responsibility for yourself can lead to many different behaviors. You may be overly concerned with external appearances or hypersensitive to social rules; perhaps you consider it necessary to be included in any invitation; you might worry constantly about doing and saying the right thing. You need external acknowledgment and validation because that's the only way you will know if you are succeeding in your goal—which is to please others and avoid conflict. But there's a catch here: if you try to feel good by always doing what you think others think you should be doing, you'll always feel bad.

For one thing, if everyone else is always right about how you should behave and what you should say, then you are never right, always wrong. You may develop a negative self-image; perhaps you constantly criticize and demean yourself. If someone around you is sad or angry or withdrawn, you assume it's because you've done something.

Also, the critical messages of your parents have become so ingrained, you continue to apply them to your own behavior even though they don't fit. Frequently when my clients start working on parental issues, they become blocked because of the pain associated with having to look at what their parents said about them.

There's nothing wrong with developing a sense of yourself from reflection and appraisals of others. This is how we all learn who we are in relation to others. But in your family of origin the distorted dynamics prevented you from getting a clear image of yourself and filled the void with negative messages.

Instead you developed a self-image based on the needs and expectations of others. This self-image may even help you deny codependence. After all, you may appear successful, competent, well liked. But inside you are lonely, unhappy, or hurt.

Needing a High Degree of Control

You may have grown up in a family in which you learned to control the expression of your feelings to avoid anger and rejection. You had to control people and circumstances to create a safe environment. If you could perfectly control your feelings, your environment, and the people around you, you could protect yourself from feeling pain.

As an adult, if you continue to maintain control, you can avoid feeling the deep pain that you've carried for so long. But when a person acts unexpectedly, when things don't go according to schedule, when an unpleasant feeling is evoked, the old wounds are open and hurting again. You need to have control to survive.

This has been expressed by my clients in many different statements: "I hate feeling out of control." "If I'm not in control, it's frightening." "I've always got to be in control." The need for control surfaces in many different ways: endless to-do lists, rigid rules for behavior, the need always to be "right," fear of change, adherence to habits and meaningless rituals. What's behind all of this controlling behavior?

Not having control is equated with being open, vulnerable, exposed to the environment. When you were out of control emotionally in your childhood, it was painful. You were ridiculed, criticized, ignored, screamed at, possibly even hit. You quickly learned how to protect yourself. Control your own feelings, and no one would see the unacceptable ones. Control the circumstances—make sure the chores are done, come home too late to encounter anyone, or read a book—and you could shield yourself from anger. Control the people around you—figure out what they want and then give it to them—so you would never have to be vulnerable again. In these ways your inner feelings wouldn't be touched and your self-image was maintained.

I recall one of the first statements of one of my clients, Martha, a 40-year-old woman, who said flatly during our first session, "I cannot lose control." She came to see me because her whole world was falling apart: she had several serious medical problems, her relationships weren't working, and she was depressed. Yet she was struggling desperately to maintain the happy-go-lucky, "everything is just fine" attitude she had adopted in childhood. She had been taught as a child that it was wrong to have negative feelings. So when she felt sad or angry or jealous, she smothered the feeling. If she saw someone else in pain, she flew to the rescue and was not satisfied until she had made the person happy. It was several months before she could relinquish a part of the control she wielded over her self, her feelings, and others.

Manipulating Others to Do Things Your Way

Giving in to the will of others, putting others ahead of themselves, being eager to please—codependents are such nice people. How could they possibly be manipulative? Codependents have a hard time seeing themselves as manipulators. But control extended outward becomes manipulation.

Often codependents have an equally hard time distinguishing between direct, healthy, assertive behavior and manipulation. One of my clients, Terry, told me; "When someone else lets me know what he wants, especially if he makes a direct request, I feel obligated to provide it. I don't think I have a choice, really. So, for instance, if my boss asks me to do something I don't want to do, I say yes, but I try to get back at him somehow, maybe by sulking or doing the work more slowly than usual. Maybe even visibly suffering to make the point that I'm being asked to take on more work than I can possibly do."

Terry's martyr role is one frequently adopted by codependents, as are the roles of caretaker, rescuer, and victim. Playing a role is one way to control others. Manipulation is a protective mechanism—it prevents you from looking at yourself and your own behavior. Playing a role is an essential part of the protection mechanism and becomes a shield and armor against a display of real feelings.

It's not hard to understand why codependents find it necessary to manipulate others. This behavior is a survival pattern used to protect old emotional wounds from being touched and feelings from being revealed. Naturally this behavior doesn't work. Many codependents tolerate situations and relationships that are painful, even toxic, because they feel in control in these relationships.

If you are codependent, you have carefully established an acceptable self-image that represents many of the behaviors and values that were acceptable during your childhood. To maintain this image you get other people to behave in ways that will protect you from the truth of your inner pain. You associate with people who play familiar roles or whose behavior is predictable, people you can manipulate to assure that your masks and roles are not pierced.

We try to hide our manipulative behavior by developing an acute sensitivity to other people so that we're constantly involved with their problems and issues. To be honest, I've found that this sensitivity is really a way of avoiding intimacy. By focusing on the other, you avoid revealing yourself. You avoid being truly known.

If you play the role of caretaker or rescuer, you use this sensitivity to help other people. It looks like you're encouraging change. Actually you are trying to get someone to behave the way you want him or her to behave, a way that will protect you and your feelings. You're being dishonest, trying to achieve your ends through indirect means rather than directly expressing your concern.

Denial and Delusion

We've looked at two of the major themes of codependence: a dysfunctional orientation toward others and a need for control. A third major theme—denial—is the flip side of control. Refusing to look at the painful truth of our reality requires us to control our feelings, perceptions, and thoughts.

Do you frequently make statements like "I know things will get better when he/she goes to counseling" or "As soon as I make enough money, I'll be happy"? Facing reality as it exists is difficult for codependents. It may mean facing repressed feelings of guilt, shame, and abandonment, making difficult decisions or acknowledging what appear to be mistakes.

If you are codependent, you became adept at denial at an early age. It was a survival mechanism that allowed you to tolerate exposure to harmful life experiences, situations, and people. Back then you had no choice. You had to find ways to ignore your pain since you couldn't leave. However, as an adult you continue to use denial and live in delusions. You find it difficult, if not intolerable, to accept reality because to do so is to shatter your dreams, dispel your delusions, and bring you face to face with the very things you want most to avoid.

I know this experience intimately. For five years I refused to listen to the advice of counselors, friends, and family who warned me about the emotional and psychological abuse I was suffering in a relationship. Their perceptions were unacceptable to me. I thought that if I paid attention to them, I would have to end the relationship. What was really unacceptable were the feelings of loneliness, abandonment, and anxiety that I felt whenever I did try to break away. I was involved in a codependent relationship. I needed her to maintain my addictions and avoid my inner feelings.

So I deluded myself into believing that I could convince her to love and accept me if I did the right things, found the right words, became the person she wanted me to be. I refused to look at the stress I had created for myself, refused to admit to myself that I was powerless to control her affection for me.

How do codependents deny the reality they are experiencing? One way is through total immersion in self-help books, seminars, and workshops. Constantly studying the latest techniques for improving relationships, they believe that with enough effort and affirmations they can achieve happiness and prosperity.

I recall one client, Cynthia, who was involved in an intense personal growth program that taught her how to release herself from her old programming and develop new tapes for success, wealth, and inner peace. Unfortunately the program was based on controlling feelings and creating images of how other people should treat her.

After two years of work Cynthia could see that her life had changed externally somewhat. She had more friends, a more active social life, and a blossoming career. Yet she was still lonely and unhappy inside. However, in this program, to admit to such feelings was to admit defeat. Her codependence was, in fact, being supported by a program of self-help that was based on denial of feelings.

It's difficult to accept that a job isn't working, that a relationship is destructive, that you are addicted to a chemical, food, or sex, or that codependence is "killing" you. You prefer the delusion: "Someday my boss will notice me and give me a raise," "Someday she'll treat me right," "I can quit anytime I want."

As a codependent you prefer to believe that things will get better "if only" you can figure out exactly how to change the world. It's sobering to realize that the only thing you can change is yourself.

Obsessive Thinking

Codependents are often obsessive in their thinking. They obsess about minor things and major things, about people, about decisions, about something as simple as a conversation with a friend or an associate. They worry about the future and think regretfully about what happened in the past. No matter what the object, the obsession has one purpose. Like an addiction, it focuses all attention on something external, contributing to self-alienation.

Obsessive thinking is familiar to you if you've ever sat home alone wondering about the significant other in your life. Will she call? Where is he? What is she doing right now? If the person you love is in a relationship with someone else, you may imagine them together. Images of the two of them crowd your mind, becoming more real than your present reality.

Another form of obsessive thinking focuses on regrets. You find yourself constantly churning over events and details of conversations, asking yourself "What if?" and lost in the fantasy of "If only I had . . . , then things would be different."

When you're obsessing, you may feel as if your whole being is centered in your head. Your mind races with thoughts, ideas, and images. Like any addiction, obsessive thinking interferes with your ability to feel your own feelings. By directing your thoughts outward, you avoid looking at yourself.

Difficulty Making Choices

Everyone has to make choices, but for codependents this experience can be particularly painful. Clients describe the experience of decision making with vivid metaphors—for instance, "being trapped between a rock and a hard place."

Any decision can evoke these unpleasant feelings, from something as simple as choosing between two entrees on a menu to something as complex as a job choice or pregnancy. When both choices seem equally appealing or equally undesirable, codependents get stuck.

"I'm stuck with no place to go."

"There's just no way out of this mess."

"I'm damned if I do and damned if I don't."

This problem is intricately intertwined with many of the other characteristics of codependence.

The ability to make a choice comes from an awareness of your own needs and values. If you're not aware of your own values and needs, what possible criteria can you use for making a decision?

The decision-making process is experienced as dangerous. After all, when you make a decision, you take a stand; you risk having an opinion. If your main motivations are pleasing others and avoiding conflict, you risk offending someone or being confronted when you make a decision. One of my clients said, "I know I have to make a decision, but I want somebody else to make it for me. I just don't want to look back and think I was wrong or made a mistake."

If you have no internal standards, if other people and outside circumstances determine whether you are right or wrong, how can you possibly assess the consequences?

And if in your family of origin decisions were made on the basis of an addiction or a system of rigid rule, or they were made to avoid conflict or minimize stress rather than reflecting the needs of individual family members, how could you learn to make decisions in any other way?

It's much easier to avoid the decision-making process, perhaps with obsessive thinking.

Either-or thinking and discomfort with ambiguity are typical of codependents, who prefer to believe that things are either right or wrong. After all, if there's a choice between right and wrong, the choice is pretty obvious. But this doesn't help them make decisions, since they have difficulty deciding which is which. Entering the gray area would require looking at their own feelings and noticing the consequences of their choices.

Being in that gray area of ambiguity brings up uncomfortable feelings, like being powerless and out of control. So codependents rely on the safety and security associated with black-and-white, right-or-wrong thinking. Unfortunately this conflicts with the ability to make good decisions. Decisions are made quickly or are based on old beliefs about what's right just to minimize the discomfort associated with decision making.

Being Out of Touch with Feelings

This is a crucial component of codependence, as you learned in the first chapter. Getting in touch with your feelings is the crucial component of recovery and is central to your health and emotional well-being.

If you habitually suppress feelings, you gradually lose the ability to experience them. Eventually you may be unable to identify them, name them, or express them. Paradoxically the more pleasant feelings of joy, affection, and creative exuberance get buried along with the disowned feelings. Your ability to feel good is distorted by behavior used to avoid feeling bad.

Often when I ask my clients what they are feeling, they say "I don't know." They are telling the truth; they are genuinely unable to feel their own feelings or recognize what a feeling is. They may have no words to associate with the feelings they feel or a very limited vocabulary containing only a few words, like *happy, sad, hurt,* and *angry.* Sometimes they gaze off into the air and say something like "I think I feel sad." Other clients will get a glazed look in their eyes; they appear to be daydreaming. They are clearly no longer present in the room. When I ask what's going on, they'll shake themselves a little, as if awakening from a trance.

I know where they've been. It's what I call my "black hole," a place where I retreated whenever I was close to experiencing some painful feeling. Because I felt overwhelmed—long-buried feelings have a lot of intensity—I would dissociate myself from my feelings. Waverly describes this experience as "climbing a ladder of thoughts, going up far away from myself." Others have experienced this place as a room or basement to which they could retreat for safety.

Before recovery I avoided feelings of despair, depression, and anxiety. I wanted nothing to do with the discomfort and inner pain they caused, so I trained myself to be out of touch with my feelings. Yet it is these feelings that often cover up the deeper hurt that needs to be healed—old feelings of being rejected, abandoned, and inadequate.

Being out of touch with feelings has another important consequence: it allows you to maintain the status quo. In contrast strong feelings provide the impetus for change and action.

In recovery I learned to welcome the sensations of feelings. Even though my feelings continue to be a source of pain, they also provide an indication of growth and healing, pointing the way on my path of recovery. As I learned to face and heal these feelings, I discovered feelings of happiness and inner peace. I didn't realize how alive and joyful I could feel until I was in recovery.

Addiction to Sensations

Codependents are highly susceptible to addictions and compulsive behaviors. We are drawn to addictive substances and processes, because they alter our moods and keep us out of touch with our real feelings. As you will see in Chapter 4, addictions to sensations have a distinct purpose—they create a feeling of life in our bodies. Although it's a false feeling of life, it's often better than no feeling at all or the feelings of depression, despair, and anxiety.

Notice that I make the point that codependents are addicted to *sensations*. Some people like the feeling of excitement and the high they get from intense emotional relationships, caffeine, working hard, sex, or drugs like cocaine. Other people prefer the soothing sensations they associate with alcohol, food, television, or marijuana. Some like the sensation of spacing out derived from psychedelic drugs or daydreaming. Over time the need for something that alters your moods and feelings can become the basis of an addiction.

One of my clients, Herb, was an avid exercise enthusiast, running and exercising about 90 minutes every day. Obviously he was in fine physical condition, but the rest of his life was in a shambles. He had lost two jobs in the past four months, and none of his relationships with women ever lasted longer than two months. He started counseling because he was lonely. When we looked at his relationship pattern, I pointed out to him that his life was structured around exercise. There was no room for other people or even other needs.

"When I exercise," Herb said, "I can escape all the bullshit and loneliness. I don't need anybody when I run."

"What happens if you don't run or exercise every day?" I asked.

"I get depressed and irritable" was the reply.

"Perhaps," I suggested, "those feelings are genuine, and you run to escape from them."

Herb couldn't accept this idea immediately, but over the next few months he gradually realized that his obsession with exercise was contributing to his loneliness and was his way of staying out of touch with real feelings that needed to be experienced and felt.

As a society we associate the word *addict* with alcoholics and drug users. Gradually we are beginning to recognize the existence of other addictions, such as the addiction to work. In truth *many* substances and processes are used to alter moods and escape from reality.

One of my clients was surprised to discover that he was addicted to X-rated movies and videos. Whenever he felt lonely, depressed, or sad, feelings that occurred often, he would go see an X-rated movie or rent an X-rated video, which would distract him from these feelings. However, like Herb, he wanted to get over his loneliness. I pointed out that his method of coping with loneliness isolated him even further. It was not just a way to cope with emotional pain; it was also destroying his ability to develop and maintain relationships and undermining his self-esteem.

Another client said he liked arriving late to whatever he had scheduled, because he liked the adrenaline rush, the feeling of excitement it gave him. As we pursued this further, he revealed that he often felt anxious before social events and appointments. He was nervous about his performance, afraid of the disapproval of others, and anxious about whether he could meet his own expectations. If he was late, his adrenaline would be pumping and he'd feel "on top of things," working at his maximum efficiency. Then he wouldn't have to feel the anxiety. Like many other people who say they put things off until the last minute because they work better under pressure, he was using pressure to overcome his feelings of fear and anxiety and to function better.

Addictions are cunning, powerful, and baffling, and they form a major part of the codependent life-style.

Denying Reality with Fantasies

Fantasy is another effective escape from pain, a way of numbing yourself to a reality so painful you don't want to experience it—a destructive relationship, another job loss, another failure to win approval from someone important to you. Fantasy not only destroys your ability to experience the present; it also can numb you to actual or potential danger in a relationship or situation.

As a child I had many fantasies that are typical of a child raised in an alcoholic family. I imagined what life would be like when my dad gave up his bizarre behavior. I dreamed about the vacations we would take, the friends I would invite over, the baseball games my dad would attend.

Many clients tell me about the ways they coped with unpleasant and tense family environments. They dreamed up imaginary families. One woman found solace in the fantasy that she was adopted and that her real parents would come to claim her someday. Others created special rooms in their imagination, where they could retreat when threatened. Some used movies, television, or books as a way to escape.

Fantasy was important to us when we were children. It enabled us to survive the painful reality and confusion of our homes. As adults we continue to use fantasy to keep out of touch with painful feelings. Ironically doing this only contributes to our unhappiness, since fantasies often enable us to stay in physically and emotionally damaging situations and relationships.

Veronica was living with a man who constantly downgraded her. He made disparaging comments about the way she looked, and he behaved rudely around her friends and family. Veronica was supporting him, and he made only feeble efforts to get a job and contribute financially to their relationship. He disappeared for hours at a time without any explanations but kept track of her every movement. Veronica spent a lot of time crying from loneliness and humiliation.

Yet Veronica never considered breaking up with him because she believed they were "soul mates." She could point to a series of incredible coincidences that proved they were meant for each other and had a special psychic bond. She focused on the good things that were going to happen once they got married, once he got a job, once they bought the house of their dreams. She imagined them entertaining their friends together even though he disliked her friends and she disliked his. She imagined them happily raising a child together even though they had totally different philosophies about child rearing and totally different values. Her fantasies blinded her to the painful reality of the relationship. Once she gave up her fantasies about how things would change and looked at what she had, she realized that she didn't want to continue the relationship.

Unrealistic Expectations

If you are codependent, you are a survivor. You survived in a family that threatened your sense of existence. Now you have a high tolerance for pain and stress, despite the physical, emotional, and psychological toll it takes. You can handle, even triumph, in difficult and challenging situations, and you expect the same from others.

Many of the roles associated with codependence contain a streak of this perfectionism. Are you the hero who constantly strives to excel or the martyr who is always suffering because other people don't meet your expectations? Do you see in yourself the workaholic who takes over and does the job because no one else can do it as fast or as well as you can?

If you are codependent, you probably find yourself frequently involved in challenging situations. You are used to facing difficult situations and feel uncomfortable when things are too easy or running too smoothly. You may commit yourself to a number of projects, then feel upset when you're unable to complete all of them. Without a sense of your own limits you have difficulty assessing your abilities and often seriously underestimate the amount of time it will take you to complete a task. You may feel that your energies are scattered and you are being pulled in many different directions.

Your unrealistic expectations then become part of a vicious cycle. Overcommitted, overworked, overstressed, inevitably you fail to perform up to your expectations or to meet the commitments you've made to others. Different people react to this situation in different ways. You may work harder, work longer hours, and get tired and stressed. Or you may find ways to manipulate the situation so that you don't have to complete the project. Or you may procrastinate and then, when the deadline is inevitable, push yourself into a panic-driven last-minute rush of activity. None of these solutions is truly satisfactory. You can't do your best work when you're burned out or working at midnight. You can't feel a sense of accomplishment if you're always leaving projects undone.

Shame is one of the painful feelings commonly suppressed by codependents and is a close relative of low self-esteem. Unrealistic expectations, requiring perfection and external approval, lead inevitably to failure and then to shame and low self-esteem. Rather than reassessing their expectations, codependents castigate themselves for not being able to carry out the impossible tasks they demand of themselves—for instance, being in an intimate relationship when they have not yet learned how to trust themselves. Codependents fear what they perceive as potential embarrassment and the shame of not "doing it right." They worry about hurting the feelings of others, about possible rejection, all experiences that maintain low self-esteem.

Low Self-Esteem

Low self-esteem seems inevitable when you look at the other characteristics of codependence. Yet this is a characteristic that people frequently disown. If you believe in the competent, well-liked self-image you've constructed, or if you can point to the success of your roles and masks, you may be unaware of the inner reality of low self-esteem that they conceal.

Often clients tell me that they have high self-esteem, that they are able to meet any challenges. On further exploration they realize they are talking about an inflated self-image or a high degree of self-confidence founded on a specific technical or intellectual ability. They discover that they are driven by perfection and are extremely demanding of themselves. What they consider high self-esteem is based on their ability to meet their own unrealistic expectations and is conditional on successful performance and the approval of others.

Self-esteem is both a feeling about and an attitude toward yourself. To esteem yourself is to have unconditional positive regard for yourself, both your positive qualities and those you consider negative. Unconditional positive regard means accepting yourself, and that includes your feelings.

As you review the characteristics of codependence described in this chapter, what is your reaction? Do you judge yourself harshly, or can you accept these behaviors as possible avenues for growth and change?

Self-esteem is not based on things that you do or things you own. It's based on an honest appraisal of yourself and your limitations.

Problems with Intimacy

If you've followed along with all the descriptions of codependent characteristics above, it should come as no surprise that codependents have trouble with intimacy.

Intimacy requires an ability to be honest with yourself and others, honest about your feelings, thoughts, and fears. It requires the willingness to be open and vulnerable; it means giving up control and manipulation. It requires a strong sense of self, not sacrificing your own interests and needs in an attempt to please the other. Above all it requires a sense of trust and safety, feelings that were absent in your family of origin.

If you identified with some of the characteristics above, you were brought up in a family that trained you in how not to be intimate. You learned to suppress your feelings. Although you may have been told that "honesty is the best policy," you suffered emotional, psychological, or even physical abuse when you were honest. You were brought up to obey certain rules—rigidity, isolation, silence, the denial of "negative" feelings, an emphasis on social conformity—all of which prevent the development of intimate relationships.

It is probably too much—another unrealistic expectation—to hope to develop and maintain intimate relationships until you are in a recovery program. How can you hope to become intimate with someone when all of your attempts to reveal yourself in the past were fraught with pain, confusion, and disapproval?

So what sorts of relationships do codependents have if they are unable to develop intimate relationships? Often a shared addiction becomes the basis for relationship, an addiction to a substance or to sex, chaos, or excitement. Sometimes mutual fantasies, dreams about the future, are the focus of the relationship rather than the here-and-now. Or a relationship is built on talking about intimacy and analyzing behavior.

Intimacy with others can occur only when we are able to be intimate with ourselves. This is something that codependents have not yet experienced. We repress our painful feelings and thoughts, preferring to maintain our self-images rather than have to face the inner truth that they conceal.

Chronic Ailments and Physical Illness

The life of a codependent is stressful. Repressing feelings, constant vigilance, and addictive behavior, combined with the legacy of a dysfunctional family, all contribute to a variety of stress-related illnesses. As you will learn in Chapter 5, our bodies suffer greatly under the impact of codependent behaviors, resulting in weakened immune systems, accident-proneness, psychosomatic illness, and depression. Codependents extend the same unrealistic expectations they apply to their behavior to their bodies, expecting them to suffer years of abuse and stress without consequences.

The physical illnesses that plague codependents are not always serious ones. Not at the start anyway. Persistent coughs, frequent bouts of flu, fatigue, skin problems, and a variety of other minor physical ailments can be ignored. Yet the cumulative stress of the codependent life-style eventually takes a greater toll. If you are 25 and reading this book, you may think this characteristic doesn't apply to you. If you are over 40, you probably have an entirely different view.

As part of my assessment with clients I ask about medical history. Sixty percent of my clients report a variety of medical problems, ranging in severity from frequent colds to gastrointestinal problems, psoriasis, hearing problems, nervous tension, and anxiety. Although these seem to be unrelated, unsevere conditions, there is a pattern that reveals the underlying stress of the codependent life-style.

When I reviewed my own medical history, I thought it was fairly normal. I had had a few surgeries, back problems, cuts and bruises, acne, problems sleeping, intense energy, periods of fatigue and depression. Nothing seemed that serious, but it was. My life-style was wearing out my body, and I was just ignoring it. Denial and delusion played their part. I wasn't aware of the stresses I placed on my body, and

I deluded myself into believing simple solutions like a change of diet and a vacation would solve my problems.

In Chapter 5, we'll look at how a codependent life-style affects your body and some of the serious medical consequences of codependence.

Assessing Yourself

As you read the first two chapters, you probably began to think about your own codependence. The chart that follows is designed to provide a more precise tool for your self-evaluation and a direction for growth.

Compare the characteristic typical of codependence on the left with the qualities on the right, then circle the number that indicates your current position on this spectrum.

Your rating may vary somewhat, with much higher scores on some characteristics than on others. Many people find they have greater difficulty with certain themes of codependence—for instance, relationships or control issues—than with others. Noting your strengths and weaknesses accurately will help you develop a personalized recovery program.

Before you begin to use this chart, you may want to make a copy of it so you can assess yourself again at periodic intervals. This practice, which I recommend, will give you a sense of your progress and allow you to pinpoint the areas in which you still have challenges to meet.

Don't be alarmed if your self-assessment reveals a high degree of codependence. You have successfully accomplished one of the most difficult steps toward recovery—honest identification. In the following chapters you will find the information you need to take the next steps—understanding how you became codependent, how it impacts your life today, and how you can recover your sense of self.

What is Codependence?

Codependence Self-Assessment Chart

#		1	2	3	4	5	6	7	8	9	10	
1.	I focus attention on others.	1	2	3	4	5	6	7	8	9	10	I focus attention on respecting myself and others.
2.	I give up my personal interests and needs.	1	2	3	4	5	6	7	8	9	10	I acknowledge and act in accordance with my personal interests and needs and am willing to examine them in relation with others.
3.	I base my responses to others on fear of rejection or anger.	1	2	3	4	5	6	7	8	9	10	I am willing to relate to others honestly despite the possibility that I might experience anger or rejection.
4.	I work hard to get others to do things my way.	1	2	3	4	5	6	7	8	9	10	I am honest, direct, and assertive in expressing myself and respect the rights of others to feel and act differently.
5.	I don't acknowledge my values.	1	2	3	4	5	6	7	8	9	10	I respect my values and beliefs and am willing to explore them in the light of new information.
6.	I base my self-image on what others think and say.	1	2	3	4	5	6	7	8	9	10	I have a deep sense of self based on my awareness of my feelings, my needs, and interests, and I recognize how my behavior impacts others.

7. I often fantasize about how people or things will change.

1 2 3 4 5 6 7 8 9 10

I am in touch with the reality of the current moment and know the only changes that can occur are within me.

8. I am out of touch with my feelings.

1 2 3 4 5 6 7 8 9 10

I am aware of my feelings and express them effectively.

9. I am addicted to the sensations associated with alcohol, drugs, food, sex, work, adrenaline rushes, intense intellectual effort, or intense emotions.

1 2 3 4 5 6 7 8 9 10

I allow myself to experience a wide range of feeling sensations, including pain and joy. I choose not to alter my feeling states or stimulate feelings with addictions to sensations.

10. I need a high degree of control.

1 2 3 4 5 6 7 8 9 10

I allow the natural flow of events to occur and take responsibility for myself in the flow.

11. I have trouble with intimate relationships.

1 2 3 4 5 6 7 8 9 10

I recognize that intimacy requires self-disclosure and self-awareness, and my relationships reflect my ability to be intimate.

12. I have low self-esteem.

1 2 3 4 5 6 7 8 9 10

My self-esteem grows stronger and more secure as I experience and express my feelings and inner truth.

13. I have unrealistic expectations.

1 2 3 4 5 6 7 8 9 10

I am aware of and respect my own limitations and those of others.

What is Codependence?

14 I take responsibility for others.

1 2 3 4 5 6 7 8 9 10

I am willing to communicate and act honestly, accepting the responses I receive while recognizing how my words and behavior may influence others.

15 I have a history of minor chronic ailments or serious physical illness.

1 2 3 4 5 6 7 8 9 10

I take care of my body through a program of physical and emotional health.

16 I find myself thinking obsessively.

1 2 3 4 5 6 7 8 9 10

I can let go of situations, events, and people and experience peace of mind.

17 I have difficulty making decisions.

1 2 3 4 5 6 7 8 9 10

I make decisions based on my needs and values and trust my own decision-making process.

18 I live under a high degree of stress, but I deny it and delude myself.

1 2 3 4 5 6 7 8 9 10

I acknowledge that denial and delusion cause stress and am willing to explore and change my beliefs and life-style to reduce my stress level.

3

·······

How Codependence Develops

I N YOUR FIRST AND MOST basic social unit, your family of origin, you develop beliefs, attitudes, and opinions about yourself, others, and the world. To a great extent these views become a part of the way you live the rest of your life, although they can be changed.

I don't believe that a codependent worldview is the inevitable result of certain childhood experiences. The fact that your parents had difficulty with intimate relationships does not mean that you will be unable to develop intimate relationships. You need not be a victim of your upbringing, nor should you use it as a scapegoat. However, I do believe that your family of origin greatly influences your thinking and way of being and acting in the world as an adult. You can have a more fulfilling and less painful life today by exploring the strategies you developed for coping with problems in your family of origin and recognizing how those strategies still affect your behavior. This work will help you begin to *differentiate* yourself from your family. Even if you left home at an early age and haven't had any contact with your family members since then, if you are at a loss when it comes to feeling good, your family of origin probably still influences your present behavior.

Consider how a seed becomes a plant. Given enough light, water, and nourishment, the plant grows naturally to its full potential. The same plant, struggling to grow in adverse circumstances—poor soil, inadequate light, not enough water—will not be able to reach its full potential. As the plant struggles to get its needs met under deficient conditions, its natural growth is distorted; it may stay small and weak or become unnaturally spindly.

34

A child who grows up in a healthy environment, whose major needs are met by his family, will naturally learn to develop his full potential, like the lucky plant in our example. But many of us did not grow up in healthy families. Our needs were not met; we grew up starving for attention, affection, recognition, love. Because it was so hard to get our needs met in a natural and direct way, we developed sophisticated, complicated, and distorted ways of getting our needs for nurture met.

A plant has very few needs—light, water, and food. Human beings have many more—physical safety and security, food, sleep, love, recognition, self-respect, and competence. Abraham Maslow ranked these needs in a hierarchy based on their necessity, which is reproduced below:

Hierarchy of Needs

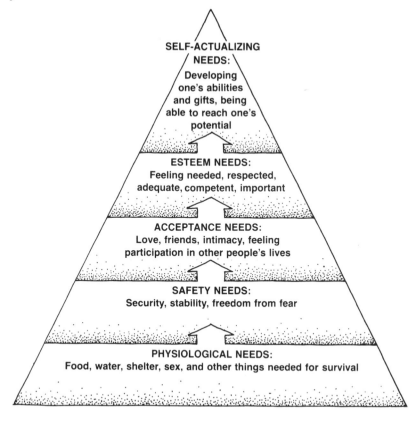

SELF-ACTUALIZING NEEDS:
Developing one's abilities and gifts, being able to reach one's potential

ESTEEM NEEDS:
Feeling needed, respected, adequate, competent, important

ACCEPTANCE NEEDS:
Love, friends, intimacy, feeling participation in other people's lives

SAFETY NEEDS:
Security, stability, freedom from fear

PHYSIOLOGICAL NEEDS:
Food, water, shelter, sex, and other things needed for survival

The needs at each level must be met before effectively moving to the next level.

Primary needs are those needs that must be satisfied for the individual to survive—nourishment and physical safety and security. On a higher level are acceptance needs, necessary for healthy social development—feeling loved and loving. Higher-order needs, such as competence, self-expression, and self-actualization, can be met only when the needs below them on the hierarchy have been satisfied.

Were Your Needs Met?

The world of a child is small. Whatever kind of family you grew up in, there were only a few significant others—your parents, your siblings, perhaps a close relative, possibly a stepparent—who were responsible for meeting your needs for many years. Were they able to fulfill your primary needs? If one of your parents had a serious addiction problem or a severe mental condition or if you grew up in a house full of violence and physical abuse, your basic needs for security and nourishment weren't met. It's hard to feel loved or loving when you're scared of dying.

But even if your primary needs were met, what about the needs described below?

1. When you talked, were you acknowledged and believed? Acknowledgment and trust are necessary for the development of self-worth. If you were ignored or belittled, you may have grown up believing that what you had to say wasn't very important.

2. Were you allowed to express your opinion about important family issues and matters even when your viewpoint was different? If you could assert your own opinion, you learned to value your uniqueness. If you were expected to confirm with family norms and never deviate from the common viewpoint, you may have learned to value your opinions only when they agreed with others.

3. Did you feel loved? Did you receive plenty of physical affection, acceptance, and recognition? Studies have shown that loving touch is essential for survival; babies who are deprived of physical contact are more likely to be sick, small, and slower to develop emotionally and physically than babies that are cuddled and held. If physical contact was frowned on in your family, you may still be uncomfortable with your body, unable to read its helpful signals of both pain and pleasure.

4. Were you allowed to express your individuality through your gifts, interests, and feelings? If you were encouraged to explore things that interested you, do things you enjoyed, and express your feelings, you were given a rare gift—the ability to experience your own being. If, however, your parents frowned on your expression of

your talents and discouraged you from pursuing your interests, you lost contact with an important part of yourself, the inner self that contains the passions and gifts that make you unique. If your parents also let you know that they did not want to hear about your feelings—particularly those they found unacceptable, such as anger, jealousy, sadness, disappointment—then you learned how to suppress these feelings, perhaps to the point where you no longer experience them.

5. Were you encouraged to try new things? If you were allowed to experience stimulation and challenges, you developed a clearer sense of your abilities and greater confidence in new situations. But if your parents discouraged new endeavors in favor of doing things as they've always been done or sticking with what you know, you may be handicapped when faced by any one of the many changes life brings, since you have no practical experience in facing new challenges and no confidence in your ability to do so.

6. Did you trust your parents and the other close members of your family? Did they trust you? If your parents were honest about their feelings and told you the truth about uncomfortable situations, you learned to trust your own perceptions of reality. "Dad is acting strange and, yes, Mom, tells me he is acting strange, so I guess I can be guided by my feelings about people" is the statement of a child who has learned trust. By contrast, consider this statement: "Dad is acting horrible and weird, but Mom acts like it's okay and, in fact, tells me he's under a lot of pressure, so I guess it's okay for him to act that way, and I guess I shouldn't trust my feelings, because obviously I don't know everything that's going on." If you were brought up in the second kind of family, where feelings are denied and reality is ignored, you long ago stopped trusting your feelings and were thus cast adrift in a confusing world where you can rely only on the opinions of others for your understanding of reality.

7. Did you feel safe? Were you able to experience security through structure and reliability? If your parents were relatively consistent, if you were able to count on things being a certain way and people responding to you in certain ways, you felt safe, and safety is necessary for every kind of exploration and self-expression. If your experience in your childhood was one of unpredictability, if you never knew how your parents were going to act, you were so busy trying to figure out what was going on that you may have lost all sense of self and become focused entirely on their behavior. Perhaps your parents were consistent, but in an unhealthy way, maintaining overly rigid standards of behavior. In this case you may fear change and feel anxious in new situations, watching to try to figure out the rules so you'll know how to behave rather than acting spontaneously.

Martin Seligman, famous for his research on learned helplessness, describes childhood as "the dance of development." Healthy development requires a sensitive response to your needs at various stages from one or both of your parents. If your parents were occupied elsewhere—if the family energy was centered on an addiction, or coping with the current crisis, or keeping up a good image—you had no partner for this dance. In such a family both parents are often unavailable or simply too exhausted and depressed to interact with their children.

An essential ingredient in healthy families is their ability to validate the feelings and thoughts of each member of the family. Unhealthy families criticize, deny, or make shameful judgments of feelings or thoughts when these do not fit the parents' expectations. The quantity of the time one or both of your parents spent with you as a child may have been significant. But if a lot of that time was focused on controlling or shaming what you felt and thought, then you were exposed to an environment that was toxic to your growth as an individual. This factor is often confusing to people who are just beginning to explore codependence. They question how their family could have been unhealthy when their mother was always available and father provided well. A healthy or an unhealthy environment is not so much a matter of time, finances, or availability—although these are important—but of how honest you could be in expressing your feelings and your perceptions.

If you grew up in a healthy family, your needs were met to a great degree. You were treated as an individual, and your individuality was nurtured through acknowledgment, recognition, and acceptance. Don Wegscheider in his book *If Only My Family Understood Me* describes the characteristics of a healthy family. If you were raised in a healthy family, you would have learned:

1. to negotiate with family members without fear of put-downs
2. to say yes or no without fearing rejection
3. to ask without demanding
4. confidence in the stability of relationships within the family
5. to show feelings of all kinds without fear of damaging or losing your relationships
6. to develop specific relationships with individuals in your family
7. confidence in the honesty of family members and in their trust of you
8. to celebrate, play, and have fun together.

If you grew up in a healthy family, you learned to accept your experiences and the sensations of your feelings as part of yourself. You learned that it's okay to acknowledge and express your thoughts, your needs, and, most importantly, your feelings. In this nurturing environment, like the seed under ideal circumstances, your real self and the unique gifts and talents found within it were nurtured and their expression encouraged.

Sounds pretty unrealistic, doesn't it? If you grew up in such a family, you probably wouldn't be reading this book right now. Most of us did not grow up in healthy families. We come from a variety of backgrounds, from families that were severely dysfunctional and from families that seemed perfectly normal, families in which there was no active addiction being practiced by any family member and no obvious abuse.

Your Place in the Family System

Until fairly recently people with psychological problems were treated as individuals. Then, about 25 years ago, therapists, realizing that symptoms that were alleviated by individual therapy recurred when the person returned to the family context, began working with the entire family unit. New approaches and concepts are still being developed in this exciting and rapidly growing field. Although the strategies that are used to treat families differ, the basic metaphor that underlies family therapy is the comparison of the family to a system or a process.

One of the images I use to explain the term *family system* is that of a mobile. Each piece in a mobile has its place in relationship to the others in a state of relative equilibrium. When the wind blows the mobile, all of the pieces shift yet return to the same positions. If you change the way one piece is balanced, the whole mobile shifts to compensate for the change. A family forms a similar system and is involved in the same process. Each member plays a role that is balanced with those of the others in a state of equilibrium. When one family member changes, the entire family must adjust.

Have you ever wondered why it is so hard to change your behavior? Perhaps you've had the experience of returning to visit your family and being surprised by how readily you shift back into a familiar role or an old way of behaving. You are part of a very powerful system that may resist your changing because it alters the balance of relationships and roles. Before you know it, you are acting like a child again.

One of my clients described the atmosphere he felt when he was around his

40

R E C L A I M I N G   Y O U R   S E L F

family in this way: "It's like going into an ether that affects how you act, think, and feel." Other clients have described the same experience as "like being in a swamp" or "being stuck in quicksand." The family system consists of a set of relationships in a state of equilibrium. When you reenter the system, the old state returns—it can function even despite a distance of thousands of miles.

I remember the experience of my client, Ralph, who had been working on his recovery program, which included individual therapy and Al-Anon meetings, for about nine months. Our exploration of his experiences within his family of origin was thorough, and he fully understood the impact these experiences had on him. When he decided to fly to Cleveland to visit his family at Christmas, he said, "Now that I'm in recovery, I can take care of myself and, most of all, be myself."

Because I knew how difficult such reunions can be, particularly during the holidays, when the family system seems to operate at its most intense pitch, I cautioned Ralph to set aside time for himself and locate some Al-Anon meetings he could attend. Although alcoholism was not a problem in his family, the Twelve-Step approach was very beneficial for him.

Ralph called me about three days after his return from Cleveland, asking to see me as soon as possible. He sounded anxious and edgy. When he entered my office, I was surprised by the strained and tired look on his face.

"It's crazy," he said abruptly, waving his hands in the air. "I went back there, and . . . my God, it's crazy!"

"What's crazy, Ralph?" I asked. He was breathing rapidly and looked like he might burst into tears at any moment.

"For the first couple of days I was in Cleveland," he said, "I did okay. I found an Al-Anon meeting and went to it, and it seemed to help. But then"—he paused and shook his head in amazement—"something happened. There I was, doing all the same old stuff—shutting down, arguing, siding with my dad against my mom, shouting at my mother. It got real crazy. I tried to tell them about codependence and recovery and"—he looked horrified—"they got mad at me for saying there was something wrong with our family." He shook his head again and sighed. "I feel like I'm back where I was nine months ago—confused, exhausted, and lonely."

When I asked what he had done for himself since his return, he said, "Nothing. I just go to work and come home. I feel so bad, so depressed about what happened."

Ralph and I spent the rest of the session exploring the ways he could resume his recovery program and find his own equilibrium again. As the session came to a close, he said, "You know, I think I finally understand that I can't change them. The only person I can change is me. I guess that's a valuable lesson to learn."

In my work as a therapist I often see my clients hesitate when we begin to explore family-of-origin issues. Some say they've already worked out their relationship with their families—they just don't see them or contact them. Others say they don't want "to dredge up the past," because they want to live in the present. Some say they see no point in looking at their families because they can't change what happened in the past anyway.

But those past events are still affecting you today. One of the pioneers of psychology, C. G. Jung, wrote: "The more intensely the family has stamped its character upon the child, the more the child [the adult child] will tend to feel and see its earlier miniature world again in the bigger world of adult life."

Observing Family Rules

Many family therapists have noticed that families seem to operate as if following a set of unwritten rules. As you read the lists of rules in this section, consider which ones were rules by which your family of origin abided.

Claudia Black, one of the pioneers of the ACOA movement, summarizes these rules most succinctly with this trio of injunctions: "Don't talk. Don't trust. Don't feel."

Merle A. Fossum and Marilyn J. Mason, in their book *Facing Shame: Families in Recovery*, describe the rules that occur in shame-bound families:

1. Control. Always be in control of all behavior and interaction.
2. Perfection. Always be "right." Always do the "right" thing.
3. Blame. If something doesn't happen as planned, blame someone (self or other).
4. Denial. Deny feelings, especially negative or vulnerable ones like anxiety, fear, loneliness, grief, rejection, need.
5. Unreliability. Don't expect reliability or constancy in relationships. Watch for the unpredictable.
6. Incompleteness. Don't bring transactions to completion or resolution.
7. No talk. Don't talk openly and directly about shameful, abusive, or compulsive behavior.
8. Disqualification. When disrespectful, shameful, abusive, or compulsive behavior occurs, disqualify it, deny it, or disguise it.

Wayne Kritsberg in *The Adult Children of Alcoholics Syndrome* condenses these rules into four: the rules of silence, isolation, denial, and rigidity.

The rule of *silence* means that certain things cannot be talked about. The family secret—alcoholism, perhaps, if there is a practicing alcoholic in the family, or gambling, or drug use—is protected. Sometimes the family secret is a secret of shame from the past. Silence puts distance between reality and the experience of it. The rule of silence is finally being broken by people who have experienced incest and physical abuse in childhood. Without the rule of silence these two damaging and abusive experiences may not have occurred.

The rule of *isolation* prevents family members from speaking about family matters to outsiders. "We don't air our dirty linen in public." "Blood is thicker than water." "We take care of our own; we don't need anybody else." "We don't want anybody to think we have problems, do we?" These mottoes prevent children from getting an outside or more objective perception of what is happening in the home. The rule of isolation also applies to relationships within the family. One of my clients expressed this with a powerful image: "Growing up, I had to make it on my own. Now my soul feels lost in a desert of self-reliance."

The rule of *denial* dictates that family members cannot admit that there are problems in the family. Addictive and compulsive behaviors are ignored. Anything that causes stress or imbalance in the family system is not recognized. Likewise feelings, particularly disturbing feelings such as anger and need and pain, cannot be acknowledged. Family member have to deal with such feelings alone and in silence.

It may seem paradoxical that dysfunctional families are both rigid and unpredictable, but the two are closely paired. *Rigidity* develops in response to unpredictability and translates in adults to a need for control. How do you deal with unsettling and upsetting events if you are unable to talk about them or resolve them? You must develop rules that guide your behavior, rules that are shared, implicitly, with other family members: "We've always done things this way." These rules become part of the structure of the family. Spontaneity disappears; family members are unable to act out of their genuine feelings. When something goes wrong, it's because the rules weren't followed, and blame can be assigned. At the same time, the rules imply that perfection is possible: everything would be just fine if everyone obeyed the rules or played his or her role properly.

All families have rules by which the family system is maintained. These rules, many of which you are probably not aware of, still affect you today. In recovery you will be examining the rules through which your family controlled the expressions of feelings and honest communication among family members. Developing new, healthy rules for yourself is one of the adventures of recovery.

Playing Your Role

Family therapists have also observed that children in dysfunctional families often adopt, or are assigned, roles to play. Every family is different, and in some families roles overlap somewhat. Still you may be able to recognize yourself in one or more of the roles described below. As we saw in the section on the family system, you may continue to play your childhood role even as an adult, particularly when you are around your family.

Family Hero

Usually the oldest child, the family hero takes over the responsibilities abdicated by the parents, working hard to maintain the image of the household and to shine forth to the outside world as an emblem of the normality of the family.

If you are the family hero, you may have surpassed the achievements of your parents in terms of schooling and work. You are so busy that you never have enough time to do all the things you have to do; you never have time to do things that please only you, which is okay with you since when you relax you feel guilty. When there's a crisis in the family, you're called to fix it. If someone in the family is too weak or too poor or too scared to carry out a task, you do it for that person. Despite the fact that you are always busy, however, you never feel you've done enough. And, although you get praise for your achievements, you begin to feel that you are valued only for your performance. One of my clients put it this way: "There was no room for me—only for the things I could do."

Caretaker

This role is similar to that of the family hero. Like the family hero, the caretaker always puts the needs of others first, feeling responsible for the happiness of others. If you are a caretaker, your friends always come to you to talk about their problems, but you never reveal your problems to them. You feel you must always be perfect; you are deeply ashamed of and try to conceal your feelings of weakness and doubt.

People who go into helping professions—for instance, therapists, social workers, and nurses—are often people who learned the role of caretaker in their family of origin. Caretakers are usually empathic people who are able to elicit deep self-disclosures from others. Unfortunately caretakers feel comfortable only when providing help to others. Because they are unable to express their own feelings of weakness and insecurity, they may not be able to tolerate similar feelings in others and may rush in to suggest solutions before all of the pain has been revealed. If, in addition, they prefer to avoid conflict, they may be unwilling to confront others and end up enabling addictions and codependent behavior.

Perfectionist

A similar role is played by the perfectionist. If you play the perfectionist role, you believe that everything should always work perfectly, other people should do what you know is best, and there's "a place for everything and everything in its place." Your main goal in life is being right. You get upset when you make a mistake or when things don't go according to your plans. Spontaneity is impossible for you. You'd rather follow a rigid schedule than have some unplanned event interrupt and disrupt your life.

Black Sheep

If you saw the movie *La Bamba*, then you saw a good illustration of two roles that often exist in dysfunctional families. Ritchie Valens was the family hero, living out his mother's dreams of ambition and prosperity, buying her a house so they could live like normal people, always being nice. His older brother—an alcoholic, a biker, a wife-beater, a disgrace, unable to hold a job—played the complementary role of the black sheep.

In the dysfunctional family there are real problems, but these problems can't be discussed. Blame for the problems of the family is focused and projected on whichever child adopts the role of the black sheep, or scapegoat. The black sheep acts out, is wild, runs away from home, flaunts the family's conventions. Like every role, this role has rewards and penalties for the child who adopts it.

The black sheep, the rebel, the scapegoat, the victim—there are only a few shades of distinction between these roles. It's easy for members of a dysfunctional family to focus their anger on the black sheep—"If he would only behave . . ."

—who thus becomes the scapegoat. And the child who accepts this responsibility, of personifying the family's disowned negative aspects, can quickly become the victim. The victim expects to be excluded or mistreated, and sure enough, this happens over and over again, in many different relationships and arenas, at work, in groups, in personal relationships with spouses or children.

Combine victimization with self-righteousness, and you get the martyr, who suffers for others. When the chicken is passed around the table, the martyr always takes the wing. If someone has to stay to answer the phone when everyone else goes out to lunch, the martyr will volunteer. Martyrs believe that life is suffering and start worrying when things go too smoothly.

Lost Child

Often a middle child, who can't compete with the high achievements of the family hero and doesn't wish to suffer the disapproval directed at the black sheep, the lost child simply withdraws and becomes invisible. The lost child is secretive and adept at not drawing attention. One of my clients described his childhood by saying "I felt I lived under fire, so I learned to live in secrecy, in my own foxhole." This may be the child whose nose is always buried in a book or who is constantly daydreaming.

If you were a lost child, you are used to being in the background, to being overlooked. You dress and behave in ways that will not attract attention. You feel acutely uncomfortable when the spotlight is on you. You deflect attention from yourself by giving credit to others.

Clown

Often a younger child, the clown gets by with humor, diverting attention from the serious problems of the family by acting silly. Or the child acts as the family mascot by being adorable and cute and lighthearted. Sometimes this role demands that the child be helpless, innocent, or naive, always in need of guidance from the other, more practical members of the family.

If you became familiar with this role as a child, you may continue the same behavior as an adult, cracking jokes when the atmosphere is thick with anxiety or diverting attention by performing. You may be very good at asking others for help, to the point where you need other people to perform the mundane tasks of life—fixing the car, balancing the checkbook, paying the rent.

* * *

No individual ever completely embodies any of these roles. Sometimes children switch roles or take up a role left behind by a departing sibling. Usually my clients can identify with two or three roles and can recognize those their siblings chose.

Children and adults in healthy families also adopt roles. We all play roles throughout our lives. In dysfunctional families, however, people tend to become equated with their roles. Behavior is orchestrated carefully to conceal painful secrets about the reality of the family. The rules of behavior are often unstated, and one of the rules is to keep the secret. It's much easier to maintain this deception if everyone has a clearly defined role. Whenever you have a question about how you should behave, you have only to glance at your script—"Oh, I'm the clown. I better start cracking jokes so no one notices that Dad is three hours late"—to find out how you should act. These roles provide a sense of identity and a formula for behavior that you can use to get your needs met—at least partially. Unfortunately, the better you learn your part, the more likely it is to persist in your adulthood.

Identifying Dysfunction

Often it is very difficult for adult children of dysfunctional families to identify the dysfunction within their family of origin. Remember that denial is one of the hallmarks of codependence. As a child you were trained to ignore the signs of problems and to repress your uncomfortable feelings about the reality of your family.

I remember my work with Roy, a 29-year-old accountant, whose four-year marriage was disintegrating. His worry was obvious throughout our first session. Both he and his wife, Sheila, a nurse, were committed to the marriage. But the way they argued frightened them.

After several sessions their relationship had stabilized somewhat and we were able to begin family-of-origin work to identify the patterns of intimacy and conflict that both brought to the marriage. Sheila readily acknowledged the difficulties with relating she had learned growing up in a strict and rigid Fundamentalist family. But Roy couldn't discern any problems in his family. According to him, they were all very nice and his childhood was ideal.

Both Roy and Sheila said that they saw little conflict between their parents, but Sheila was able to recognize that it existed. "I felt it and knew it was there," she said, "but we weren't allowed to talk about it." Roy was firm in his opinion that no one in his family ever experienced anger.

One afternoon, after about 10 sessions, they came in for their appointment, and I noticed that Roy was visibly shaken.

"I got a call from my dad this morning," he said. "My mother was just admitted to a drug treatment center." It was obvious he still had trouble believing what he had heard. "My dad said she's been on medications and tranquilizers for 20 years or so." He paused a moment, then shook his head and said with amazement, "No wonder our house was so peaceful!"

For Roy this information was liberating. With his view of his family shaken, he became more willing to really explore his childhood experiences.

For many of us identifying family dysfunctions and doing family-of-origin work is threatening and unwelcome. One client expressed his feelings this way: "Out of sight, out of mind." Not necessarily so. Your family had an impact on you, an impact that affects you throughout your life. Breaking the code of silence is the beginning of freedom and individual identity.

The Inner Child and the Adult Child

One of the major therapeutic concepts of the ACOA and codependence movements is the concept of the wounded or inner child. Although it is not a new concept, it has become an important tool in the healing and recovery process.

The inner child is that part of you that never grew up, because you had to suppress it. It may be the child who was abused but who learned to dissociate from the abuse. It may be the part of you that was never expressed because of your role; if you were the clown, your inner child might be sad or scared or hurting; if you played the role of the hero, your inner child might be needy and ashamed. Your inner child knows the feelings you've disowned, dismissed, or ignored.

The process of maturation is marked by a series of developmental stages. The progression is basically one through which we move from psychological dependency to psychological self-sufficiency. In order to fully make this transition, we need to be supported and coached. This means having an environment in which our observations, thoughts, and feelings are validated by people important to us. This validation allows us to experience ourselves as being in touch with reality and to develop a sense of mastery over our own lives. Unfortunately, most of us were not supported in this natural growing process. Thus, a part of us—our emotional part—never grew up. To be a mature adult means being aware of both thoughts and feelings and being capable of expressing these in a self-sufficient manner. The recovery plan in this book provides the tools and resources to be your own supportive coach in the emotional growth process that you did not experience as you matured physically.

At the same time the concept of the inner child has become important, the term *adult child* has become common. The adult child is exactly that: a person who has reached adulthood physically but has the emotional experiences and relational skills of a child.

This is what happens to the inner child of a codependent: that inner child gets left behind, is hidden, ignored, locked in a dark closet, while the codependent forges ahead, creating a self that will seem competent, capable, and mature to the outside world.

How Codependence Develops

We push away the feelings of the inner child, using the defensive behaviors we learned to protect ourselves as children. The feelings of the inner child are buried, yet these are the feelings that need to be healed if we are to recover from codependence.

In a passage in my journal I commented on the feeling of being alienated from my inner child: "I am afraid to be like a child—to be free, unchained and creative, to be in awe of life. I am bound up by my adult expectations and norms. This chained-up feeling, this fear, only forces me to do what others want, to be what others want. I want to be free."

Many people find it difficult to make contact with the inner child. But once they do, the recovery and healing process often progresses much more rapidly. The experience of one of my clients, Katherine, reveals the profound influence of this contact.

Katherine was a petite, 38-year-old woman who wore her blond hair in a mass of waves framing her fine-boned face. She had been sober for four years and had been involved in various forms of therapy. She was experiencing the kind of emptiness and despair I spoke about in Chapter 1. She contacted me after reading about codependence. She thought the theory of codependence provided her with an explanation of the source of these feelings and a way of healing her past.

After the first three sessions it became apparent that she had a sexual addiction. It had been disguised during the time she was drinking because she blamed alcohol when she woke up and found herself in bed with a stranger she had picked up at a bar the night before. But this pattern continued after she stopped drinking—only now she called it her need to be nurtured. This feeling came on her in the evenings.

"Sometimes I'm fine," she explained. "A good book or a TV show will keep me occupied, but other nights I feel sad and forlorn, and the later it gets, the worse I feel. Those are the times I call Bobby. I can't help it. We never talk. He just comes over, and we jump into bed, and for a little while I don't feel those terrible feelings."

I referred Katherine to Sexaholics Anonymous; I generally recommend the Twelve-Step programs as an adjunct to therapy. At the same time, we explored her childhood in our sessions and she realized that she had been sexually abused by her mother.

It was our 11th session, and Katherine told me that she had called Bobby the previous night because she couldn't handle being alone.

"Katherine, you know what you're doing to yourself," I said. "You have a network of people you can contact to help you."

She nodded grimly. "Yes," she said desperately, "but it's the only way I know to get away from it."

I was startled by her emphasis on the last word, but I also felt that something important was happening.

"You've never told me about it," I said. "What is this 'it'?"

She stared at me pensively, then blurted out, "It's the ball and chain." She twisted in her chair and looked back over her shoulder as if she would see a ball and chain on the floor behind her.

"Can you tell me more about it?" I asked.

"The ball is heavy," she said in a hollow voice, "and the chain is attached to my ankle."

I understood that whatever the ball and chain represented, it was significant. I asked her what it represented, and she shook her head mutely. I asked her how it got there, and she shrugged her shoulders.

"Can you cut it off?" I asked.

"No, I just try to stay away from it," she said quickly.

"Could we try an experiment to find out a little more about it?" I asked.

"Depends on what it is."

"Well, I'd like to create a ball and chain here in the office and have you walk around with it and see what it feels like."

"That sounds okay," she said.

Since I don't have a ball and chain in my office, I improvised one, using a pillow from one of the chairs that was fastened around the middle with the belt from my trench coat. Katherine tied the other end of the belt around her ankle and began walking around the office slowly, dragging the pillow behind her.

"What are you feeling?" I asked.

"I have to get away from it," she said in a lamenting voice. "I've got to get away from it." But she never looked back.

To amplify the heaviness of the ball, I told her I was going to hold on to the belt. She nodded in agreement, then struggled to move forward as I held the belt.

"This is just what it feels like," she said. Her arms were stretched out on either side of her, thrashing the air in her attempt to move forward. "I feel stuck. I've got to get away from it."

I asked her to turn and look back and tell me what the ball and chain represented. She did. Nothing.

"I can't see anything," she said. "I just know I have to get away from it."

I asked her if she was willing to trade places, to become the ball and chain. She agreed, and we traded places. Now the belt was fastened to my ankle and she held the other end, preventing me from moving away from her.

As I struggled to move my leg, I asked Katherine, "Why are you holding me like a ball and chain?"

She burst into tears and cried out: "I need you! I need you! Don't ignore me." Tears poured down her cheeks, and she sat on the floor, her arms hugging the pillow, sobbing.

"Who are you?" I asked gently.

"I'm scared and sad," she said. Her voice was the whimper of a child.

A few moments passed, and then Katherine lifted her head and looked at me with eyes still filled with tears and a look of astonishment.

"It's me as a little girl," she said. "I've been running away from the hurt little girl in me. I never knew that! I never knew that."

Tears continued to run down her cheeks, and she clasped the pillow to her chest and hugged it close, as a mother would hold an injured child.

After some time had passed, we discussed what had happened and how Katherine could begin to care for her wounded inner child.

The next week, when she came into my office, she looked markedly different. Her eyes were clear, and she met my gaze directly.

"I know I'm not all fixed," she said with excitement, "but so much has changed in just one week. I know what I've been doing all along. I've been treating my little child just the same way my mother treated me!"

She had been ignoring her inner child's sadness and fear and using her addictive sexual relationship with Bobby to violate the frightened child within just as her mother had violated her body when she was a child. Now that she understood this, she could choose to protect the little girl within from abuse. It would require a great deal of work, giving little Katherine the care she needed, but it would be a start toward healing the wounds of her childhood.

As Katherine discovered, we often treat our inner children the same way our parents treated us. If we were ignored, dismissed, abused, rejected, criticized severely, or discounted, we tend to treat our inner child in exactly the same way.

Often the experience of this inner child is captured only in memories or trapped behind persistent feelings or psychosomatic pain, such as a lump in the throat. The gradual disclosure of the inner child's trauma will permit release and result in new ways of being and new feelings for the adult.

Children who grow up in dysfunctional families are not allowed to grow up emotionally or are not taught how to do so. Although they may develop normally toward intellectual and physical maturity, their emotional life is stunted. When intellectual and physical maturity exceed emotional growth, the inner child, who is so immature, must be ignored and repressed. But the grief of the inner child never goes away. It is carried as a legacy that calls out to be healed.

In the next chapter you'll see how your childhood experiences are the root of the vicious cycle of codependence and how the process of recovery can free you from that vicious cycle.

4
. . . .

The Road to Recovery

ONE OF MY CLIENTS SAID to me, "I've always been on top of things, but there is a self-destructive part of me that I try to run from and hide from others. It's a part of me that keeps me stuck doing things that don't make me feel better, but I keep on doing them. Why?"

Another client described his response to situations as if he were a computer. "It's like I'm hard-wired or have a cassette inside of me that tells me what to do. I really wonder sometimes if I have any choice about what I say or do. It seems completely automatic."

Both of these individuals were describing the effects of the repetitive and self-fulfilling cycle of codependence. Understanding how the cycle works will help you move along the road into recovery.

Codependence begins with childhood experiences. For various important reasons—reasons that differ depending on the circumstances in your family of origin—you start covering up and denying feelings. You develop beliefs, self-messages, and behaviors to help you avoid your feelings. Those beliefs and self-messages are lived out and reinforced by life experiences, becoming self-fulfilling prophecies.

As an adult you continue to function in many of the same ways you adopted as a child. Your patterns of behavior become more strongly rooted as they are repeated again and again. In effect you re-create your childhood experiences by using your old patterns and reactions to avoid uncomfortable feelings. No matter how diligently you try to change your thoughts and beliefs, the underlying conflict and buried feelings still resonate within.

In Chapter 1, I made the point that experiencing your feelings was the key to being yourself, to changing and growing as a person. You will see in the first half of this chapter why this is so. The road to recovery involves deep and lasting change at the foundation of beliefs and self-messages—the buried feelings of childhood.

The following examples tell the stories of three individuals who were able to identify the feelings that were at the roots of their codependence during recovery.

When Will I Be Enough?

Jenny is a 37-year-old sales representative for a printing company. She was married once and, since her divorce four years ago, has had two significant but painful relationships. Jenny first learned of codependence when a friend suggested she attend a Co-Dependents Anonymous meeting (you'll hear more about this organization later).

"My friend just straight out asked me, 'Why do you always apologize for everything as if it were your fault?' She told me I always seemed to be blaming myself for everything that went wrong. I realized that she was right even though I didn't like to hear it."

After several months of attending meetings, Jenny began to recognize the origins of her codependence and how it dramatically affected her life. Her parents were social conformists. They insisted that she always do everything according to what other people expected. It didn't matter how Jenny felt or what she wanted. It was more important to please other people by behaving in socially appropriate ways. She remembered huge battles with her mother over what she wore, how she fixed her hair, whom she chose as friends, whether or not she said hello to the right people after church on Sunday.

"There was really no room for me to be me. They praised me only when I acted the way they thought I should act," Jenny said. She grew up in constant fear of feeling inadequate or ashamed, the primary feeling experiences of her childhood. To avoid these painful feelings she naturally developed certain self-messages and behaviors, and the cycle of codependence began.

Childhood Experiences

"My parents were always ridiculing me, but in very subtle ways. It seemed like caring. They would say things like 'We only want what's best for you,' but they were constantly undermining my self-confidence by telling me that they knew how to do things right and I didn't. I never felt like I could do anything right, and I still don't at age 37. There's always this feeling inside me that I'll never be good enough."

Social conformity

These experiences created **feelings** for young Jenny:

Inadequacy, shame, hurt, guilt

Because these feelings couldn't be expressed, Jenny pushed away her feelings. She describes developing "a steel wall against their words."

Yet these feelings and experiences had an impact on Jenny, as seen in the **beliefs**, **behaviors**, and **self-messages** she developed:

Some of Jenny's **beliefs:**
"No matter what I do, it's never enough."
"People love you only when you do things right."
"People like you only when you do what they want you to do."

Some of Jenny's **self-messages:**
"I have to work hard to be loved."
"I have to look like I'm in control."
"I'm tough; what people say won't hurt me."

Behaviors:
The hero role
The nice girl
Controlling

Adult Experiences

As an adult, still trying to avoid those painful feelings from childhood, Jenny tried to prove to herself and others that she was adequate. "I've really tried to control everything in my life and make it perfect," she said. "I get uptight if I'm just five minutes late. I'm always nice and polite, and I get a lot of things done to try to get people to admire and respect me."

While trying to escape from her feelings and fears, Jenny built up a tough steel wall that shut out not just her parents but also her own feelings. As you will see in the next three chapters, this way of dealing with bad feelings only makes things worse.

Keep Them Happy

Warren had begun focusing on other people from an early age. "I learned as a child how to please people and make them like me. When I was in my twenties, I read the book *How to Win Friends and Influence People* over and over again. I practiced using the suggestions in it to convince people to like me. What I realize now is that I was really afraid of people and of conflict.

"I try to stay out of other people's way. I just can't say no or create any trouble, even when someone does something that hurts me. It's too scary."

Warren is now 42 years old and works as an engineer for an airplane maintenance crew. He was married once and now lives with his girlfriend. He wants to get married again, but he's afraid of making the same mistakes he made in his first marriage. With his first wife Warren withdrew or covered up his feelings at any sign of conflict. Although he always gave in, he resented the fact that his wife controlled the relationship. He grew to believe that she didn't care about him because she never guessed how bad he was feeling. The relationship died slowly. The pain Warren felt after his wife left compelled him to seek out counseling. He realizes now that he wants to be able to deal with conflict directly and honestly. Warren believes that working on his codependence is the most important contribution he can make to the success of a second marriage.

Childhood Experiences

Warren was raised in an alcoholic and physically abusive home. He has vivid memories of his father coming home drunk and lining up the kids to decide who needed to "get a whipping for being bad." This situation went on throughout his childhood and early adolescence. Warren's first memory was of a beating he received one day because he started crying after being told he couldn't go out and play.

**Physical abuse,
alcoholism,
high stress,
anxiety**

These experiences created many **feelings** for Warren:

Terror, anxiety, fear, hurt, anger

Warren adopted certain **beliefs, behaviors,** and **self-messages** in response to these feelings and circumstances:

Beliefs:

"Other people have power over me."

"Doing good things for people and being good makes them happy."

"The world is a dangerous place."

Self-messages:

"I have to please people to be safe."

"If I get too close to people, I'll be hurt."

"Always be in control."

Behaviors:

Controlling

People pleasing

The victim role

Adult Experiences

For Warren the repeating cycle of codependence had its roots in the life-threatening experiences of childhood. To avoid conflict, he tried to maintain control of people. At any sign of conflict he felt the same fear he felt as a little boy, the fear that he might die. And he employed the same defenses he used in his childhood: he tried to placate the person who was angry or leave the scene of the conflict.

Do Anything You Want, But Don't Leave Me

At age 29 Gene has just celebrated his fifth anniversary in Alcoholics Anonymous. He began drinking at age 12 "to keep up with friends and feel like part of a group" and hit the bottom at age 24. He feels grateful to AA for helping him achieve five clean and sober years. Still Gene is concerned about his repeated failures in relationships and has begun exploring his codependence.

"Since I've been working on my codependence, I've really seen how needy and dependent I have been with women. Once I get in a relationship, I'm like a fly on flypaper. I get possessive and demanding, but I try not to let the woman know how desperate I'm feeling. I feel like I would do practically anything to keep her from leaving me."

Childhood Experiences

Gene grew up in what he calls "a good family." "We didn't fight and my parents never argued. They did have some strict rules about things. We weren't supposed to be sad or angry. I remember when my grandma died when I was nine. My mom told me that I should be happy because Grandma was in Heaven. But I felt really sad."

Gene recalls a threat his mother used a lot. She would tell him: "If you don't stop doing that, I'm going to give you away!" Gene remembers how he felt when she said that: "She seemed so serious. I would get really scared. Then, when I was about 12, I stopped believing her because she never did it. That was about the same time I started drinking."

Emotional oppression, control, rigidity, denial of feelings

These experiences created strong **feelings** for Gene:

Gene developed certain **beliefs, behaviors,** and **self-messages** as a result of these experiences:

Fear, anxiety, confusion, rejection, abandonment

Beliefs:
  "Feelings don't matter."
  "Be nice or pay a price."
  "People will leave you if you tell them how you feel."
  "If people don't like something you do, they leave you."

Self-messages:
  "What I feel doesn't matter."
  "I have to keep a stiff upper lip."
  "It's important always to be nice."

Behaviors:
  Controlling
  The nice guy
  Manipulation

Adult Experiences

Gene's alcoholism from age 12 to 24 helped him avoid his feelings of abandonment and rejection. When he began recovering from alcoholism, he used relationships as another way to avoid his feelings. When he started looking at his codependence, he saw that some of his problems had their roots in the terror of that little boy who thought his mother was going to give him away. "I've managed to stay away from the hurt and loneliness inside me," said Gene, "but my running away only made it worse. Now I'm beginning to see what I've been doing to myself. Now I know what my neediness is all about."

The Vicious Cycle

In the section above you saw how three different people developed ways of dealing with uncomfortable feelings they experienced as children. Jenny worked hard, Warren practiced pleasing other people, and Gene drank. In addition, all of them used controlling behavior, one of the predominant yet subtle characteristics of codependence. These defenses were developed to protect them from reexperiencing those old painful feelings. When Gene stopped drinking, he quickly came up with a new behavior—obsessive attachments to women—to protect himself from feeling those old feelings.

The beliefs developed as a result of the painful experiences of childhood become self-fulfilling prophecies. For example, Jenny believes that people like her only when she does what they want her to do. Whenever somebody around her rejects her or becomes displeased, she looks for the reason in her own behavior. She invariably finds something she did wrong because she's looking for it. Thus her belief that she must behave correctly all the time is reinforced.

Codependents use defensive behavior and beliefs to protect themselves from the feelings of the past and from situations or relationships in the present that might evoke similar feelings. Jenny has to keep working hard or she'll feel inadequate. Gene feels desperate about holding on to a romantic relationship because if the woman leaves him he will feel those horrible feelings he experienced as a young boy: rejection, abandonment, and fear. When someone gets angry around Warren, he immediately begins placating the person because he wants to avoid reexperiencing the terror he felt as a child when his father was in a rage.

Unfortunately these behaviors don't work. Jenny still feels inadequate, as evidenced by her constant apologizing. Gene is haunted by fear of rejection. Warren is terrified of anger. The vicious cycle of codependence keeps them locked in a self-perpetuating, unhealthy way of living as shown in the diagram below:

Codependence begins with:

CHILDHOOD EXPERIENCES—experiences, like those shown in the box below, that are painful or confusing.

> High stress, rigid controls over emotional expression, denial of reality, high tension, chemical dependency or other addictions, physical abuse, sexual abuse, rigid attitudes, shaming, religious indoctrination and control.

Childhood experiences lead to:

FEELINGS—the felt experiences that you did not express, that had to be repressed, that were not allowed.

> ashamed, hurt, afraid, anxious, fearful, angry, terrified, rejected, confused, resentful, disappointed, abandoned, sad, inadequate, helpless, dumb, abnormal

Feelings lead to:

BELIEFS—the attitudes and opinions you developed about the world, other people, your own life, and who you are.

> "People can't be trusted."
> "Life is a struggle."
> "The world is a cruel place."
> "Powerful people are dangerous."
> "Men/Women will never listen to me."
> "Life is against me. My needs are never met."

> "When you let people get close, they abandon you."
> "Expressing feelings is wrong."
> "When you're perfect, you're okay."
> "If you want to be loved, don't tell anyone how you feel."
> "When people are mad at you, it's okay for them to hit you."
> "To be accepted, you have to be nice."
> "People will always let you down."
> "Feelings don't matter."
> "People are lazy."
> "You can't control what happens to you."
> "Never be too happy, because it doesn't last."
> "Needing something is selfish and bad."

Beliefs lead to:

SELF-MESSAGES—what you tell yourself about your own capacities, skills, personal worth, etc.

> "I am not capable. I am dumb. I can't do it."
> "I'm a loser."
> "I have to be quiet."
> "I can't be me. I have to hide my _____ ."
> "I have to help everybody."
> "I have to be happy."
> "I am not lovable."
> "I can't share my feelings."
> "I am helpless to change my life."
> "I need to _____ ."
> "I am at fault. I don't deserve happiness."
> "I better not to be too (happy, successful, etc.)."
> "I'm selfish if I take care of my needs."
> "I don't count."

ROLES AND MASKS—behaviors you assume that either hide or confirm your self-messages:

> Hero, Caretaker, Rescuer, Enabler, People Pleaser, Black Sheep, Clown Mascot, Rebel

As you live in the world, you inevitably encounter:

LIFE EXPERIENCES—encounters with a world of changes, choice, other people, etc.

> Rejection, problems with intimacy, relationship ends, conflict, success-failure syndrome

Life experiences lead to:

FEELINGS—the feelings you have as a result of your life experiences, which are denied and repressed.

> ashamed, hurt, afraid, anxious, fearful, angry, terrified, rejected, confused, resentful, disappointed, abandoned, sad, inadequate, helpless, dumb, abnormal

The denial and repression of these feelings supports and reinforces your childhood experiences and original beliefs and self-messages. Through the cycle of codependence you treat yourself the same way you were treated as a child.

There is only one way out: feeling the feelings that were originally denied. This is the paradox of feeling: you must feel those feelings to feel better.

I know many people who've tried to feel better by reframing their beliefs or giving themselves new self-messages. I tried those things, too. But will telling yourself "I am fine just the way I am" change your behavior? I don't think it will, even superficially. You've built an entire system of defenses on top of those old feelings. Changing the shape of the structure doesn't affect the feeling that is the foundation.

Until you bring that feeling to light, you can't change the choices you made and beliefs you developed in response to those feelings.

The progression described above depicts the degenerative process of codependence. Codependence, which results from focusing on the needs of others or controlling others to avoid feelings, has an adverse effect on a person's physical, mental, and spiritual well-being.

You *can* intervene in this self-destructive and degenerative process. That's what this book is all about—supporting you as you intervene in the vicious cycle of codependence. The choice to change is a choice to grow.

The Choice to Change

Why do this? Why start on the road to recovery? The promise of feeling better is tantalizing, but the prospect of the work to be done and the pain to be endured can be daunting.

I have always been interested in the reasons people choose to change, to take responsibility for their own lives and their own personal growth. What factors influence a person to undergo the painful process of personal transformation? I'll share with you my own experiences and the stories of others in the pages that follow.

Usually the journey begins with the realization that life just isn't working, despite all the defenses that have been created and maintained, despite determined willpower to succeed, despite all external signs of success and achievement. A misery sets in that is unique for each individual.

Perhaps a death, divorce, job loss, physical or mental illness, or another mental traumatic event brings a person face to face with the pain inside. For some it's the sobering realization of a chemical addiction. For others it's the hurt of repeated failures in relationships. For those who are fortunate these experiences bring an awareness of the discomfort deep within. They feel something inside calling out for recognition and expression. Or they sense an inner emptiness and despair.

Few people readily admit that their life isn't working. In giving up your attitudes and ways of being and acting in the world, you surrender the defenses you developed to survive. This means changing yourself without a clear sense of what will take its place.

The motivation that compels you to risk this radical change doesn't come from outside. It comes only from within. No one changes for something or someone else.

Real change happens only when you are ready to take responsibility for your own life and its expression.

When Things Fall Apart

The cycle of growth begins when things fall apart. This disintegration happens internally at first and perhaps invisibly. But at some point in time it is reflected in the outside world. Sometimes suddenly, sometimes gradually, you realize that life just isn't working despite the tremendous effort that you've put into keeping things together. These are some of the warning signs that signal this failure: a series of job losses, the dissolution of a significant relationship, physical problems such as chronic or serious illness, and mental and emotional disorders like depression and anxiety. All the props and defenses you've used to keep things together crumble, and you face the stark reality: to continue to live in the same way would be miserable and perhaps disastrous.

It took a dramatic and almost total disintegration of my life before I was able to make a total commitment to change. Some of us have to make this choice several times before we really choose to heal ourselves.

For three years I had been pursuing a recovery program (or so I thought), but I wasn't satisfied with the changes I had made. For one thing, I was involved in an emotional roller coaster of a relationship. So I decided to try a geographical solution to my problems: I moved halfway across the country. I'm amused now when I think of the events that transpired within the next 18 months, events that led me to the bottom. But it wasn't very funny then. In fact I was miserable. I found I couldn't escape my problems just by moving. Instead they got worse—drastically.

I moved back across country and got reinvolved in the same relationship, only this time it was more problematic and more painful than before I had left. The denial and dishonesty inherent in the relationship began to taint all the areas of my life. Eventually I hit bottom. I felt what Lorie Dwinell, an expert on the grief process and adult children of alcoholics, describes as "the bankruptcy of will-power." Bankruptcy was a good metaphor for my entire life. I was bankrupt in every way—financially, morally, spiritually, emotionally, and physically. I was living dishonestly, denying my true feelings, refusing to look at reality, anesthetizing myself with lots of sex and fantasies of change. I even started smoking a pipe: it helped me avoid my feelings. After hitting the bottom, I wallowed there in a swamp of frustration and helplessness for several weeks. I can recall a very vivid scene that symbolizes this bottom for me. I needed a place to stay during this period of transition and my only option was to stay with a friend. I ended up sleeping on my futon beside his washer and dryer in his basement. All my degrees, training, and workshops had not prepared me for the feelings of loneliness, despair, and abandonment I felt. I wanted out of my present pain, but I didn't want to experience the pain I knew was within me or the pain of changing.

Then I realized that I did have a choice. I could continue to live in pain or decide to change. But this sense of choice faded. It was a strange and unsettling experience. For a month or so I wavered back and forth between knowing and not knowing, deciding to change and deciding to continue as I was. This feeling of uncertainty was just as terrible as the pain I had felt before. It eased only gradually as I recognized that the choice was really between living my own life or dying a slow death.

The choice may seem obvious, but many people choose a slow death. What do I mean by a slow death? For me it meant denying my inner reality and suppressing my feelings of anxiety and fear by anesthetizing myself with work, fantasy, sex, tobacco, alcohol, and prescription medication. Or I could choose life, which meant experiencing and healing my emotional pain and giving up my fear of being alone, of being rejected, of "hurting" other people. I'm glad I chose life.

Breaking Up Is Hard to Do

For many individuals the loss of a significant relationship is the event that precipitates change. Sometimes it brings to light a repeated pattern, a recurring failure at intimacy. At the same time it can reactivate old fears of being alone, being abandoned, being unloved. Although it's painful, it's often a turning point.

My client Karl was a good example of a codependent who used the pain of loss as an opportunity for transformation.

"I can't keep doing this to myself," said Karl emphatically during our second session together. The breakup of a relationship coupled with chronic health problems (intestinal pain, headaches, and fatigue) had brought him to the brink of despair. When he mentioned to a friend that he was having thoughts of suicide, she recommended that he contact me.

After an initial phone evaluation during which I determined that suicide wasn't an imminent danger, I set up an appointment with Karl. During our first session I learned more about him. He was a 39-year-old restaurant manager with a history of abusive relationships, chronic headaches, and poor eating habits—he practically lived on coffee. His girlfriends typically treated him badly, comparing him unfavorably to other men, ignoring him at parties, and generally treating him as if he didn't matter. He was feeling depressed because his most recent girlfriend, Julie, had announced three weeks earlier that she didn't want to see him anymore.

It was during our second session that Karl announced, "I can't keep doing this to myself." Then his eyes filled with tears, and he buried his face in his hands and sobbed silently for a few minutes.

"You're in a lot of pain," I acknowledged when he looked up at me, his face still wet with tears.

Karl nodded and said, "Something has to change. Julie and I broke up four weeks ago, and I feel like I'm dying inside without her. I just want to go out and find someone else to take her place."

"What happens if you don't?" I asked.

"I don't know," Karl replied. "I've always done that before."

"How many times have you done this?"

Karl sat quietly for a few minutes, staring at the floor. I noticed that his hands were tightening into fists. When he spoke, his voice was tense and strained.

"I've done that more times than I can count," he said. "Since my marriage broke up 10 years ago, I've had countless affairs and women. I've never been without a woman."

I asked him if he was aware of his tension, of how his hands were clenched into fists, and shared my perception that he looked as if he wanted to attack something.

"That's right!" he said with some intensity. "I feel like I want to tear something apart, but I don't know what it is."

"How long have you felt this anger?" I asked.

"I don't know," he said. "I feel like this only when I'm not in a relationship."

We sat and looked at each other for a few minutes. Finally I spoke: "Karl, I think you have a choice here. You seem to have some strong and painful feelings that you're able to cover up by immediately getting involved with someone else."

Karl sighed. "It's true," he admitted. "I feel like I'm chasing after something I can never quite get or like I'm running away from something. It's like being on one of those treadmills, the ones they use for mice, constantly spinning but going nowhere. Something has to change or I'll go crazy."

I told Karl that he could get off the treadmill, but it meant breaking his usual pattern and accepting the feelings he wanted to run away from.

Karl made the choice to change. Although he was successful in his work, the painful and repeated failures of his personal relationships and his increasing fear about the implications of his health problems motivated him to change. He began attending Co-Dependents Anonymous meetings and continued with individual counseling too. He learned how to spend more time alone and to acknowledge his feeling of loneliness, one of the feelings he had been avoiding.

The loss of a significant love relationship is not the only type of relationship loss that can trigger change. Difficulty relating to a child, the ending of an important friendship or repeated failures at friendship, and recurring unpleasant experiences with co-workers can also be motivators of change. But because intimacy is both so desired and so difficult for people who try to avoid feelings, the pain of failure in an intimate relationship is more often the crisis that stimulates change.

When two people enter into a relationship, they bring their families with them. If either was raised in an unhealthy family, he or she brings along the unsatisfying ways of relating learned in childhood. The struggle for love and acceptance goes on following the same patterns. Margaret and Jordan Paul in the title of their book *Do I Have to Give Up Me to Be Loved by You?* summarize the dilemma of a relationship in which both partners believe they must give up their true selves and pretend to be someone else to be loved. Such a relationship is laced with self-sacrifice, denial, need for control, fear, and defensive patterns.

Perhaps you recognize your relationship or your pattern in relationships as unhealthy. You can choose to continue as you have been, knowing, as you alone know so well, the price you are paying. Or you can choose to change. You probably feel that you will lose an important relationship or experience terrible loneliness if you make a change, and this may be true. What's on the other side of your willingness to risk loss, however, is the ability for a truly mature and intimate union with another.

As you work your recovery program that is provided in Part Three you will develop a greater sense of self-sufficiency and emotional maturity. These two benefits of recovery will enable you to develop new, healthy relationships in which the fear of loss is not nearly so threatening. The loneliness that you may experience during recovery is due, to a great degree, to the changes you are making and what you are leaving behind. However, these changes will support you in creating relationships that are truly affirming of you.

Living in Quiet Desperation

Both the circumstances described above—things falling apart and the loss of a significant relationship—can be fairly dramatic heralds of the need to change. Less dramatic, but perhaps more profound, is the realization of inner pain.

Many people live what Thoreau describes as "lives of quiet desperation." If you are one of them, you know something's wrong, something's missing. You know you're scared and confused. You sense that there should be something more to life. You move quietly through your days, doing your duty, being nice to other people, performing competently at your job and in your relationships. Inside you are crying. Occasionally the tears may turn to explosive anger.

Carol was one of my clients who recognized the need to change because of her deep and bitter dissatisfaction with her life. A marketing representative, single and in her early thirties, Carol attended one of my workshops on codependence and called me several weeks later requesting an appointment. She wanted to come in for an assessment and some help in making a few decisions.

Within a few minutes after our session started Carol's anger came pouring out. "I've always done what other people wanted me to do," she declared, "but it's a sham or an illusion, because I'm not happy. I'm pissed!"

She sat on the edge of her chair, her hands clenched as she described the life she had created to make herself look good and keep up a front.

"You've forged quite a life for yourself, Carol," I observed.

"I've forged a forgery!" she exclaimed. "And I won't do it anymore. I may not know what normal is, but I know what it isn't. I had to be a pretty little 'thing' all the time for my dad. I couldn't be me. And even though he's dead, I still keep doing the same thing. I hate what he did to me."

"What do *you* want to do?" I asked, emphasizing the word to make the point that she did have a choice.

"You know, from what I heard you say about codependence and what I've read, I know I'm a real people pleaser. But all along I've been losing touch with me. That's what I want! Me!"

"How do you know you're out of touch with yourself?" I asked.

Carol didn't have to pause to think about this. Her words burst out in rapid fire: "Because life wasn't meant to feel like this. I'm always struggling, always feeling worried inside, always trying to figure everything out. I'm miserable."

Carol looked at me, took a deep breath, and then began to cry. She was beginning to feel the pain that lurked behind her life of quiet desperation.

Another client, the adult child of an alcoholic, told me: "By the time I was 30 I was feeling so unnatural—emotionally, socially, spiritually, in my career—that it was too painful to ignore."

The pain is always there, no matter how much you try to cover it up with compulsive work, intense but unsatisfying relationships, and other addictions. It was this pain—the pain of being out of touch with my reality and my feelings—that I was attempting to avoid for most of my adult life. It was the pain that Karl was fleeing when he rushed into a new relationship as soon as the current one ended. It is this pain that others try to drown with alcohol and drugs.

After Sobriety

For some people the choice to change is made after experiencing a period of recovery from addiction. One of my clients, Wayne, a 27-year-old graduate student, had been involved in Alcoholics Anonymous for three years. He was sober but not better. As he said, "I'm in the program, but after three years of sobriety my life isn't any better. I don't drink. But my relationships suck, and I'm not as happy inside as I know I can be." Giving up the substance he used to deal with his inner pain didn't release the pain.

Recovery from an addiction does not always take care of the problems that prompted the addiction. Sometimes giving up an addiction that has been used for emotional numbing makes the underlying pain clearer.

Starting Down the Road to Recovery

Although you may sense there is something better ahead when you make the choice to change, you are really venturing on a path that leads directly into the unknown. You don't *know* what lies ahead. There is no promise of success or guarantee of happiness. You must rely on your faith that something better exists.

Most of us don't undertake this journey lightly. We are driven to it. But the choice to change is always ours. As one of my clients said during our first session, "I don't want to do this. But I have to. And I'm going to. I've used everything I could to try to control my life, avoid pain, find joy. Nothing works. Well, it's time to change my ways—because, though I hate to admit it, they don't work. So, what do I do now?"

It's never too late to begin the adventure of recovery. I recall a 65-year-old woman who came up to me after one of the codependence workshops I lead. During these workshops 40 or 50 people spend a day taking a good hard look at codependence in their lives. What happened in their families? What were the addictive and dysfunctional processes? How could they reclaim some of what they lost or buried?

She had been rather quiet during the workshop, so when she looked me straight in the eye with an expression of defiance, I wasn't sure what was going to happen.

"You know something?" she said. "For years I've wondered why I always have to put on my best face at church. I'm always happy, always smiling. I've never questioned it. It was just the way it was and what you're supposed to do. Well, I'm tired of it—faking a smile when I don't even want to be there. I don't know if it's too late, but I'm not going to do it anymore. I want to be real."

She nodded, satisfied with herself, and set off across the room with a determined stride. She was just beginning to explore her own feelings and interests and needs, beginning the exciting journey of recovery.

Recovery from codependence *is* possible. In fact I believe it's the most important and challenging activity anyone can undertake in life, for it is the process of recovering and reclaiming life. The degenerative effects of codependence can be reversed and redirected into wholeness. Balance and integrity can be restored. It is ultimately the choice we make, the prize we claim, to live in truth to ourselves.

Recovery as Process

Since I use the word *process* frequently in this book, I invite you to consider the meaning of the word while reading this dictionary definition:

> a natural, progressively continuing development marked by a series of gradual changes that succeed one another in a relatively fixed way and lead toward a particular result or end.

I'd like to share my understanding of the recovery process by examining more closely the different components of that definition.

First, recovery is a **natural** process. Think about what happens when you cut yourself. First you feel pain, a signal that sets in motion protective mechanisms. Then the wound is cleansed by the flow of blood. White blood cells rush in to protect you from infection. A scab may form to protect the cut during healing. All of this occurs naturally.

A similar process occurs when you are ill. The more you cooperate with and support the natural healing process, the faster your recovery.

The natural process of recovery involves feeling the pain and healing the wounds of the past. To do so you must create an atmosphere that fosters health, giving up substances and behaviors that are unhealthy and giving yourself the time and compassion necessary for healing.

Recovery **continues progressively** over time. It is not instantaneous. How long does it take? It's different for everyone. Once you start a recovery program, you will gradually notice changes in your self and your life. True recovery is a lifelong process. If you want to become the self you were created to be, you will commit yourself to an ongoing process and live your life one day at a time.

The recovery process is **marked by a series of gradual changes.** There isn't necessarily a moment when you can say "Aha, I'm cured!" Most likely you won't even notice your progress except by comparison when you look back at what you thought or how you reacted to people or situations several months earlier.

Recovery occurs in a **relatively predictable fashion**, which is reassuring since you thus have some information about what lies ahead.

During recovery you move from a state of dis-ease to a state of health. The word *health* is derived from the same root word as *whole*. If you are going to recover and experience health, the process must be holistic and take into account the whole of your being.

Plato knew the wisdom of this when he said, "The great error in the treatment of the human body is that physicians are ignorant of the whole. For the part can never be well unless the whole is well."

As you will see in Part Two, I have developed a framework that will help you understand the effects of avoiding feelings. This simple framework focuses on three dimensions of being: physical, mental, and spiritual. It provides a way of understanding what the pain of healing is all about, how you sabotage yourself, and where the roots of your true self are buried.

I believe that recovery is an integrated process of physical and mental healing coupled with reclaiming your inner self and spirituality, as shown in this equation:

Recovery = (healing your mind + body) + reclaiming your inner self

Reclaiming the inner self brings about a spiritual transformation. This does not mean a religious conversion but a deeper and more loving acceptance of one's self.

Edward Hays, a priest and mystical storyteller, describes the significance of this in his book of stories *The Ethiopian Tattoo Shop*: "To find oneself is to find the real self, the divinity dwelling deep within. . . . To choose to be me is the most redemptive and revolutionary act anyone can perform."

Recovery into Wholeness

The more informed you are about the process of recovery, the better prepared you will be for the experiences you will encounter.

A program of recovery involves a lot of hard inner work. It takes courage to face the dark side of your self, your internal demons—your anger, your fear, your resentments, your controlling behavior. You may have to face the wrath of family members or a partner as you differentiate yourself from the old system. You may have to say farewell to friendships that are no longer life-giving. You may have to give up a job that is no longer fulfilling. Perhaps the most frightening aspect of recovery is the feeling of psychic death: you may have to die to the self you now know.

Clients often admit that dying to the self (or identity they've created) is something they understand the least. Most would give up friendships that aren't healthy or face the wrath of family members if it meant developing a strong sense of self. But the death of the identity they have known is daunting. You will more fully understand the willingness to die to yourself as you experience the gift of rebirth that is part of recovery. Remember, the self that is dying is the one you have created to please others. The self that comes to the surface in recovery is the one that has been in you all along. The recovery program in Part Three will support you as this old, unreal self dies and the rebirth of the new (but always present) self unfolds. This rebirth, like the shedding of an old skin, will reveal to you the richness of your true inner self.

Part Two provides a framework for codependence that forms the foundation for the recovery program described in Chapters 8 through 12. After reading Chapters 5, 6, and 7 you will fully understand the price you are paying for your codependence and the prize awaiting you in recovery.

PART TWO

· · · · · · · ·

The Impact of Codependence on the Three Dimensions of Being

─────────

5

· · · · · · ·

How Codependence Affects You Physically

THE PHYSICAL DIMENSION is the most tangible of the dimensions of being. Through your body you experience life and all the pleasure and pain associated with it. Through your senses you perceive the world. With your body you express yourself in the outer world.

Your body acts as a conductor for information about the environment and situations in which you find yourself. This information is interpreted by your mind; almost simultaneously, your perceptions evoke feelings. These feelings are tangible realities experienced through the medium of your body. Experts estimate that our bodies are made up of 99 percent water. Picture the ocean, which moves and rolls with waves. Your body is similar—it moves and rolls with the sensations of feelings. Feelings are living realities. They are the result of changes in the biochemistry in our bodies. Like the tides and currents of the ocean, our feelings come and go. We can experience storms of feelings like rage and anger, deep currents of joy, or waves of sadness.

Before I began a recovery program focusing specifically on codependence, I read a lot of books that told me I would feel better if I could get in touch with my feelings. *What* feelings? I could talk about my feelings as if I knew what I was feeling. In truth I didn't even know that I didn't know what I was feeling. My feelings were mostly in my head in the form of thoughts about what I should be feeling. When I did experience feelings, they were usually so powerful that I was scared of getting emotional and being out of control.

This is a common experience for codependents. The experience of being raised in a dysfunctional family teaches you to suppress your feelings.

Feelings Are Real

Sensed feelings, the feelings our bodies experience, have tangible qualities. They can be described in tangible terms like other concrete objects. Feelings have depth, density, volume, and viscosity. They can be fuzzy, bright, warm, cold, deep, prickly, tingling, red, or square.

My clients have shared with me many wonderful descriptions of feelings. One woman described the feelings associated with the perfectionist role she played: "I feel heavy, weighed-down." One client described his experience of anxiety as "a thousand bugs crawling under my skin." Another described the sadness and loneliness she felt in the evenings as a "thick, dark, icky feeling." One client said that jealousy felt "like a hot branding iron in my chest." Other clients talk about a narrow band of feelings, as if measuring their pitch and volume and range on a oscilloscope.

Feelings seem to occupy a space in the body that I call the *inner feeling space*. Although feelings can be felt in many parts of the body, most people experience feelings in the torso or trunk—the place where we carry our feelings. This part of our body, from the esophagus to the bottom of the lower intestine, is lined with billions of nerve cells whose purpose is to pick up the biochemicals that induce emotions. It is no wonder that clients who describe their feelings often place their hands over their heart, chest, or stomach. One client would grab his throat when he felt sad. It helped him relieve the heavy sad feelings that were there. The most familiar gesture I see is a client placing a hand over the solar plexus in response to fearful or anxiety-producing thoughts. These gestures are, quite literally, a response to a biochemical experience of fear and anxiety felt in his solar plexus. So I visualize the inner feeling space in this part of the body.

The body is a wonderful source of self-awareness and identity if you pay attention to its messages. There is no real distinction between your feelings and your body. When you feel good, you know it, because you feel good in your body. If you've ever lost someone you loved, you know that the pain is deep and physical.

St. Augustine, writing about his life before his conversion to Christianity, described his feelings when he lost his lover with these powerful words: "When they took her from my side, . . . her with whom for such a long time I had been used

to sleep, my heart was torn at the place where it was stuck to hers, and the wound was bleeding." Notice that he does not say "it was as if my heart was torn." No, his pain is physical because feelings are physical. They cannot be experienced except through the body.

Knowing What Feelings Are

Jael Greenleaf describes the consequence of growing up in a family in which feelings are altered or suppressed in an article in *Co-Dependency: An Emerging Issue*: "As parents suppress their feelings, they cease to discuss them and the children do not develop an adequate vocabulary of feeling words to describe their emotions. Feelings that cannot be named, cannot be talked about."

You may not recognize certain feelings because you have no words for them. For instance, if you never saw enthusiasm or exuberance expressed in your family, you may not be able to experience those feelings. I remember the amazement and look of delight on the face of one of my clients as she realized that the strange new feeling she had been trying to name was serenity. She had never felt it before.

You may have other problems with feelings that were considered "bad feelings" in your family. You may know all about indirect, manipulative, toxic anger, the kind that turns into resentment and is expressed through complaints, but if you've never seen direct, honest, outspoken anger, you may be unable to experience it. In fact, when you do feel a surge of anger, it may feel so alien that you feel you are possessed by something outside yourself. Or you may know anger only as a dangerous and destructive force instead of as a natural feeling that can be expressed in healthy and effective ways.

Painful feelings—feelings of rejection, abandonment, loneliness, hurt, sorrow, and fear—are probably the most problematic for you if you grew up in a dysfunctional family. Your parents may not have expressed these feelings for themselves. They certainly did not want you to express them.

If your feelings are not valued or acknowledged or expressed, if you learn to deny them and suppress them, eventually you may learn to believe that you do not have any feelings at all.

The Wounds of Childhood

As a child you experienced many painful feelings. You felt these painful feelings physically. I call this process *suffering the wounds of childhood*.

I once saw an episode of childhood wounding that made such a deep impression on me that I wrote a story about it:

A SIMPLE STONE ON THE BEACH

Sunny skies, warm breezes. The noise of adults and children playing in the surf of Hawaii. Snorkeling gear flopped on feet and dangled on necks. Music. Picnics.

The family in front of me had just fitted their snorkeling masks on their faces. I drifted off for a half hour. When I awoke, I saw them again. Father, mother, young boy about eight, and a girl of six. She had just found a little shiny stone on the beach. She brought her trophy, carried proudly in her little hands, to display it to her parents.

"Look what I found!" she exclaimed. Her smile radiated with the glow of her achievement. "I want to take it home!"

"No! Put it back!" said her father, his words shooting out like a dart aimed at a target.

She flapped her arms wildly for a few minutes. A grimace of pain washed over her face.

"Please. I found it!" She held it up to show her father—a stone about a half inch in diameter.

"I said, 'No!' Now put it back." The words bit into her. "Get ready to go. I'll either take you or the stupid stone."

She turned away from him, her shoulders slouched, resigned to her task, saying good-bye to the treasure she had found on the beach, thousands of miles from home.

I felt so angry after witnessing this scene that it took me several hours—after working out my feelings—to regain my emotional equilibrium. I realized I was watching the infliction of a wound, a wound of confusion, hurt, and shame. And I realized that this wound was probably only one of thousands of wounds this little girl would suffer during her childhood. I wondered if she knew what she had done wrong. *I* wondered what she had done wrong. I guessed that her hurt would be buried, like many other wounds, as she learned how to survive the pain of being alive.

Many children suffer similar wounds in childhood. But if you grew up in a dysfunctional family, you were wounded repeatedly, and you were not allowed to express your pain. Because the pain was so unbearable, because you needed to survive, you learned to suppress or deny your painful feelings. But they could not disappear entirely. Feelings are real. They are tangible. They are associated with a biochemical response. So where do they go when you suppress them or deny them?

Numbing the Inner Feeling Space

When you suppress your feelings, you push them—along with the biochemical energy associated with them—into your inner feeling space.

As you fill up this inner feeling space with the painful feelings and inner tension that must be suppressed, your inner feeling space becomes a dense mass of stuffed feelings. Scars form to defend the unhealed emotional wounds of childhood. Your inner feeling space becomes clogged.

You may forget about the wounding process, but your emotional body is marked by the scars. Your body does not forget the emotional wounds of childhood. Dr. John Bowlby, expert on the effects of deprivation and loss on children, believes that emotional neglect in childhood creates "scar tissue" in one's feelings, seriously handicapping an individual's ability to respond to others, to feel closeness, and to participate with satisfaction in social activities.

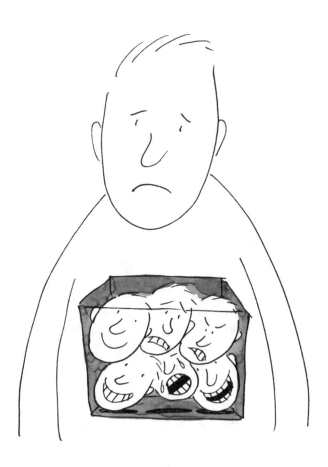

I often compare this process of suppressing feelings to the operating of a garbage compactor. To survive the pain of being alive you stuff feelings into your feeling space just as you would compact garbage into a compactor. As more and more feelings are suppressed, the "garbage" becomes a thick, dense mass. Your feeling space is stuffed with the hurt of the past.

Your feeling space is like a transmitter that gives you emotional information about experiences in your life so that you can respond appropriately. When this space becomes clogged with unexpressed feelings, its ability to function is significantly reduced. The feeling space is then hampered in transmitting to you information about your internal and external experiences.

It becomes dead space. Codependents frequently describe their inner lives as bleak, gray, dull, flat, monotonous, empty. This may be in contrast to an external life full of busyness and activity. When asked to describe their feelings in response to some recent pain or childhood trauma, they often say they feel "nothing" or "numb." Although these words describe the codependent's feelings, they more aptly describe the deadness of the inner feeling space.

To simulate the experience of being a child who must deny or suppress his feelings, you can do this exercise. You'll need a willing partner. As you do this exercise imagine what is happening inside your body as the biochemistry of feelings surges through you. The billions of nerve cells in your feeling space will be saturated with biochemcials. Ask yourself what will happen to these biochemicals, to your nerve cells and your muscles after you have finished the exercise. This exercise provokes the stress response which you will learn about in this chapter. Without resolution of the feelings you will essentially be doing the same you did as a child—stuff the feelings and the biochemicals associated with them into the tissues of your feeling space.

The diagram below shows the positions you and your partner take.

Your partner, who will play the part of a barrier to your getting your needs met, stands with one foot behind the other, braced to provide more resistance to your attempts to get past. You place the palms of your hands against your partner's palms, as if playing pattycake. Your goal is to get to a place about two or three feet past your partner; this place symbolizes the fulfillment of your need as a child for love and affection. To do so you will have to get your partner out of the way. Your partner's job is to prevent you from getting your needs met. You and your partner will probably be fairly evenly matched. But you weren't evenly matched when you were a child trying to get your needs met by the adults in your life. So get down on your knees so you can really feel the difference between your ability to get what you need and your partner's ability to frustrate you. Remember that your partner represents the barriers that got in your way when you tried to get your needs met. These barriers could have been parents, siblings, or friends. As adults we are often our own barriers.

When you try this exercise, you will feel certain sensations within your body as you try to get past your partner. After two or three minutes you may feel frustrated and angry. This is an exercise in experiencing the feelings of a child who could not get her needs met. As an adult doing this exercise you can express your anger or frustration. So remember you are doing it as a child. If you continue for 10 to 15

Simulating the Unresolved Feeling States of a Child

Your partner simulating the barrier

You, on your knees as the child, pushing against the barrier

minutes, you will probably get pushy or want to quit. As you do this, you will get a faint glimpse of the painful experiences you had as a child trying to get your needs met.

Feelings and Addictions: Suppressing

Paradoxically, when you've been forced to suppress feelings as a child, feelings seem dangerous to you as an adult. You may take over your parents' role and force your *own* feelings back down, because that's what you've been taught to do. Addictions are often used to help suppress feelings. As one client explained:

"Whenever I get angry, that's when I get the urge to have a cigarette. It's almost as if when I draw the smoke down into my lungs, I push the angry feelings down, too. I do know that I stop feeling angry when I'm about halfway through a cigarette."

Food is also used for suppressing feelings. The warm sensations of a hot fudge sundae or the creamy taste of a mouthful of cheesecake going down your throat can soothe your hurt feelings. In many families food was used as a way to control or reward children, keep them quiet, or compensate for bad feelings. We learn very early in life about the value of food to fix a bad feeling.

On the one hand, addictions can help you suppress feelings you don't want to experience. On the other hand, addictions can be used to create excitement in your body and replace the dull sensations of the crammed feeling space. This seeming contradiction—addictions can help you suppress feelings and also create feelings— can be resolved. The fact is that both suppressing and replacing feelings is about avoiding the experience of your true feelings.

Feelings and Addictions: Replacing

It is through your body that you experience your own aliveness. Even if you have dulled your feelings so they can barely be felt, you still must experience sensations to feel alive. At this point addictions to substances, relationships, work, etc., can become substitutes for the suppressed feelings.

There is a tendency to think of addiction as limited to classical dependency, the abuse of alcohol or drugs. Only recently have similarities among all addictive or compulsive behaviors been recognized; the definition of *addiction* has broadened to include many substances and even processes.

Addictions can be grouped in two categories: substance addictions and process addictions. We already recognize the debilitating effects of addiction to alcohol and drugs, but there are many other substances that can be addictive, among them, coffee, cigarettes, sugar, and other food. Process addictions usually show up as compulsive behaviors; for instance, compulsive gambling or compulsive sexual activity.

Addiction to work is a process addiction. We recognize its similarity to alcoholism when we call it *workaholism* and those who engage in it *workaholics*. This addiction is endemic in American society and is even rewarded and encouraged.

Many codependents become involved in obsessive and abusive relationships. Several recent books, such as *Love and Addiction* by Stanton Peele and *Love and Limerence* by Dorothy Tennov, have looked at these unhealthy "love" relationships as addictions. Robin Norwood's insightful book, *Women Who Love Too Much*, is about the pain caused by addiction to relationships. If you remain in a relationship with someone who abuses you physically or emotionally, believing that through your efforts your partner will finally change and treat you right, if you put your partner's needs above your own and are happy only when your partner is happy, you are in a codependent relationship.

It's also possible, though seldom discussed, for a person to become addicted to an internal mental process such as fantasy. I have worked with several men who use sexual fantasy as a means of avoiding feelings or unpleasant realities. As soon as an unacceptable feeling or realization surfaces, they replace it with a sexual fantasy that absorbs their attention and prevents them from experiencing or expressing the original feeling. Other people use compulsive worrying or relentless self-analysis to distract themselves.

All addictions alter moods and provide sensations. If your feeling space is dead or damaged, you can become addicted to the sensations you feel when you use a particular drug or the emotional highs and lows of an intense, chaotic relationship. Intense intellectual activity, a sense of achievement through work, and the experience of chaos can all bring a sense of life to a deadened feeling space. One of my clients refused to give up his addictions to alcohol, sex, and intense emotions because, as he said, "I need my addictions to feel alive. I feel dead when they're taken away."

The feelings that are stimulated by addictions are usually experienced at the extreme ends of the feeling spectrum because that is the only way they can be felt.

The feeling space is so numb that it cannot register moderate feelings, only acute euphoria or deep depression.

Addictions are often interchangeable. Anne Wilson Schaef describes this phenomenon in *When Society Becomes an Addict*: "It is rare for a person to have only one addiction. Instead, the addictive person, or the individual operating within an addictive system, really has multiple addictions."

You may recover from one addiction, but unless you focus on the underlying issues of codependence, you are likely to replace it with another addiction. The core of wounded feelings that the addiction is being used to avoid must be exposed and healed, or relapse into addiction is likely.

Mental Feelings

Addictive behavior is one of the ways codependents try to compensate for their deadened inner feeling space. Mental feelings are another. When you are asked how you are feeling, do you have to stop and think about how you're feeling? Do you describe your feelings by starting your sentences with a phrase like "I think I feel" or "I feel that"? If so, you are describing mental feelings, not sensed feelings that are experienced through the body. When expressing a feeling to someone else, do you say something like "I feel you're being cruel"? This is not a feeling; it's a thought or an opinion about the other's behavior. It does not describe your felt experience.

I can easily tell the difference between mental feelings and sensed feelings by watching my clients. Lisa, for example, a 30-year-old secretary who had grown up in an alcoholic home, told me that her mother never arranged birthday parties for her. She related this in a neutral voice as if she were talking about something that happened to someone else. When I asked her what she was feeling, she tilted her head up and fixed her eyes on a point in space near the ceiling. She seemed to be searching for something, so I asked her what she was looking for.

"I'm trying to find the feeling," she said. Like so many codependents, she was reaching out for a mental feeling, a thought of a feeling that would correspond to an event.

"Don't look up," I suggested. "Look down." Suggesting that she look down was a way to reorient her search for a thought of a feeling to the sensation of a feeling in her body.

Within a few seconds she began to breathe rapidly, and her hands clenched the arms of the chair. As I encouraged her to really feel what she was experiencing, she broke into tears and sobbed quietly. When she was able to speak, she described a tense, constricted feeling she felt in her chest and a sadness she didn't know was there.

Two Consequences of Deadened Inner Feeling Space

Pushing Hot Buttons

When feelings are stuffed, the sensations of feelings cannot flow through your body naturally. Your emotional wounds can become hot buttons, areas that are so built up that when they are touched through actions or words of other people, they trigger painful shock waves way out of proportion to the event. When one of your hot buttons is touched, you may feel it as a jolt or as heat or as an area of intense energy that seems to radiate throughout your body. Hot buttons release such a large amount of pain and energy because they are tied in to all the pain accumulated during a lifetime.

Inventorying Hot Buttons

The term *hot button* describes an intense emotional response. These responses often indicate childhood wounding experiences that are calling to be healed. Deep feelings of dread, fear, or anxiety are clues of deep wounds. Couples often learn each other's hot buttons and push them in arguments. When one of your hot buttons gets pushed, it feels as if someone has gone into you and touched a hurting spot to which you react in defense and pain. Events, situations, and thoughts can also push hot buttons in us.

Hot buttons usually involve a strong reaction to another person's behavior. These reactions are attempts to defend and protect the emotional wound that has been stimulated. Like any unhealed wound, it is only natural to want to protect it from further injury. Although hot buttons vary considerably from person to person, there are some common ones that I have noticed. These examples show up most often in intimate relationships. They include hearing words directed at you that are negative labels (i.e., nag, bastard, bitch, stupid) or sound judgmental; being ignored by someone you are talking to; and observing body language and facial expressions that seem to indicate disapproval. Feelings of sadness, fear, guilt, shame, and despair often precede the hot-buttoned anger. You will learn in Part Three of this book to open up your hot buttons and find your fears and feelings.

Body Armoring

As your inner feeling space is filled with stuffed feelings, your body becomes a dense area of hurt. Your muscles may tense to protect your wounds, and you may develop body armoring. Wilhelm Reich, who pioneered the use of bodywork in psychotherapy, called the muscular rigidity that often accompanies defense mechanisms "character armor." He showed his clients how to release the tension in their bodies. The release of tension was often accompanied by a vivid reliving of a past experience or the reexperiencing of a repressed emotion, almost as if the memories and feelings were stored within the muscular tension. His work inspired other body-oriented therapists and teachers, such as Alexander Lowen, Moshe Feldenkrais, and Ida Rolf.

During my recovery, as I learned to express and release more and more of the feelings that were stuffed into my feeling space, I become aware of an area of tension that felt like a band of steel around my chest and stomach. Although this band was so tight that I found it difficult to breathe, I was also aware that it held me tight and protected the hurt within my body.

The Wounded Inner Child

You met the inner child in Chapter 3. How does the inner child feel? I first encountered my inner child in 1980, although I didn't know just what it was at the time. I was attending a workshop on grief and loss during which I was asked to draw a time line showing significant events in my childhood. I noted several childhood illnesses, two of which were life-threatening, the theft of my bike, the death of my dog, and the confusion and fear over my dad's drinking. As I worked on my time line, I was amazed by the intensity of my feelings of anger, sadness, and despair. Where did they come from? The workshop facilitator made a comment about the losses I had suffered as a little boy, and I realized that my childhood had been very painful. Inside of me I felt the hurt of that little boy.

How did I know that I wasn't feeling normal adult emotions? I felt very young, very hurt, and very little as I experienced these deep feelings. The feelings were out of proportion, inappropriate for me as an adult, but completely appropriate for a young child.

My second experience with the inner child occurred in 1982, when I saw a movie about an alcoholic family. As I watched the film, my stomach became increasingly tense, and I found myself physically reliving my experiences as a child, but my memories were vague and confusing. When the film was over, I was in such physical distress that I called a massage therapist. As the therapist massaged my tense stomach, images from the past floated into my mind and I vividly relived experiences from my childhood. I saw the kitchen table and the empty seat waiting for my father. I felt again the shame I had experienced at family gatherings because of my father's drunken behavior. I recalled lying in bed, night after night, waiting for him to come home. As the therapist worked, I wept, overwhelmed by the deep hurt and pain of the little boy within.

Alice Miller in her insightful book *The Drama of the Gifted Child* talks about "The Lost World of Feelings":

> . . . a child can only experience his feelings when there is somebody there who accepts him fully, understands and supports him. If that is missing, if the child must risk losing the mother's love, or that of her substitute, then he cannot experience these feelings secretly "just for himself" but fails to experience them at all. But nevertheless . . . something remains.
>
> Throughout their later life, these people unconsciously create situations in which these rudimentary feelings may awaken but without the original connection ever becoming clear.

These feelings that couldn't be experienced in childhood are buried deep within. They are frozen in time and space and buried in your emotional memory bank.

During recovery you will work with your inner child, learning to reparent your emotional self, to provide the empathic, attentive environment that was lacking in your past. In this way you allow your inner child to express painful emotions so that your old wounds can be healed.

Experiencing the Pain of Codependence

Unfortunately for most codependents the feelings that first come into awareness— after years, maybe decades of suppressing all feelings—are the painful feelings of grief, anger, sadness, and despair. The pain associated with codependence is very deep and very real, like the pain of a genuine physical wound. When my clients begin a recovery program and start experiencing those painful feelings that have been covered for so long, the hurt is felt deep within the body. Clients frequently describe a painful feeling that has no bottom. This is often the point at which individuals are tempted to return to their old codependent behaviors, because they want to avoid this pain. One of my clients described this pain vividly during his fourth session with me.

When I first met Bert, a 35-year-old banker, he was dressed conservatively in a dark gray blazer and matching pants, a narrow tie, and a neatly pressed white shirt. The same meticulousness that he exhibited in his attire was apparent in his explanation of why he had come to see me. During his first session he described his recovery program as if it were the fourth on a list of things he does daily.

"I do affirmations, I run when I get angry, I keep busy, and I go to ACOA meetings just to know I'm not alone," he said briskly.

"What are you recovering from?" I asked.

"I know I'm codependent," he responded immediately. "My family was screwed up, and I don't want to live like them. But nothing seems to work."

After three sessions we had developed some bonds of trust and openness, and Bert no longer seemed as nonchalant and in control as he had earlier. He swayed in his chair. His eyes brimmed with tears.

"I don't want to feel this pain," he said. "Life was easier before I started doing this inner growth. I don't want to try drinking. I've done that. Sex doesn't work. Nothing takes away the pain."

"What's the pain like?" I asked.

He curled his fingers like claws and dug them into his stomach. As he drew them toward his sides, as if pulling himself apart, his face was contorted with pain. He looked like a creature from a horror movie. "I feel like I'm being ripped apart, in my stomach," he said. "It feels like my life is draining out of me. What can I do to relieve this?" he asked me desperately, his voice rising as he spoke. "I just don't want to feel this."

For Bert and thousands of other codependents, the pain is very real. It hurts as much as any physical wound—worse than a cut, as nauseating as a migraine, as aching as an abscessed tooth. And, even worse, it feels unending. My own pain felt like a deep, dark well with no bottom. And I've heard my clients describe it with similar phrases: "like a bottomless pit," "like a dark, oily swamp."

As I sat with Bert, knowing the pain he felt from my own experiences, I also knew that I could not take his pain away and wouldn't if I could. Feeling the pain is part of the recovery process, an important part of the redemption of the inner child. Just as wounds will not heal when they are kept covered, the pain of childhood cannot be assuaged by kind words, reassurance, or the bandages of compulsive behavior and addictions. The wounds can heal only when they are brought into the light. As the pain is reexperienced, the wound drains of its festering contents.

My first real awareness of my feelings as physical realities occurred at a bodywork workshop. I had just finished doing a movement that was intended to express my grief, when I felt a deep pain in the middle of my chest. It felt as if my chest had been slashed open with an ax. After checking with my doctor, who told me there appeared to be no physical cause for my pain, I spent the next two weeks letting myself feel the painful feeling. I tried to discern what the pain was expressing for me and finally realized that it represented my sadness and my grief. The tight band around my chest, which had protected me and restricted me for so long, had broken open, unleashing the pain within. I had survived this first internal breakthrough, and this encouraged me.

I was determined to continue allowing myself to experience feelings. Sometimes I did—sometimes I didn't. I had learned to identify two basic feelings: grief and sadness. I went on to explore anger, my feelings of abandonment and helplessness, frustration, shame, and others. Like an emotional archaeologist, I explored gradually, over the course of six years, the recesses of my feeling space.

I continue that process on a regular basis as a key element of my recovery program. In Chapter 10 I will discuss a variety of ways you can get in touch with your feelings, allowing them to come forth and pass through you.

Feelings, like any other living reality, want to be recognized, given space, and acknowledged. After years of being denied they will find some way to get your attention—sometimes expressing themselves through illness or depression.

Living in Chronic Shock

We tend to think of feelings as part of our emotional reality, but feelings also have a physiological component. When you experience a feeling, you are experiencing a biochemical phenomenon within your body.

Imagine that you experience a need to be acknowledged for your achievements by a significant other, like the little girl on the beach. You act to fulfill this need, as she did by displaying her rock for her father's approval. When the need is not met, or when it is met, as in the little girl's case, with a highly negative response and hostility, you experience certain biochemical reactions.

You must perceive and interpret an event as a threat before you react to it physically. But if you were raised in a dysfunctional family, sensitive to every nuance of the environment, limited in ability to interpret what's going on because of the rules of silence and denial, you are more likely to perceive threats in the environment than other children. It doesn't matter whether the threat is real. The perception of a threat is enough to cause the physiological stress responses.

George Engel and other stress researchers list the following events that lead to stress responses:

1. Perceived or actual loss of a person, object, or activity in which we are psychologically invested
2. Actual or threatened injury or damage to the integrity of our body (e.g., injury) or to our self or self-esteem
3. Actual or potential frustration of what we perceive to be our basic needs and drives
4. Ambiguous or incomplete perception or information leading to the belief that something might be a threat or danger

The little girl on the beach was experiencing all of these threats—a perceived loss of a person (her father would leave without her) and the actual loss of an important object (the stone), damage to her self-esteem (her father would not acknowledge her achievement), frustration of her basic need to be acknowledged, and confusion as to why her innocent desire to take a rock home with her provoked her father's hostility.

Your body responds in certain predictable ways to any stress. First you perceive an actual or perceived threat in your environment. The degree of danger that the threat represents to you is based on a multitude of factors, including childhood experiences, the amount of repressed feelings, your physical condition, and your personal beliefs and values.

Once a stimulus is experienced as a threat, your hypothalamus, which influences the physiological responses of your body, is activated. It secretes a chemical that activates the pituitary gland, which in turn secretes the hormone ACTH (adrenocorticotropic hormone) into your bloodstream.

ACTH stimulates the production of both cortisone and adrenaline. These hormones affect your body in a number of ways. Your breathing pattern changes—you take frequent, shallow breaths. Your blood pressure elevates, and your heart rate increases. Your body is preparing you to fight or flee. Muscles tighten throughout your body, resulting in neck and shoulder soreness and low back pain if prolonged. Digestion slows down and stops; the immune system is suppressed while the body mobilizes to respond to the present emergency.

If you grew up in a family that discouraged expression of feelings, you weren't able to express and release the pent-up feelings and energy you were experiencing. The muscles that contracted stayed contracted as long as the situation continued. When the situation changed—perhaps you turned and walked away—the physical state of your muscles and the chemical preparations your body made in response to danger were left essentially in place and unresolved. The feelings associated with the perceived threat were suppressed and stuffed into the inner feeling space. If you experienced frustration of your needs frequently, a chronic state of tension developed within your body.

Wayne Kritsberg in his book *The Adult Children of Alcoholics Syndrome* asserts that over 50 percent of all children from alcoholic families are, to some degree, in chronic shock. All of us experience some traumatic events in our childhood. What's different for a child from an alcoholic—or any dysfunctional—family is the way those events are interpreted and resolved by the family. Alcoholic and all dysfunctional families operate according to the rules of rigidity, silence, denial, and isolation. None of these provide an appropriate way for a child to work through and resolve a traumatic experience.

Kritsberg believes that chronic shock develops whenever a person experiences a catastrophic event and is unable to resolve the physical and physiological effects of that catastrophe.

What exactly happens when a person goes into shock? Shock is caused by the bodily responses described above, which slow or stop the circulatory system, draining blood from the heart and brain. The corresponding emotional state is one of shutdown or numbness. If you ask someone in this condition how he is feeling, he will probably say he feels fine, but you will notice a glassy or vacant look in his eyes. This is a natural response to an emergency situation. It's what happens *after* this initial state of shock that makes the difference for resolution.

Some time after the shock the feelings that have been suppressed begin to reemerge. At this point the person needs to talk about his experiences. This won't happen in a dysfunctional family. Left alone in silence, the child can interpret the event only from her limited perspective. Often she assumes that she was somehow at fault. The problem is denied. It must not be talked about either in or out of the family. The child is offered no reassurance, no support, no explanation. The shock cannot be resolved, but it must be dealt with. Usually the child forgets what happened or becomes emotionally dissociated from it. This emotional numbness continues throughout life. No one who is suffering from unresolved shock can function in a healthy way.

If you grew up in a dysfunctional family, you are still feeling the effects of the traumatic experiences you lived through. You learned how to deal with stress in ways that helped you to survive but did not release you from the effects of the trauma.

For one thing, the physiological components of the shock experience still exist within the body and often surface as stress-related diseases: lower back pain, neck and shoulder soreness, allergies, headaches, and gastrointestinal problems. We can see why these physical symptoms would be common complaints for codependents. They are derived from the natural physical response of the body to trauma— increased heart rate, decreased disgestion, tightened muscles, suppressed immune system.

The Cumulative Effects of Stress

If you grew up in a dysfunctional home, you experienced thousands of episodes of high stress. As a result your body is always prepared for defensive action. You are hypervigilant and hypersensitive. For instance, shallow breathing is a natural physiological response to perceived threat, the "fight or flight" situation. It is also a noticeable phenomenon in 100 percent of the clients I see.

When you feel threatened, safety is of utmost importance. But as you learned in this chapter, the perception of a threat to your self-image or self-esteem as well as to your body will stimulate the stress response. By slowing down and deepening the rapid shallow breathing that marks the stress response, you can become conscious of your body's feeling state and relieve the tension in your body. Shallow breathing or holding your breath in a state of fear is the way you spent much of your life in your dysfunctional family.

A client was asked once by a counselor to come up with an image of herself as an animal. She compared herself to a deer in the forest. "The deer," she said, "is always tense and poised for danger. Just the slightest hint of trouble, a smell on the wind, a rustle in the bushes, and she's gone."

When her counselor asked her to follow up on this image and imagine a place where the deer could be safe, she considered several possibilities—a zoo, as the pet of nice people, on an island with no predators—and then dismissed them all. She said sadly, "There's no place the deer can be safe. Because even if she were safe, she wouldn't know it. She believes she's in danger. That's her mode of being."

Pioneering stress researcher Hans Selye emphasized that when your body is in a state of stress—for instance, because of a perceived threat to your self-esteem—it is less able to defend you from germs and other external threats. As Dennis Jaffe explains in his insightful book *Healing from Within*, "Research suggests that people may develop chronic diseases after they have worn themselves out with long-term emotional stress."

We can put feelings out of our mind, but we cannot put them out of our bodies. The energy and chemical correlates of trapped emotional reactions stay alive and "scream for release." Sooner or later uncomfortable feelings are exchanged for uncomfortable symptoms as victims of repressed feelings become plagued with a variety of emotionally related physical problems and diseases.

Diseases and Codependence

The chart below shows the progressive and chronic diseases that are the result of stress-related illnesses. How many of these symptoms of stress have you experienced?

Jaffe describes the psychological correlates of several of these diseases.

For instance, he discusses the results of research by Herbert Weiner on people with ulcers. Weiner found that these individuals had intense psychological needs to be loved and cared for, but these needs were chronically frustrated. They also repressed anger, were withdrawn and inhibited, and believed they were unable to get their needs met. Jaffe says: "These studies are only suggestive, but they add to the growing body of evidence linking unmet needs to subsequent helplessness and disease."

Jaffe also reviews the conclusions of a study by W. J. Grace and D. T. Graham that looked for the emotional correlates of 12 diseases suffered by 128 patients. They found that diarrhea was related to wanting to end a particular situation or get rid of something or somebody, while constipation was the disease of patients who grimly persevered through a seemingly insurmountable problem. Patients with asthma and hay fever were faced with unpleasant situations that they wanted to avoid. Patients suffering from a painful skin disease felt frustrated and "picked on." Nausea and vomiting occurred when patients wished something hadn't happened. Migraine headaches occurred after an intense effort to complete a task. Hypertension was the disease of individuals who were hypervigilant and worried about possible threats. Low back pain usually indicated a desire to do something involving the whole body, like running away. Jaffe points out that this study is particularly useful because

The Physiological Results of Unresolved Stress

INITIAL

CARDIOVASCULAR	MUSCULAR	HORMONAL	RESPIRATORY	GASTROINTESTINAL
high blood pressure migraine headache palpations	tension headache tension backache	skin problems obesity thyroid problems	asthma hyper-ventilation	irritable stomach irritable bowel constipation gas nausea

CHRONIC

CARDIOVASCULAR	IMMUNE	HORMONAL	NEUROLOGICAL	GENITO URINARY	GASTROINTESTINAL
increased heart problems stroke heart failure	reduced resistance to infection, colds, flu, cancer	hair loss menopausal problems male impotence	anxiety phobias obsessions depression psychosis	kidney damage	ulcers

LEADS TO

EXHAUSTION

HOPELESSNESS

HELPLESSNESS

DEATH

Grace and Graham demonstrated the pathways by which emotions can be translated into body language, particularly when the individual does not think it safe to admit or act on these feelings. My experience suggests that such patients do not initially want their attitudes to become conscious, and look instead for alternate solutions to them. So the feelings simply simmer in hidden anger, frustration, helplessness, anxiety, or pain.

Other studies discussed in *Healing from Within* link acne with the feeling of being picked on or nagged at, while rheumatoid arthritis has been associated with frustration over unfulfilled ambitions.

Jaffe concludes:

> . . . many of the most common and chronic diseases occur when a person is unable to deal effectively and adequately with something he dislikes. Disease seems to result when a person inhibits an effective response to the events of his life.

Lawrence Hinkle conducted a study of 1,000 telephone company employees and compared the 10 healthiest individuals with the 10 who were most frequently ill. Dennis Jaffe summarizes the conclusions of Hinkle's study:

> In a sense, healthier people are more "selfish." . . .
> By contrast, less healthy people are unable to articulate their personal needs. They are most accustomed to living for others and they often do little for themselves, even at levels of basic hygiene and adequate rest. In treatment, they are, as MacLean [researcher on the connections between brain structure and emotions] suggests, initially unable to pinpoint their feelings, frustrations, anger, or depression.

Sounds like a description of a codependent, doesn't it?

Recent research on cancer is coming up with a picture of the type of person most likely to get cancer, and again the description resembles codependence. When Lydia Temoshok, a psychologist at the University of California School of Medicine in San Francisco, interviewed melanoma patients in a search for similarities among them, she found a distinct personality type, which she named a Type C personality. Type Cs always have to feel happy and be in control. Their dominant characteristic is the nonexpression of emotion; they refuse to express any negative emotions. Sound familiar?

The correlation of cancer with codependent behavior may have a great deal to do with the effects of living under constant stress. The biochemicals that your system produces under stress, the corticosteroids, also inhibit the immune system. Furthermore, body chemicals that are released in stress situations—epinephrine and norepinephrine—inhibit the production of interferon, an anticancer substance produced by the immune system's T cells. Every time you tense up in anticipation of a perceived or real threat, you weaken your immune system, which is then less able to protect you from disease.

Codependence is a degenerative process. If you deny your body's experience of reality and suppress your biochemical responses, you damage your body. You lose the ability to recognize the signals your body uses to warn you. And you restrict your experience of life. As your body suffers more and more from the stress of containing unexpressed feelings and unreleased chemicals, you weaken your immune system and increase your chances of suffering from a serious disease. Codependence is not just a psychological concept—it can cause an actual life-threatening disease.

Edrita Fried writes in her book *The Courage to Change:*

Feelings are an absolute necessity for self-renewal which, in turn, banishes fatigue and dangerous boredom. They provide a strong biological-psychological balance and offer crucial guidance in the pursuit of and discriminant participation in human relationships, without which self-image, self-esteem, and the maintenance of cooperation go awry.

She goes on to say that

persons who have "lost" their emotions have forfeited the mechanism that can steer a relatively safe course through life.

Your fluid and open feeling space, with its billions of nerve cells, is intended to be a channel of vital information about your perceptions and experiences of life. If an external event or interaction makes you sad or happy, angry or joyful, you know it by your feelings. If a thought makes anxious or glad, the same thing happens. Your feeling space also gives you a gut sense of things. The expression "gut sense" describes a felt sense in your gut about something or someone. It is a biochemical experience of something your body is trying to communicate to you, whether you are consciously aware of it or not. Your feeling space becomes numb, dead, or frozen as a result of codependence.

The body is damaged by unresolved muscle tension and unexpressed feelings, manifesting themselves in rigid body posture, chronic ailments, and serious illnesses. This process has a significant influence on your mental and spiritual dimensions, which will be described in the next two chapters.

6

· · · · · · ·

Codependence and Your Mental Dimension

I N   T H E   1 7 T H   C E N T U R Y
Descartes wrote, "I think, therefore I am." His insistence on the primacy of the mental dimension has become a given in Western culture.

As you learned in the preceding chapter, if you were raised in a dysfunctional family you became alienated from the signals of your body and unable to experience any sensations except those of extremes. This suppression of important information from the physical dimension is often accompanied by a great reliance on the mental dimension for a sense of identity and a way of forging an existence in the world. In fact intellectualization is a common defense against feeling.

The mental dimension does have a physical correlative—the brain, the locus of mental activity.

Unlike the physical dimension, which is tangible and visible, the mental dimension is intangible and visible only in its products and results: scientific achievements, intellectual accomplishments, creative expression and manifestations in the concrete world—buildings, bridges, computer systems, organizations, balance sheets.

Communication is one of the primary and most important functions of the mental dimension, although we also communicate with body language. Communication is at its best when it's rooted in the physical dimension and uses concrete and sensory images, descriptions of feelings and sensations and images. I had a hard time writing this chapter because the language used to describe the mental dimension is, of necessity, abstract and theoretical. If you notice a difference between the writing in this chapter and the previous one on the physical dimension, you are experiencing the difference between the two dimensions.

All of the dimensions of the body are meant to work together in harmony and health. But the degenerative process of codependence causes separation and distortion, and this is particularly evident in the functioning of the mental dimension. Like many codependents, you may believe you have no problems in this dimension: you exercise your intellect, visualize your goals, make plans, and exert your will toward accomplishment. The distortions that codependence creates in this dimension are subtle and difficult to recognize at first, precisely because codependents tend to be mental over-achievers and our culture values mental achievement.

Many codependents (like me) overinvest themselves in the mental dimension. After all, if you can't rely on your body and your feelings for information about yourself, you must get this information from somewhere else.

As a child you learned to use your intellect to analyze what was going on. "Mother doesn't like it when I act this way. Let's see what happens if I act another way." "Dad sometimes hits Mom when he's drunk, but Mom says it's because he's under a lot of pressure, so maybe if I could figure out how to ease that pressure for him, he wouldn't hit her anymore." You focused on gathering information about what other people were doing, ignoring how you felt, and practiced behaviors that helped you survive. You could avoid feeling pain by using your mind.

If you were successful, you may have learned how to act to get some of the love and recognition you desired. But at what a cost! Because your parents responded only to your assumed behavior—the behavior you engineered to get your needs met—they were loving and recognizing only your assumed identity. Your real needs were still unmet. You wanted to be recognized and loved for yourself, the self that had all those feelings and opinions that you believed couldn't be expressed.

Constructing the Personal Self

Everyone develops an identity, which I call the *personal self*. Your self-image is included in the personal self, but the personal self is more than the self-image. It is the self you constructed out of your experiences, the composite of your beliefs, defenses, ideas about yourself, your self-image, and much more. You developed your personal self through your experience of your own inner and outer realities and your experiences with others. It is distinct from the inner self, the true self, which I will describe more fully in the next chapter.

If you grew up in a healthy family, your personal self is simply a window through which your inner self radiates and manifests your talents and essence. In other words there is little disparity between who you are, who you think you are, and how you feel. You can express yourself and respond to life freely. However, if you grew up in a dysfunctional family, your personal self is not a window to your inner self, but rather a curtain hiding it. The personal self becomes the primary source of your identity since you are out of touch with your feelings and the inner self. Your choices for self-expression and responsiveness are limited to those options that are compatible with your personal self.

If you are codependent, your personal self was created as a defense against the pain you experienced in childhood. You can hide behind this constructed identity, ensuring that others cannot see your pain, even trying to convince yourself that you feel none. Your personal self becomes concerned with control—of feelings, the environment, other people—and focused on external recognition and validation.

The smiling face is a typical mask for codependents, the persona of the person who believes he must always be happy and optimistic despite difficult experiences. I know this mask well. It was a part of my own self-image. I believed it was necessary to smile even when I felt miserable inside.

If you grew up in a dysfunctional family, you probably learned to believe that you had to give up a part of yourself to prevent the rejection and avoid the pain that you sensed was inevitable if you revealed your true self and your feelings. To help illustrate this process I lead participants in my codependence workshops through an exercise similar to the one described in the preceding chapter on the physical dimension. In that exercise you experienced the frustration of trying to get your needs met while your partner prevented you from getting past.

This exercise begins in the same way. Assuming the same position with your partner, facing each other with palms pressed against palms at shoulder height, try to get past your partner, who tries to prevent you from doing so. After about 30 seconds of pushing you can go around the barrier, but you must leave behind some token of yourself, perhaps a watch, a ring, a sweater, your shoes, an earring, or a belt. Having left behind a part of yourself, you are now permitted to walk around the barrier. Your partner can pick up and keep the token you left behind (at least until the end of the exercise, when you get it back).

If you were a child, you would have this experience again and again. And the part you give up would be more important to you than a ring or an earring. And you wouldn't get it back. As a child, you learned how to get your needs met, at least partially, but to do so you had to give up a part of yourself, deny your needs, and hide the pain you experience.

One of my clients, Georgia, was raised by parents who were obsessed with rigid religious practices and ideals. In her family spirituality was associated with the mental dimension; the physical dimension was scorned. Georgia was not allowed to feel—let alone to express—anger. Whenever she felt sad or hurt, she was told she had no right to feel sad. She was shamed for "feeling sorry for herself" and told that God in his wisdom had some purpose in mind. So she learned to deny her feelings, because they were wrong, bad, even evil. She could only be happy and nice, and those feelings got her the "love" and "recognition" she craved. In exchange for approval and a sense of belonging she had to deny the reality of her experience.

And Georgia's childhood experiences are mild—though nonetheless damaging—compared to those suffered by children who are physically or sexually abused. The processes used to survive the pain of a dysfunctional environment, processes such as dissociation from feelings and psychic numbing, are complex and powerful.

Your self-image can become inflated by alignment with the role or roles you learned to play in your family. Think of the family hero, whose superhuman self-image is based on his or her accomplishments and success. Or the martyr, who feels noble because of the sufferings he or she endures on behalf of others. The victim has adopted helplessness as part of his or her self-image.

As you developed your self-image, you also developed patterns of thinking and beliefs that supported it. For example, suppose you believed that expressing your feelings of anger would cause rejection. Since you were afraid of being rejected, you never expressed anger and were always accommodating to others. Because you never tested your belief against reality—or perhaps you did once or twice and found to your horror that you were right; Mother did reject you when you got angry—you continue to be accommodating, believing that you had to be to protect yourself from rejection. Gradually you stopped feeling your anger. Perhaps you made it go away by using your intellect: "Getting angry won't accomplish anything." "Why should I get angry? I know he's always late." Now whenever you are in a situation in which you might experience anger, your mind reinterprets the situation so that feeling angry isn't even a possible option. You become, in the words of the Italian poet and novelist D'Annunzio, "a magician caught in the spells of his own weaving."

When you are out of touch with your feelings and your inner self, the personal self takes on an exaggerated importance in your life. It becomes the source of your identity and the means by which you relate to others.

Unfortunately the personal self you constructed was based on your experiences in a dysfunctional family. As a result the personal self does not really meet your needs for love, acceptance, and recognition. When you do receive love, you are likely to feel it's undeserved. When you receive recognition, you discount it, because you know, deep inside, that you are not being recognized for your true feelings and real self.

Robert Subby and John Friel, writing on "Co-Dependency: A Paradoxical Dependency" in *Co-Dependency: An Emerging Issue*, describe this vicious cycle: "By doing only what we think others want us to do, we deny ourselves and become divided inside. . . . Denying who we really are prevents us from ever knowing if those people close to us really care about ourselves."

Paradoxically every compliment, every award, every sign of respect you receive creates a further gulf between your personal self and your inner self. After all, if you got these compliments, awards, and respect for acting in a way that isn't natural, you believe you must continue to deny your real self to continue receiving recognition. You fear that you might accidentally reveal your real self and experience rejection, so you work harder at manipulating your behavior and hiding your feelings. This is why codependents, who are often likable, successful, high achievers, get so little pleasure from their successes and popularity. I constantly hear my clients say the same things: "I feel like a fraud." "I feel empty inside."

One of the biggest challenges of recovery is figuring out how to get authentic recognition, recognition for your real feelings and thoughts, for who you really are. When your primary source of recognition comes from what you do rather than who you are, it's difficult to give up "doing"—even if you recognize that no matter what you do, your real needs for acceptance and love will not be met or even acknowledged. But continuing the false "doing" can block the healing process. People in recovery often question their jobs, career paths, and relationships and find that they have made many life choices that reward and acknowledge them only for the achievements of their assumed self-identity. The impact of this realization can be overwhelming.

The Mind's Distortions

Here's how some of the functions of the mental dimension help contribute to the distortion of codependence.

Intellectualizing

Ideally your intellect helps you analyze and evaluate your experiences. You can apply your mind to physics, chemistry, or mathematics or use it to understand and explain human behavior. You can use it to reflect on your own behavior or that of others. It is intended to be used—with the other mental functions and with the other dimensions—to promote your health and growth.

Unfortunately, for many people the intellect becomes the primary function used to get needs for acceptance and recognition met. You saw several examples of this while looking at the construction of the personal self. You use your intellect when you formulate beliefs, such as "if I get angry, they will reject me." You use your intellect when you analyze the results of your behavior—for instance, "Aha! I knew it. I spoke sharply to her, and now she avoids me. My anger must have caused her rejection." And you use your intellect to frame self-messages to apply to your own behavior—"I must never, ever get angry again."

In my private practice I have worked with many people who are recovering from codependence. Several rely on intellect and willpower for achievement and a sense of satisfaction. Intellectual activity becomes a defense mechanism and is used to avoid pain, the emptiness of loneliness, the fear of failure, dissatisfaction with success on someone else's terms.

One of my clients, Barry, fit this pattern. He came to see me because he wanted to recover from codependence. One of his initial goals was to become more spontaneous and playful. Barry was very clear about how he used his rational intellect and logical processes to avoid feelings.

"When I start feeling fear, confusion, pain, or indecision, all the stuff that little boy feels," he explained, "I just go inside my head." Barry sat down and, lifting his right thumb to his mouth, tilted his head back, as if drinking from a bottle.

"What is that?" I asked, puzzled.

"It's my addiction," he said. "I don't drink, but I might as well. I use my mind to do the same thing—get me out of pain. When the little boy in me wants to play and just do something, because it's fun, I analyze it carefully to see the costs and benefits. It's got to have a positive outcome, show a profit, for me to do it."

"What about just enjoying yourself?" I asked.

"I can't do it," Barry said, shaking his head. "I have to be able to justify everything I do intellectually; there has to be some other benefit."

The intellect is a powerful weapon in the battle against feeling. As you saw in Chapter 3, many codependents employ the intellect to try to identify feelings, looking for answers or searching for explanations rather than experiencing the sensations of feelings. Talking about feelings is a defense mechanism that protects them from feeling or expressing them.

This is especially true of intellectual achievement. In our society intellectual achievement and academic excellence are encouraged and held up as standards of success. This overemphasis in our culture reinforces false "doing" by a codependent. Earlier in this chapter I mentioned that many codependents have been brought up to believe they can get recognition and love only for their accomplishments.

Several of my clients have described being pushed into careers by their parents or being expected to bring home excellent grades if they wanted recognition. Of course intellectual achievement may be your true gift; learning and involvement in an academic environment may be your real avocation. But in some dysfunctional families parents push academic achievement on their children. If you grew up in one of these families, love was withheld or you were ridiculed when you did not achieve the grades and awards your parents wanted. You've probably read newspaper accounts of a serious manifestation of this problem: high-achieving teenagers who commit suicide because of a bad grade or failure on a test.

Using intellectual achievement as the sole standard of worth not only leads to denial of real feelings, needs, and talents but also robs you of a precious part of yourself.

If your true gifts and interests were belittled or ignored, you probably still feel a sense of inner loss. You gave up something very important—your gifts and passions—for success in an area that meant little to your real self.

Imagination and Fantasies

The power to imagine is one of the great gifts of the mental dimension. Using your imagination, you can create works of art, experience the beauty of music, and take a trip to the moon or beyond. You can envision the future, imagine an ideal world, and visualize dreams for yourself. Functioning at its best, your imagination provides a way for you to express and experience the creative aspects of your being. Harvey Milkman and Stanley Sunderwirth in their excellent book on addiction, *Craving for Ecstasy*, describe the beneficial uses of fantasy:

> The basic function of imagery is to explore our relationship to the world. We develop specific mental pictures of who we are, which become a kind of personal identity, uniting our past experiences with our intended actions. By imagining, we can work through painful memories and sufferings or formulate models of enchantment through which we will soar to blissful heights with our lovers, family, or friends. The emergence of new ideas from the reshaping of a multiplicity of past events, in a sense, becomes a vast additional source of knowledge. Fantasy, the wellspring of creativity, may be thought of as a piece of God.

But the imagination can become distorted by codependence and become addictive, feeding into denial systems that keep you stuck in harmful behavior patterns and unhappy relationships, altering moods and keeping you out of touch with reality.

Fantasy is an important part of life in childhood. But children growing up in dysfunctional families often learn to rely more on fantasy than other children because they need it so desperately to escape from pain. There are many different ways to use fantasies to avoid pain: daydreaming about future accomplishments that will bring recognition, escaping into a book and thus leaving the current painful reality, imagining getting revenge for wrongs suffered, creating an imaginary playmate who is the one who is always bad. One of my clients imagined that she was adopted and developed an elaborate fantasy about her real parents and when they would come to reclaim her. This fantasy allowed her to survive the misery of her family life by dismissing it as irrelevant and helped her deal with the pain of not being valued by imagining that the parents who would truly value her had yet to appear.

Milkman and Sunderwirth describe how fantasy can become addictive:

> When imagination is more satisfactory than direct action in the alleviation of perceived threat, we begin to tread on the road of harmful consequences. With each experience of pleasure or removal from pain, the probability of seeking out an imaginary solution increases. Indeed our work, love and play

may progressively falter as the result of an increasing reliance on imaginary pleasures. . . . Harmful effects may be overwhelming when an entire society relies on fantasy as a means of coping.

Many addictive relationships are rooted in and nurtured by fantasy. Fantasy was one of the most significant ways I escaped from the painful realities of a codependent relationship. I imagined the vacations we would enjoy together, the way we would live, the children we would have. My fantasy was based on the romantic concept of love extolled by popular songs and the media. Wrapped up in my fantasy, with my head in the clouds, I could ignore the pain I was experiencing in this relationship.

Many people get caught up in fantasies about relationships, looking for a "match made in heaven" or thinking they have found their "soul mate." Popular songs, movies, videos, dating services, personals and workshops and books on finding the "perfect partner" all foster this fantasy. Clients frequently tell me they've found the ideal mate, adding that the relationship will be perfect "once I've convinced her that I love her" or "when he stops [drinking, working so hard, going out with other women]" or "when he realizes I'm the one." Meanwhile, the fantasy keeps them stuck in destructive and often abusive relationships.

I have also seen beneficial fantasy techniques, such as creative visualization, distorted by codependents, who add them to the arsenal of strategies that keep them out of touch with reality. These people (I was once one of them) are more interested in changing their external environment than in altering their own behavior.

My client Cynthia, introduced in Chapter 2, is a good example. When she initially called me for an appointment, she said she was upset and depressed about her life. She wanted to know why she wasn't creating more wealth and joy in her life when she was following all of the right formulas, attending a mind-power group, and focusing on her goals. She used an arsenal of motivational techniques to pump herself up for both her work in sales and her efforts toward accomplishing personal goals. Every day she spent some time staring at her treasure map, a collage of pictures of the things she wanted, and reciting affirmations. She had attained some of her goals but still was depressed.

Cynthia was clearly using fantasy, like a drug, to deny her feelings and her reality. Focusing her imagination and her attention on externals—her appearance, how others perceived her, her goals, the future—kept her stuck in denial and delusion.

Many codependents indulge in "magical thinking." They believe they can find an instant solution to their problems. Any book, process, seminar, or workshop that promises quick results is appealing. There is no magical process, and therapists don't have the answers either. There is nothing magic about recovery; it's just hard work.

Inability to complete things is another trait of codependents. I believe this characteristic also arises from a dysfunctional use of the imagination. Fantasy gets us in over our heads, committed to activities and projects that we cannot complete because they are beyond our abilities or don't acknowledge our limitations. A friend of mine, who was doing research for a historical novel she was writing, kept delaying returning an overdue three-volume set to the library because she was going to complete taking the notes she needed in just another week. Finally she sat down and began timing herself and then realized that at her current rate, it would be a year before she was finished with one of the three volumes. Her optimistic vision of the ease and speed with which she could complete her tasks had to give way to the unpleasant reality of a substantial overdue book fine.

Willpower Runs Amok

Willpower is another mental function that is often abused by codependents. Willpower, by focusing energy, allows us to achieve great feats and overcome overwhelming odds. Willpower combined with the power of the mind can achieve great scientific and intellectual advances. Willpower combined with the power of the body can perform amazing athletic feats.

Willpower, like the other mental functions, can be used disadvantageously when it's developed as a means of escape from the painful realities of a dysfunctional family. And the mere fact of surviving childhood in a dysfunctional family means that you exercised a high degree of willpower, so you might also be prone to misuse it, especially if you played the role of family hero as a child.

I recall a conversation I had with an investment banker about the issues facing adult children of dysfunctional families and the roles that develop in these families. He listened to me so intently I thought he was reflecting upon his own childhood. And when he started to speak, I anticipated a personal revelation.

"Those family heroes you're describing," he said. "They must have pretty strong willpower. I bet they're real drivers."

"Yes, typically, they are," I replied. "I know because I was a family hero. Always working hard, trying to get recognition. I did it as a boy, as a teenager, and in my adult career."

"This is very interesting," he said with excitement and regret in his voice. "I wish I had known this ten years ago." He gazed off as if looking into the distant past.

"Why? Are you a family hero? Would it have changed your life?" I asked.

"No, not that. I don't care about that," he said, dismissing the personal with a wave of his hand. "Ten years ago when I was a stockbroker managing a small office, I could have hired eight or ten family heroes, created a competitive office, and then set them loose to beat each other. I'd have made a lot of money."

The relentless exercise of willpower in the pursuit of success is one of our most highly valued cultural norms, associated with words like *drive, succeed, win, compete*. We celebrate the accomplishments of individuals who have willpowered their way to the top, not looking at the toll they pay in addictions, stress-related diseases, neglected personal relationships, and unfulfilled desires.

From my work with clients and my observations of my own behavior, I've learned that there is a direct relationship between willpower and control. Control is one of the core issues of codependence. It is based on a fantasy—the belief that we can control someone, something, some process that is outside of ourselves. Willpower can blind us to the reality of the situations around us and keep us locked on a treadmill of activity that is the hallmark of the compulsive nature of addiction.

The trap of willpower was clearly illustrated one evening in one of the codependence recovery groups I lead. One of the group members, Maureen, described a message that she heard frequently as a child: "You can do it! You can do anything!" As Maureen reflected on her life, she saw a connection between this message and the way she was living.

"When you're told you can do anything," she said, "even if you know you can't, how can you ever learn about limits? I had to do it all. I just couldn't let people down. But nobody knew that inside I felt like a failure, like it wasn't true. And I've never been seen as me, because that is who I am, someone who's just fooling everybody. I don't want to keep on doing everything!"

Maureen's comments struck a common chord. Within a short period of time several group members had described similar experiences.

"I'm always trying to do what other people want me to do," said one of them. "If they tell me they think I can do something, I'll do it, whether I want to or not, because I'm afraid of disappointing them." The feeling that flavored the disclosures was a mixture of insight, excitement, anger, and frustration.

This belief, that one can do anything, is based on reliance on willpower. In truth we cannot accomplish everything we want. External circumstances do affect us. And so do internal ones. A codependent cannot will recovery any more than an addict can use willpower to overcome addiction.

In Alcoholics Anonymous there is a saying that addiction is "willpower run riot." Most actively practicing addicts believe that they can stop at any time. They believe that willpower is more powerful than the addictive process. Recovery requires more than willpower. That's why the first step in the Twelve-Step program is surrender, the surrender of willpower to a higher power.

Recalling Memories

Memory is the storehouse of words, ideas, and images from the past. It provides you with a sense of history, relationship, and place in the world and a sense of how you've grown and changed. Memory is a rich source of information vital to your sense of self.

Unfortunately this resource is often diminished by the experience of growing up in a dysfunctional family. There are obvious reasons why this would be so. Amnesia and emotional numbness are normal responses to trauma, part of the shock process that protects the body from overwhelming pain. But as we saw in Chapter 5, children raised in dysfunctional families frequently remain in chronic shock because they are never given the opportunity to release and express their feelings about the traumas they have experienced. When I ask my clients about their memories of the past, they often say, "My childhood is a blank." Painful experiences and wounds have been blotted out. If any images can be recalled, they are usually only pleasant ones.

Retrieving memories is an important part of the recovery process, but it can be difficult and requires time, patience, and support. Sometimes I have to work backward with my clients, moving from the present to the past, looking for the roots of current attitudes and behaviors in the past by asking "Does this remind you of something? Is this an old feeling?" I have found that you can't force memories to come. You must work with memories in the same way you work with the inner child, by inviting them and being open to moving into the deeper realms of memory.

In recovery you'll retrieve many memories in the process of healing your inner child, and you'll discover that your painful and hidden memories can be gifts. Memory is your link between the past and the present. Without it you cannot access the important experiences that have shaped your personal self. Without it you have a vague or distorted sense of your own history.

Memory is linked intimately with feeling. In fact memory is one of the ways in which the physical dimension and mental dimension are linked. If you have an intense response to something that is happening in the present, particularly if your feeling seems "out of proportion" to the actual event, you may be responding to something in the past.

Other times this process works in reverse. Exploring your memories can evoke strong feelings. While recalling incidents from your past, you may experience the strong feelings associated with them. For instance, often when I hear the music of the sixties I can recall images from my lonely search for acceptance and companionship as well as times when I was embarrassed by my father's behavior. A few years ago I wouldn't let myself feel these feelings. Now much of the pain has been removed, and I can feel acceptance and love for the young person I was back then.

While working with memories, the pain that can emerge can be overwhelming, especially if you feel a strong need to be in control of yourself. In Chapter 10 I will discuss ways to work with powerful emotions that are evoked by painful memories.

Composite Picture of the Mental Dimension

As you grow from a child to an adult, you rely on your personal self and your mental functions for surviving in the world. Your life is organized around rigid structures, logical defenses, and fixed states of being.

It is this structure—with its defense against feelings, reliance on the external world, and avoidance of any painful realities—that keeps you out of touch with your feelings. Over time the mental dimension assumes more and more importance as more and more energy is invested in its functioning.

The mental dimension becomes overdeveloped to protect you from experiencing the inner wounds and pain of childhood. But this process creates great stress for the body. And the spiritual dimension, the essence of individuality, is cut off from expression. Instead of radiating your inner self through your personal self, your personal self becomes a brittle mask, only tangentially related to who you really are.

Codependence and Your Mental Dimension

7

· · · · · · ·

Losing Touch with Your Inner Self

I AM WRITING THIS BOOK for one primary purpose: to support you in reclaiming your own essential inner being. Recovery brings gifts that are more than just the absence of pain, anxiety, and paralyzing fear. The most precious gift of recovery is a renewed connection with your spiritual dimension and your inner self that resides within it.

Each one of us is seeking to feel alive. The sensations of feeling alive emanate from the essence of your identity—your inner self. As I illustrated in Chapters 5 and 6, codependence damages your ability to feel and express yourself and your essential nature. When you look primarily outside yourself to find love, recognition, and acceptance, as in codependence, you lose touch with your inner resources and the source of your life within the spiritual dimension.

What Is the Spiritual Dimension?

I see the spiritual dimension as our connection to the source of creation and life. We learn and know about the spiritual dimension through our experiences of life, which sometimes transcend our ability to understand them.

Artists, philosophers, prophets, magicians, mystics, and theologians all have tried to express the spiritual dimension over the centuries. Because it's so difficult to talk directly about a transcendent experience, metaphors and parables are favorite vehicles for conveying the truths of the spiritual dimension. Jesus Christ expressed the unconditional love of the spiritual dimension with the metaphor of a father's love for his only son and the richness of life with the image of the kingdom of Heaven. Although these metaphors and images provide a way for us to grasp important truths, they are only pale ghosts compared to the reality Jesus was trying to express.

I believe that we all have experiences of the spiritual dimension throughout our lives. Many are minor; we may not even be aware that we have experienced the transcendent. For example, we rarely give a second thought to those times when we have experienced the grace and beauty of the ordinary. At other times, a spiritual experience can be profound and literally change your life. Perhaps you were swept away on a flood of creative inspiration. Or perhaps you have experienced that mystical sense of merger when you become one with nature or another person or a group of people. I can recall very vividly an experience that occurred while I was walking with a friend through the rain forest in the Pacific Northwest several years ago. As we walked in silence, I could sense the rich stillness in the deep green of the forest, the leaves, mosses, and ferns all around me. We came upon a dip in the path, a place where the forest floor sank gradually about three feet and then climbed again. As I reached the bottom of this dell, I stopped briefly and looked around. Something shifted within me. I signaled my friend to walk on and stayed there, feeling a deep stillness within me, within my heart. The green all around me deepened to an intensity that seemed full, almost pregnant. The whole forest was breathing, and I was breathing with it. This lasted a few minutes. I finally just sat down to allow myself to be nurtured in the depths of my being by this feeling of unity and peace.

I believe we have all experienced similar sensations. These moments occur countless times a day, but we're so busy and unaware that we pass them by. Experiences that emanate from within the spiritual dimension of our being are known through our body. What the mind cannot understand—and it cannot understand a spiritual experience—the body can comprehend as a tangible feeling and transmit that feeling to us. We experience joy, love, serenity, peace, our own (w)holiness as a feeling within our body.

The form of the experience is of little importance. The spiritual dimension is expressed and experienced differently by each person. One of my clients, describing his experience of the spiritual dimension, said it felt like "a glow I can rest in." Another described "a feeling of deep warmth that moves up in me, and then I know things are going to be okay."

Opening Yourself Up to the Spiritual Dimension

Opening to increased spiritual awareness begins with noticing and honoring the transcendent experiences in your life. They may last five seconds or five days and can occur in nature or on the crowded street of the inner city. As we begin to acknowledge these experiences and sensations, we open ourselves to noticing more of the miracle of life.

The great religions of the world have attempted to develop ways to help people connect with the spiritual dimensions. Ideally religion, with its stories, rituals, and symbols, is a vehicle for spirituality. Too often, however, organized religion focuses the attention of people outward on externals—the words of the ceremony or the rules for behavior. Or through custom and habit the meaning becomes dulled. Sometimes the images used by a religion are taken literally rather than viewed as metaphors, and people envision a literal Heaven with pearly gates guarded by St. Peter. The metaphor is mistaken as the reality.

It is through the spiritual dimension *within our own being* that we have connection with a higher power. It is this relationship that is revered and celebrated in religious rituals, ceremonies, and symbols. Behind the external lies the living reality of the spirit. The spirit lies deep within each human being as well.

The spiritual dimension is everywhere, and it is within. Jesus Christ said, "The kingdom of Heaven is within." St. Augustine, one of the leading philosophers of the Catholic Church, described his search for God this way: "Too late I loved you, O Beauty, so ancient yet so new! Too late I loved you! And, behold, you were within me, and I out of myself, and there I searched for you." All the great spiritual leaders say that to know the spiritual dimension, the source of your life, look within. Once found within, you will see the spiritual dimension all around you.

Your Inner Self: Your Link with the Spiritual Dimension

When you go within to seek the spiritual dimension, you will find and experience an essence or inner core. This is your inner self, your link with and identity within this dimension of your being. This inner essence has been given many different names over the centuries. Roberto Assagioli and C. G. Jung described it as the

Losing Touch with Your Inner Self

"Self." Theologians such as Paul Tillich call it "the centered self." Others have called it the "ground of being," the "God or Goddess within," the "true self" or "true nature," the "Higher Self." I prefer to use the term *inner self*. Your inner self is like a seed that is rooted in the ground of your spiritual dimension, receiving nurture and vigor from it.

Fritzjof Schuon, who writes about world religions, describes it this way: "There is in every man an incorruptible star, a substance called upon to become crystallized in Immortality; it is eternally prefigured in the luminous proximity of the Self." The image of the star calls to mind the experience of inner light that is often a sign of the emergence of the inner self. Christ said, "You are the light of the world." Buddha said, "Be a lamp unto thyself."

Your inner self is the source of a deep and trusting identity that is true for you. It is the center of your personhood, self-esteem, and self-worth. Experiences of the inner self have tangible attributes that are felt as sensations within the body—feelings such as grounded, solid, secure, and authentic. One client said that when she touched into her inner self, she felt as if her center of gravity shifted from her neck and shoulders to her solar plexus and pelvis. She felt stable and aware of herself.

I know my inner self as an experience of a feeling of being planted solidly on the earth. I can trust this sense of my inner self. I'm frightened sometimes by what it draws me to do but it's always there supporting me, solid and strong. When you live in touch with and out of your inner self, you know you belong and you feel your belongingness on earth.

When I first began to acknowledge and feel the presence of my inner self and a spiritual dimension within me, I wrote a poem that tries to express the feeling as a metaphor. I want to share it with you, for I believe it describes the indestructible nature of the inner self. As readers, I ask for your understanding of the difficulty of trying to convey such a powerfully moving experience:

> *May my life be a snowflake—*
> *Unique in pattern from all before and all to be;*
> *Intricate in design and laced frailty,*
>   *feathers and bonds.*
>
> *Cool to the touch and yet melting with a caress,*
> *I will float down to cover—*
>   *a bough, a leaf, the ground,*
>   *a path, the ice or never cover at all.*

My melting will not be death—
*   only resurrection*
To a new pattern.
I will follow streams; I will be dew;
I will bring forth flowers
*   and I will gray the clouds—*
Ever to refresh, ever to be renewed.

To grasp a snowflake, one unique crystal of God's
*   creation is not possible.*
The touch of love melts it away
*   as I will melt when love touches me—*
*   be it flower, rock, sea or sun.*
Still I will retain
My unique beauty, my own pattern,
My very personal way.

The Inner Child and the Inner Self

It's easy to confuse the inner child and the inner self. For a few years I believed they were the same. But the inner child is only one aspect of the inner self.

When my clients ask me how they can distinguish between the inner child and the inner self, I refer them to their own experience. From my own experience I know my inner child as a delightful, spontaneous, childlike part of me. The inner child has certain characteristics and qualities, including impulsiveness, awe, trust, adventurousness, wonder, curiosity, candor, spontaneity, excitement, willingness to take risks, and playfulness.

Your inner self is your source of strength, the core of your being, your light within. Your magical, mystical inner child is your source of wonder, awe, playfulness, and curiosity.

The Relationship of Spirit to Body and Mind

The inner self of the spiritual dimension does not function independently. When you are out of touch with your inner self, you feel disconnected from your body and dominated by your mind. You don't feel solid and whole in yourself. On the flip side, when you are in contact with the inner self, the other two dimensions of your being follow in an integrated, harmonious sense of wholeness.

The three dimensions of being function in harmony, wholeness, and integrity with each other. The inner self can emerge, and the person has an opportunity to bring forth his or her gifts, truth, and essential contribution to the human community. Inner strength and courage are available through contact with the inner self and the spiritual dimension.

Codependence fundamentally damages the harmony, wholeness, and integrity of the three dimensions of being by cutting you off from contact with your inner self. How alienation from this core of your being affects the rest of your life, and your mental and physical dimensions, is the subject of the rest of this chapter.

The Physical Dimension and the Inner Self: When It Feels As If There's Nothing There

If you are codependent, you may be almost completely out of touch with your inner self. As you stuff your feelings, you smother your inner self and hinder your ability to experience it. As you repress your own desires and ignore your values to follow the wishes of others, you stop expressing your unique self. Your inner self is not lost, but you may not even know it's there.

Your inner self is not who you *think of* as yourself—that's your personal self. Your inner self is your essential identity at the core of your being. When you feel the loss of this identity you experience an emptiness within.

Have you ever asked the question "Who am I?" and been unable to find any solid answer? That's because the answer is buried deep within you. Have you ever been afraid to look more closely at yourself because you're afraid there's nothing there? Felt that life was meaningless except for the structures imposed on you from the outside? Felt unreal? These feelings are typical if you're out of touch with your inner self.

I remember one of my early sessions with Melanie, a successful conference manager in her mid-thirties. Melanie had grown up in a family addicted to social conformity. Looking good was so important that when Melanie was raped as a teenager, this trauma was covered up and never discussed.

"I've learned to pay so much attention to other people's feelings and what my

parents wanted," said Melanie about her goals for our sessions, "that I've totally ignored myself. I don't even know who I am."

"How do you know that you don't know who you are?" I asked. I've found that this self-reflective question encourages people to reach for their feelings associated with loss of self.

At first Melanie just looked at me with a quizzical and stunned expression. Then she remained very still as if exploring some internal reality.

"I don't feel like me," she said at last. "I feel out of touch with myself."

"How do you feel out of touch?" I asked. Notice how inadequate our words are here to express the feelings we both understand. I was encouraging her to have more than the words, to tap into the felt experience.

"I don't trust me; I don't trust myself," she replied with growing frustration as she grappled for a way to communicate her inner reality. She looked at me with eyes full of desperation. "Don't you know what I mean? It's like there's nothing there."

I did indeed know what she meant. I can remember one of the first times I became aware of both my inner emptiness and my inner self. I was attending a weekend retreat that focused on meaning and purpose in life. That was during my days as a hospital administrator, scurrying up the ladder of success and keeping busy trying to please everybody. I lived life automatically, trying to keep myself satisfied and out of pain. I had never seriously considered the meaning of my life. But during one presentation on living intentionally, honestly, and creatively, I felt something stir within me. Suddenly I sensed an inner void and knew that my life was empty despite all the frantic activity in which I engaged. Something yearned for expression deep within me.

But I was frightened by this experience. For the next four years I tried to ignore it, staying busy and moving restlessly from one success to another. I didn't want to pay attention to that yearning because I didn't want to change my life.

Robert May in his excellent book on religion, *Physicians of the Soul*, describes the encounter of Moses with the burning bush as a metaphor for this meeting with the inner self: "It is from within our souls that we experience God or the Self. When you have this experience, you are indeed on holy ground. You have reason to fear, as Moses did, because your whole accustomed way of life may be swept from beneath your feet. You may be called upon to perform tasks that you never believed yourself capable of."

Writing this book is an excellent example of that kind of task. I first felt drawn to writing almost 10 years ago. But as with many of my dreams, I could not sustain the energy and commitment. It was a dream based mostly on fantasy, with no ground or strength in my inner self. Still I struggled with writing as I struggled in my own healing and recovery process, keeping a journal, beginning several books. In the Introduction I said that writing this book is what this book is all about. It is the fruit of my own recovery. It represents the accomplishment of a task that I never thought I could complete. And without a sense of my inner self, it's true, I would not have been able to write it.

Heeding the Call

Sometimes you may actually hear an inward call that beckons you. Most people experience this as a sensation, an inexplicable feeling within. I remember when I first allowed myself to experience this calling. It was the time in my life when I was most alienated from my inner self. It was when I hit bottom. I knew that I had to end a codependent relationship and face my feelings of abandonment and loneliness and the fear of the dark unknown. But I couldn't move. I felt like a ghost, an empty shell.

Yet at the same time I felt inside of me a call, a deep beckoning so real that I thought of it as a voice. The quote at the beginning of the book refers to this beckoning as a "summons" that will bring you into awareness of your inner core. The word *vocation* comes from the same Latin root as *voice* and *vocal*, for that's what a vocation is—a call to self-expression and a life lived in accordance with the true self.

Like a seed, your inner self represents all of your potential, the pattern of your skills and passions that can be brought to fruition during your life. When it calls you, it calls you to be who you are in your heart of hearts, regardless of the conventions of society or the desires of your loved ones.

In my case, when my despair was greatest, I surrendered to this inner call and made the choice to change, facing the pain and beginning the recovery process. I knew not with my mind but with my heart that what I was doing was right, even though it hurt me and disappointed others. And during the years that followed my awareness of my inner self increased. I became aware of a growing sense of inner strength. It was something I had read about and prayed for but never experienced fully before.

Clients with whom I've worked who have reached the point in recovery where they feel the inner self often talk of something happening deep within. Sometimes they cry, not sad tears but tears of quiet joy, as they attempt to put this experience into words.

I can remember the change in Melanie, the woman who didn't know who she was. After several months of intense work she came into my office one day with a wide smile on her face and a twinkle in her eye. She was eager to tell me what had happened:

"I was reading about feelings and spirituality," she explained, "and suddenly I understood something. But not with my head. It was like everything lined up. It passed, the feeling, but I had it. And I know it's there. It was a sense of trust in me, an inner kind of feeling that made me feel like everything was going to be okay. It was different from anything I've ever felt before, and I want to feel it again. And I know I will."

Sometimes the call from your inner self leads you to self-expression. Your passions and interests lead you to the core of your self if you know how to listen to them. If you are true to your heart of hearts, you will be following your own path.

I finally began expressing the yearning that I had first felt during that weekend retreat and ignored for so long, by keeping a journal to record my experiences of life, a process I continue today. As I felt more comfortable expressing myself in writing, I extended my efforts, which culminated in this book. I still don't know if writing is the best expression of my inner self—I also want to learn to play the mandolin, write poetry, and paint. I do know that expressing my self through writing enriches my life and grounds me in a significant way.

The process of recovery can open the pathways again so you can experience and express your true self. The sense of satisfaction and confidence that you develop as a result will be your greatest reward.

Ignoring the Call

Codependence interferes with your ability to listen to your hearts of hearts. If you are codependent, the phrase "ignoring the call" is perhaps a little strong. Because you probably have only faintly heard the call of your inner self, you've grown adept at ignoring it.

You've already learned that an unhealthy emphasis on other people is one of the chief characteristics of codependence. This is one of the ways in which codependence damages your ability to be in touch with your inner self. As a participant in one of my workshops put it, "When you are codependent, you've lost touch with the inner pathways to spirituality because you listen only to the external." If you're preoccupied with meeting others' standards of behavior, you don't look inside for your own standards, for your own sense of inner rightness. If you're concerned with seeming normal or being liked, you'll choose to adopt the beliefs and values of those around you without checking to see if they're in conflict with your own beliefs and values.

What are the consequences of ignoring the call once it is heard? For me, it was like avoiding something that I desperately wanted. The way I dealt with this contradiction was to run into addictions that kept me numb. I have heard clients pour out tears of inner anguish as they described the ways they have attempted to ignore the call from within: "I've been asleep and wasted half my life"; "I have to feel what it would be like to really be myself before I die"; "I can't keep running from myself. It's too painful."

Ignoring the call makes a wasteland of your life, a barren experience devoid of meaning and purpose.

I Feel; Therefore I Know Who I Am

Descartes' dictum "I think, therefore I am" focuses on the mental dimension as the means of knowing you are alive. To balance this emphasis on the mind I want to propose this statement: "I feel; therefore I know who I am." Codependence hampers your ability to feel your own emotions. You can never really know who you are until you get in touch with your feelings. If you repress your values, your inner truth, and your unique talents in an effort to survive in a dysfunctional family, you cannot truly feel a sense of belonging in the world until you reclaim those values, talents, and truth found in the inner self.

The sensations of feelings are the means by which your inner self communicates with you. Have you ever had the experience of knowing something without knowing how you know it? At such a moment you have a felt sense that is tangible and registered in your body and that can carry you through a difficult situation with confidence because you trust your feelings and the truth of your inner being. It's at these times that you know who you are.

Substitutes for Ecstasy

Addictions are the most predominant way to substitute for the lost feelings of the inner self. In Chapter 6, I explained how addictions result from the compulsive need to alter unwanted moods and feelings. If you want to avoid feeling emotional pain, you can use substances or processes to change the physical symptoms of discomfort in your body. You can also use addictions to simulate the experience of your inner self in the same way.

Instead of experiencing the "natural highs" of life and the joy and ecstasy of communion with your inner self and the spiritual dimension, you can become addicted to substances and processes that only simulate these feelings. For example, the high induced by alcohol, the pleasure of sexual orgasm, the delight of good food, and the excitement of intense romance are all feelings that we naturally want to experience. They are part of feeling alive. When they cannot be experienced from a source within, we attempt to create them using something outside ourselves. What we use can become an addictive substitute for the ecstasy that the inner self alone can provide. These substitutes for ecstasy will never satisfy your deep craving for belonging and meaning and the feelings of joy and aliveness that your inner self brings.

When you inner feeling space is blocked with stuffed feelings, your inner world is lost.

The Mental Dimension and the Spiritual Dimension: Personal Self and Inner Self

As discussed in Chapter 6, if you are codependent, you are likely to overinvest yourself in the mental dimension. The result is the development of an identity I call the personal self. The personal self can also be called the ego self.

The personal self is the identity you constructed to forge your identity in the world, and it is an essential part of life. It is made up of your roles, self-image, and learned skills and traits. But it is also the source of your fears, apprehensions, and worries. It is founded in a fear-based awareness of life, possibilities, and experiences. The inner self knows no such fears.

Robert May describes the difference in *Physicians of the Soul*:

Our ego is the conscious self which we usually call "I." It is the center of the conscious side of ourselves. Most people, even most psychologists and psychiatrists, consider this "the self." Those who have made the inward journey, everyone from Dante Alighieri to Carl Jung, discover within themselves a deeper center which we have called the "Self."

The ego is little you, separate, suffering, fearful, and in a state of exile. The "Self" is the greater you who is no longer separate from, but reunited with God. The "Self" lives in an ineffable peace and joy.

Ideally, your personal self and your inner self resonate with each other. Your personal self gives intellectual expression to the creativity and gifts of your inner self. Your inner self also provides the values and truths that you use to make decisions and carry out actions.

There are essential differences between the personal self and the inner self. You construct your personal self. Likewise, you can dismantle and change it. The inner self is not constructed by you nor can you change or control it by employing the functions of the mental dimension. What is often experienced as growth during recovery is, I believe, the emergence of the inner self into awareness. The riches of the inner self are like a buried treasure that has been within you all the time, waiting for you to access them. The process of recovery, the healing of the physical and mental dimensions, helps you reconnect with the spiritual dimension.

Difficult as it is for codependents to give up control, the experience of the spiritual dimension is uncontrollable, like the visitation of grace. May calls it the "spiritual power which moves when the ego steps aside." Through recovery, your personal self is transformed so the spiritual power of your inner self can move into your awareness.

As painful wounds are healed and the ability to feel increases, as old defensive and addictive patterns of behavior are abandoned and new, more life-affirming choices are made, the layers of protection and numbness that have alienated you from your inner self dissolve.

The gifts of recovery are great. As the seed of your unique identity becomes rooted in the ground of the spiritual dimension and nurtured to full expression, you develop the ability to live in harmony with your self, nature, and others. You become capable of deep love and respect for yourself and others. You experience health and wholeness of being. You feel "natural highs" from your expressed creativity, sense of community, and spiritual growth.

The process of recovery will restore integrity and wholeness to you. By healing the physical and mental dimensions and supporting you in reclaiming your inner self, recovery brings you the harmony of being that you were created to experience. Part Three provides the plan for recovery.

Losing Touch with Your Inner Self

PART THREE

· · · · · · · ·

A Gift of Pain:
The Recovery Plan

———

8

• • • • • • •

A Plan for Recovery

*And the end of all our exploring will be to arrive where we started
And know the place for the first time.*

"Little Gidding,"
Four Quartets,
T. S. ELIOT

IN THIS CHAPTER I WILL
provide you with an overview of a recovery program that you can use as a map to
guide you on your personal adventure of recovery. I will point out some of the
landmarks that let you know you are proceeding in the right direction, warn you of
some of the pitfalls, and describe some of the experiences you may have along the
way. Recovery from codependence means getting back in touch with your inner self,
which is unique. Your journey of recovery will, of necessity, be unique too.

Consider the lines from T. S. Eliot above. You can think of your recovery
process as an exploration. What you will find, after going deep into the past and
plumbing the depths of your self, is what was there all along—your self.

There are certain attitudes that will enhance your recovery, the same attitudes
that enhance any journey of exploration.

1. **Willingness to experience change:** being open to new concepts, behaviors,
   attitudes, people
2. A **desire for truth and reality:** a willingness to look at what *is* rather than
   seeing what you want to see or imagine to be true
3. **Openness** to your inner world of feelings and experiences
4. **Commitment** to the process: perseverance, or not giving up when things
   aren't easy

The Wheel of Change and Growth

Clients often ask me to tell them more about recovery. "What happens in recovery?" "How long will it take?" "Is there any pattern?" "Are there landmarks to watch out for?" "How will I know when I've gotten there?" "How will I keep from getting sidetracked?"

To answer these questions I began searching for a concept that would help me convey my understanding of the process of recovery. I knew from my own recovery and from observing my clients and friends as they moved through recovery that there was an underlying pattern, a very fluid but still predictable succession of experiences and feelings that fall into four stages. Each stage involves a different experience, and passing through each is essential to real growth as a person. However, each of us has developed ways to block the change and growth process by avoiding and denying feelings. To illustrate how this happens, I use a circle as shown below.

The Wheel of Growth and Change

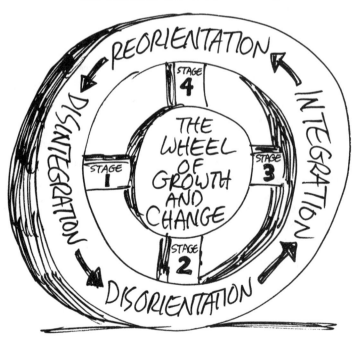

The four stages of change and growth are:

Disintegration: This is the natural beginning of the process of change. Before change occurs, something must start to come apart, to unravel, to disintegrate. It might be a significant relationship, your self-image, or work.

Disorientation: As the cycle moves from disintegration to disorientation, you may lose a sense of your bearings. Old ways of being or coping are falling apart, but you have nothing new to take their place. One client described this stage as "no-man's-land." It is usually experienced as uncomfortable, even painful.

Integration: As the wheel of change turns, you enter the stage of integration. You develop new outlooks and new ways of relating. Having successfully passed through disorientation, you begin to act on your new learning.

Reorientation: The wheel has turned full circle, and you've reached a new level. You have thoroughly assimilated the new information you gained during the cycle. You are a new and different person. Obviously this stage leads into a new cycle of growth.

In Chapter 1, I outlined the impact of avoiding feelings. I'm not talking about good and pleasant feelings. Most of us want more of those. It's the uncomfortable and painful feelings that we try to avoid and deny. It's those feelings that let us know we're experiencing distress in a situation or relationship. "Negative" feelings can be a sign that something isn't working for us.

They let us know that something is awry, that things are beginning to fall apart. They are signals of the first stage of the wheel of change and growth: disintegration. It's at this point that we are likely to try to control things around us, to fix what's wrong, to meet the needs of other people or find other ways of dealing with the uncomfortable feelings. This is where recovery starts, for this is the situation that offers us a choice to continue covering up our feelings or face them and own our own experience. To own a feeling is to name it as yours and to acknowledge its presence in you.

Many codependents about to embark on the recovery journey find the wheel of growth enhances their perspective on their own patterns of behavior. A participant at one of my workshops said, "I can see how I've used my addictions to relationships and food to avoid change and avoid feeling. I hate that place you call disorientation, so I never let go. I have to control everything." Another person provided a different perspective when he said, "I've been in recovery from codependence for two years. I've been feeling really stuck lately—like I'm getting nowhere. Now I understand that I don't have to search for things to work on. Experiences in my everyday life, like when I want control someone or deny my own anxious feelings, are valuable for my recovery. Even my frustration about being stuck is part of it. It's all part of that stage of disintegration."

Each of the four stages of the process of growth and change corresponds to a stage of recovery. As you move through these stages, you will encounter different recovery issues and challenges. Awareness of what happens in these four stages will help you prepare for what lies ahead. In the next four chapters I will discuss the different issues that come to the fore at each stage and provide the resources and skills that will be most useful for each.

The four stages of growth and change and their corresponding stage in recovery are summarized below.

Stage	Stage of Growth and Change	Stage of Recovery
One	Disintegration	Identifying and Dismantling Defenses
Two	Disorientation	Accepting Yourself and Experiencing Your Feelings
Three	Integration	Taking Responsibility for Yourself and Your Feelings
Four	Reorientation	Affirming and Expressing Yourself

The Ever-Winding Road

Recovery is an ongoing process. As you work your recovery, the wheel of growth will turn in its natural sequence. Gradually the dimensions of your being will move into integrated and harmonious alignment.

Recovery is not a simple, straightforward linear process. You won't complete all the work of one stage before moving on to another. Nor is it a process you can schedule. You will find yourself working on various issues at different times in your life. Some people need to spend a year on Stage One before gradually moving into Stage Two, and then only for brief excursions at first.

It may take years to move through all four stages to really make the deep and lasting changes you want to make. At the same time, the experience of going through these stages can happen in a very small way when you make changes in specific behavior patterns.

During recovery you identify your role and your self-messages. You also—and this is most important—become able to access deep feelings such as abandonment, inadequacy, and loneliness, that you have suppressed. As a result of this work, you should find yourself ready to try something new. And when circumstances trigger your old feelings, you will be able to accept your feelings and take responsibility for them rather than cover them up. You are then able to formulate a new belief. And this new belief will be confirmed by your experience. You have intervened in the cycle of codependence.

Of course, recovery is made up of a series of small steps, and sometimes you will make a choice that feeds the cycle of codependence again. Other times you will make the choice that breaks the chain of codependence and brings you a life-affirming experience that strengthens your resolve to continue choosing recovery. Imagine that on the perimeter of the wheel of growth are many little wheels, all strung together as depicted in the illustration on page 136.

Each of the little wheels represents a complete turn on the wheel of growth and is also part of a larger cycle of growth. It's like a tree that passes through a cycle of growth each year. Leaves die and fall away in autumn, the branches are bare, and growth is slowed to a minimum during winter, then buds form and new leaves sprout in spring, and the tree becomes a canopy of green in the summer, until the leaves start falling again. Yet this whole cycle of growth is only part of the larger life cycle of the tree, which continues to grow and expand and stretch its branches toward the sun and its roots down into the earth for nourishment over a period of many years.

The focus of the process is different for everyone. You may focus on one relationship or a particular behavior and experience all aspects of the recovery process in a short period of time. Or you may work in a more general and global way and move much more slowly. Some of my clients want to work on a particular behavior, such as people pleasing, and choose not to explore any of the other dynamics of codependence. I trust the process. I know that the wheel of growth will eventually bring them back to the point of codependent disintegration and give them the opportunity to look at what they missed the first time through.

The Ongoing Process of Recovery

Remember that your own journey of recovery will be as individual as you are. There's no one right way to recover. I'm always surprised and delighted by the variety of paths chosen by my clients and friends.

Moving Through the Dark

The overall direction of the journey of recovery is upward and forward. But sometimes, in the throes of the stage of disintegration or disorientation, painful feelings and feelings of being overwhelmed predominate.

In the throes of disintegration there's a point at which you may feel that life was better before. As one client said, "Why did I ever open up this Pandora's box? I can't go back, but going forward seems overwhelming."

One of my clients described his experience this way: "It's like trudging through a desert and not seeing an oasis anywhere." During one particularly moving session he wept because of the pain of his losses.

"My friends could always rely on me," he said through his tears. "I was always there—solid, stable, the one everyone could count on. They knew whom to call when they needed help. Now they say they don't trust me. I'm changing." He paused for a moment and wiped his eyes. "Yes, I am changing. I don't want to keep on giving advice, rescuing people. But who's going to be there for me? I feel like they have all abandoned me."

Unfortunately, when you change and discard dysfunctional roles, you may throw your relationships off balance. Some friends can adjust; others may want you to stay the same. Disorientation can mean a loss of not only internal but also external reference points.

Is this pain necessary? Isn't there some way to avoid wandering in this desert of uncertainty and doubt? If there were, believe me, I'd be able to set up a stand selling road maps of the freeway to recovery. I can tell you that I've tried countless ways that promised a quick and painless trip to recovery, and I haven't found any such shortcut.

What comforts me, and what has always helped my clients when facing the deep feelings that are part of recovery, is an understanding of the process. I expect to feel disoriented and confused and to have feelings that I don't understand and don't like. I know that as I let go and trust them, I will become stronger.

I remember a particular session with Carol, the people pleaser you met in Chapter 4 who said in describing her life that she had "forged a forgery." After we had been working together for eight months, one afternoon she came into my office, threw herself into a chair, and immediately burst into heartrending sobs. When she was finally able to speak, her first question was "Will I get through this?"

When I asked her what was going on, she said, "I feel so abandoned and alone. In my mind I know that's not true, but I feel it so deeply." Her words triggered another outburst of tears, and she wrapped her arms around herself and wept quietly for several minutes.

Although I could not reassure Carol that she would make it through, I did remind her of the cycle of growth. She was feeling what she could be expected to feel during a period of disorientation. The fact that she could feel the pain of abandonment so deeply was a good sign. I encouraged her to continue acknowledging her feelings. Only by fully experiencing them could she move on to reintegration and reorientation.

Relapse: Going Backward

Sometimes going backward is part of the journey. I relapsed, and so do many of my clients. When I use the term *relapse*, I don't mean the process of taking two steps forward and one step back that is a normal part of recovery. I'm referring to a return to old habits and patterns, including the need to control, confusion, obsessive-compulsive behavior, use of addictions as a way of coping, and inability to take care of oneself.

For one of my clients, Robert, relapse meant getting involved in an addictive relationship. Robert, who first came to see me because of his depression after the breakup of a relationship, had been working on his own recovery for a year and a half. After some hard times he began developing new friends and a social life that involved healthy people. Then he met a woman and "felt that old feeling." Within two weeks he was "lost," as he put it. He kept calling her, he had to see her, he obsessed about her. It was all very exciting and passionate. They talked about being in love and being soul mates.

As Robert put it, "It got crazy very fast. I can't explain it. All I know is that I completely lost track of myself." Although Robert felt like he was dying in the relationship, he couldn't leave it. Ultimately the woman left Robert, saying that it was all too intense for her. Robert was able to get back on the road to recovery again, with a new realization about the way it felt to be codependent.

Always be aware that relapsing into codependent behavior doesn't mean that you have failed. You can use the experience to become conscious of the pain of codependence and to gather information about the behaviors you want to change.

Getting Help for the Journey

I didn't and still don't undertake my journey of recovery alone. I need the help, support, and love of understanding friends. I need the reality check and feedback of a therapist. In my private practice I need clinical supervision. I have no desire to do recovery alone—although ultimately we are all alone on our paths.

Remember that you are changing as a result of your recovery program. Your needs for friendships will change. Old friendships may not feel right anymore and new ones may seem hard to find. There may be a period of time when you feel like you don't have any friends who understand what you are going through. Support groups such as Co-Dependents Anonymous can provide a source of new friends who will understand and support the changes you are trying to make. And as more people embark on this journey of reclaiming their lives, life-giving friendships will be easier to create.

You can't begin to deal with codependence if you have a primary addiction to alcohol, drugs, or some other highly compulsive behavior. Trying to walk down the road to recovery without ridding yourself of an addiction is like trying to cross a river in a boat full of holes. Your addiction prevents you from gaining access to the feelings you must recover for your recovery.

As long as you are practicing your addiction(s), you will not experience the depth of change and healing that is possible. Get treatment for the addiction first, the codependence second.

When you read a book on physical exercise, there's always a caveat at the beginning suggesting you check with your physician before engaging in any exercise program. In a similar way I recommend a physical self-care program as the basis for recovery. Taking care of your body is an essential part of the recovery process.

I also strongly advise you to find emotional and social support for your recovery, particularly by attending Twelve-Step meetings or working with a therapist.

Modeled after the original Twelve-Step program of Alcoholics Anonymous, self-help meetings for adult children of alcoholics and codependents are springing up all across the country. You may want to attend one of these meetings or any of the other Twelve-Step meetings to which you feel drawn. They are basically free, making emotional support for recovery available to everyone. As you move through the stages of recovery, Twelve-Step meetings provide a safe place where people will listen to you without judgment. The value of sharing your feelings at a meeting can help you work through the tough times.

Although I believe in the power of self-help groups, a trained and knowledgeable therapist can also be needed at certain times. If you experience or become aware of any of the following, you need to seek professional help:

- You are the victim of sexual or physical abuse.
- You feel depressed and are thinking about suicide.
- You are involved in a destructive relationship that you can't leave.
- You are abusing drugs or alcohol or engaging in some other compulsive behavior such as gambling, sex, work, or the pursuit of excitement.

- You are physically or sexually abusing someone.
- You are feeling immobilized or stuck in your behavior and being hard on yourself for not changing.

When choosing a therapist, bear in mind that *you* make the choice. Interview several therapists. Ask friends who are in recovery for the names of therapists they have worked with. I don't recommend randomly selecting someone. When you meet with a therapist, ask him how he has dealt with his own childhood issues and how he maintains his recovery. It is my opinion that if the therapist refuses to discuss this, you should go elsewhere. Frankly, the helping professions are a natural hideout for individuals who learned the role of hero, rescuer, or caretaker in their family. The fields of counseling and psychotherapy can be the breeding ground for codependence because of the nature of the helping process. Therapists can focus on other people's problems rather than taking care of their own. For example, if a therapist doesn't understand the process of disintegration or disorientation or know from personal experience what happens in these stages, there may be a tendency for him or her to try to stop or control the process. In this way he or she can avoid his own discomfort with the unknown. You have a right to work with a therapist who has training in and understands codependence and addiction issues and is personally working on a recovery program.

Group therapy is an alternative to individual therapy for getting support during recovery. Groups are less expensive than individual therapy and are effective in providing an environment in which family-of-origin issues are recreated.

Be careful! If you are telling yourself at this point that you can do it all on your own, you're still behaving codependently, insisting that you are in control and don't need help. You haven't surrendered. Both Twelve-Step group meetings and groups and work with a therapist have been important sources of insight and inspiration for me during my recovery. In fact, I don't know anyone who is recovering from codependence without such support.

Pitfalls

There are pitfalls on the recovery journey. I've experienced some of them and watched my clients flounder into others. If you're warned about them ahead of time, you may be able to avoid them. Here are some of the more common pitfalls:

Shortcuts

It's tempting to believe that you can find a shortcut to speed up your recovery and get you to your destination faster. Some of the shortcuts I've seen people use include meditations with tapes, subliminal programming, deep breathing sessions, hypnosis, bodywork, and any of the hundreds of other therapies on the market that promise "quick cures." This is not to say some of these therapies aren't valuable. In fact, I encourage my clients to get bodywork and do other therapies. The important point, however, is that there is no such thing as a quick cure. Recovery means surrender and letting go of control. Recovery takes time.

"I'm All Better Now"

Some people believe they will automatically be better at the end of two years, five years, or some other deadline: "Well, I've been working at this for three years. I must be cured." It's almost as if healing were a prescription. Take so many months of individual therapy, add a long-term group, go to so many Twelve-Step programs a week, and you'll stop being codependent within X number of years.

Recovery is a highly individual process. The harmful and debilitating effects of codependence heal over time. But codependent thinking never really goes away—the patterns linger within you and may be stimulated again. I believe you never really stop recovering, particularly if your goal is true self-expression and self-development. Time provides you with opportunities to deepen and expand on your earlier discoveries, but you never stop exploring and growing.

I recently had an experience that reminded me of the natural wisdom of the recovery process. In 1983 I noted in my journal a shameful and confusing sexual experience that occurred when I was seven years old. During all the subsequent years of therapy and inner work, I never touched on this issue; perhaps I wasn't ready. At a recent professional workshop I had the opportunity to really go into the feelings and the experience and heal a wound that had been festering for 34 years. I came away from this intensely aware of the depth of the wounds of childhood and strengthened by what I had experienced.

Unrealistic Expectations

Having unrealistic expectations is one of the characteristics of codependence. So it's easy to understand how many codependents assume that if they commit themselves to the recovery process, they will never be codependent again. Wrong.

Codependence is part of being a human being, just as dysfunction is part of the family process. Dr. Charles Whitfield notes in *Healing the Child Within* that codependence is endemic in the population.

Black-or-white, either-or thinking is another typical trait of codependence. Some people believe there are two ways to be: codependent and "recovered." That's a misperception. Everyone is, to some extent, codependent.

Both recovery and codependence are processes, and both imply movement. I believe that the term *codependence* is best used as a description of a constrictive process of living that inhibits your self-expression, dulls your experience of life, and alienates you from your inner self. Recovery is a process of growth and change toward greater health, expressive freedom, and a fuller life. As your recovery program progresses, you will be more conscious and aware of your feelings and thoughts. You will be less fearful and overwhelmed by uncomfortable feelings. This will support you in making better choices. I often tell clients that their discomfort will not disappear—life is filled with pain—but their range of feelings will expand in recovery and their ability to tolerate uncomfortable feelings without recoiling into patterns of fear and defense will be enhanced. Thus, life expands and becomes more of an adventure to be lived, not avoided and feared.

Labeling

As you become more aware of your controlling and avoidance behaviors, you'll see more of it all around you. As information about codependence is disseminated to a wider audience, more and more people tend to view the world through a filter that interprets every form of behavior as either "addictive" or "codependent." Acknowledging your own codependence will increase your understanding and compassion for others in whom you see the pain of codependence. Remember, your job isn't to fix them but to heal yourself. By taking care of yourself, you are providing the best mirror in which others can see their life reflected.

Loving and accepting yourself—all aspects of yourself, even those you consider "codependent" or "unhealthy"—is an important part of the healing process. I suggest you do the same when you are tempted to judge and label others. Instead of labeling and judging, get in touch with how you are feeling about those individuals, how their behavior affects you, and what you intend to do about it.

Tips for the Traveler

Before you launch into the four stages of recovery, here are some recommendations that will enhance your journey. First and foremost, you need a commitment to truth. If you aim for the truth whenever you are feeling lost in the process, you will find your direction. As M. Scott Peck says in *The Road Less Travelled*:

> Truth or reality is avoided when painful. We can revise our maps [ways of perceiving and responding to the world] only when we have the discipline to overcome that pain. To have such discipline, we must be totally dedicated to truth. That is to say that we must always hold truth, as best we can determine it, to be more important, more vital to our self-interest, than our own comfort.
>
> Conversely, we must always consider our personal discomfort relatively unimportant and, indeed, even welcome it in the service of the search for truth. Mental health is an ongoing process of dedication to reality, at all costs.

The recovery process is complex, rife with discoveries and revelations. Keeping everything in perspective as your inner truth emerges is not always easy. Here are some suggestions to help keep you on track as you regain contact with your lost inner self:

1. Develop and maintain life-giving, honest relationships.
2. Take care of your body and heed its wisdom.
3. Allow yourself time for creative expression.
4. Maintain your resolve to heal past hurts and the wounds of childhood.
5. Live at your highest level of consciousness and in accordance with your inner truth.
6. Acknowledge yourself for progress made, however small.
7. Dare to live your deepest truth at least once a day.

8. Take time for spiritual practice, which nurtures your relationship with a high power.
9. Explore, recognize, and be willing to express the gifts of your inner self.
10. Forgive yourself and others.

9

· · · · · · · ·

Stage One:
Identifying and
Dismantling Defenses

A journey of three thousand miles is begun by a single step.
Lao-Tzu

A S I W R I T E T H I S C H A P T E R ,
it is autumn in the Pacific Northwest. The trees blaze with color—red, orange, gold. Drifts of fallen leaves blanket lawns and litter sidewalks. There's a chill in the air, even when the sun is out. Usually the sky is overcast and the days are gray, sprinkled with light rains that leave the streets glistening. It gets dark earlier; the nights are longer.

If the first stage of the recovery process were a season, it would be autumn. The blazing glory of summer is fading. Soon the trees will be bare as they surrender to the natural cycle of nature. Autumn is a time of disintegration and decay. Like autumn, there may be a sense of deterioration about your life at the start of the recovery process, accompanied by feelings of melancholy and sadness. It's a time of reflection, of turning inward.

In Chapter 8 I discussed some of the circumstances that may have brought you to the point of making a choice to look at your own codependence and how it has affected your life. Stage One of recovery begins with that moment of choice when you decide that you need to change your life.

During Stage One you become aware that you've spent so much time trying to take care of others that you've forgotten how to take care of yourself. You realize that if you continue to live codependently, your life will become increasingly constricted, empty, or unmanageable. This stage of recovery requires your willingness to acknowledge the ways you have protected yourself from pain and growth and conscious awareness of the defenses you've developed to do so. The resources and exercises in this chapter are designed to be used by individuals who are just beginning their recovery as well as those who have a program under way.

Willingness is one of the key words for Stage One. Willingness doesn't have to entail a dramatic commitment to change. The leaves don't fall from the trees all at once. They drift away one by one. The willingness necessary in Stage One can be a gradual, incremental process beginning with something as simple as "being willing to be willing." Just the act of reading this book is an indication of your willingness to learn about codependence.

Awareness is the other key to your recovery. Willingness and awareness go hand in hand at this stage. Your willingness to begin the process of recovery will contribute to your increasing awareness of the extent to which codependence has affected you and of the defenses you've developed to protect yourself. You can deepen your awareness by using the tools for recovery—exercises and recommendations—found in this chapter.

Dismantling Defenses

As a codependent you have expended a lot of energy avoiding the discomfort of change and disorientation. You have built up powerful defenses. One common defense against anxiety is denial. According to the *Dictionary of Psychology*, denial is a "defense mechanism that simply disavows or denies thoughts, feelings, wishes or needs that *cause anxiety* [italics added]." Denial is an unconscious mechanism; it protects you from conscious awareness of the things that disturb you. When you are willing to become aware of those thoughts, feelings, wishes, and needs that you have hidden for so long, denial dissolves.

Codependents use many different methods of denial. Here are some of the forms of denial I've seen in myself and my clients:

Complete Denial: "I am not codependent. I do not control my feelings or other people."

Rationalization: "We're all codependent, so why bother to work on this stuff?"

Magical Thinking: "I know that once I finish school [meet my soul mate, find a new job, etc.], life will be okay."

Minimizing: "It's not that bad. It really doesn't bother me that my spouse is angry and critical all the time." Or "I've dealt with my parents. I moved a thousand miles away from them, and I hardly ever talk to them."

Spiritual One-upmanship: "I can stay in this abusive relationship because I'm learning about unconditional love." Or "No one understands my spiritual path."

Denial of Stress: "My life might be hard and my job might be high-pressure, but I can handle it."

Agreeing with Others: "It's easier to go with the flow and agree with what other people want. I don't like causing problems and conflict."

Comparing Yourself: "I'm not as codependent as other people. I know a woman who's really sick—she's been waiting for seven years for her husband to change and come back to her. I'm not that bad."

New Age Denial: "Reality is just an illusion. I can create my own world, and I can change it just by changing my thoughts." Or "My guides have told me that she will change if I do things differently."

Religion: "If I pray, God will cure his alcoholism." Or "God wants me to learn to tolerate pain, so I have to put up with abuse."

All forms of denial give us the illusion that we have control over ourselves and over reality. Several of the statements above may have sounded familiar to you. Every person uses a variety of defenses.

Addictions and compulsions are also used as defenses against anxiety. So are roles. When you give up your addictions and roles and face reality, you let go of control.

"It's All Falling Apart"

Although the decay of autumn seems like an ending, it is actually part of the cycle of growth. The old leaves that are not needed during the winter fall off the trees. Just so, you let go of your old defenses, those that are no longer useful in your life.

The first stage of recovery is a time for experiencing the disintegration that leads to change. Things fall apart, structures disappear, forms lose their shape and fall away.

One of my clients described his experience at this stage of recovery in these words: "All my illusions—I didn't even know they were illusions—are dying. Things are falling away, and I'm feeling stunned. Or scared. I don't really know how to describe it."

The illusions that were deteriorating were all those patterns of thinking and behaving that he had built up as defenses against anxiety. Your defenses are like the autumn leaves. As you let go of them, they fall to the ground and begin the natural process of decay. You no longer have the defenses you've used for so long to protect yourself from pain and anxiety. You are left bare, facing the cold winds of reality. This experience of disintegration is unsettling, even frightening.

How You Might Feel

As you dismantle your defenses, the extent to which self-negation permeates your life may shock you. You may respond by being even harder on yourself. Or you may be tempted to retreat into **denial** to numb yourself to the unpleasant shock of reality. These are normal responses and part of recovery.

A sense of **shame** can loom ominous and dark on the horizon at this stage of recovery. John Bradshaw believes that internalized shame is the essence of codependence and the fuel for all addictions. When Bradshaw talks about shame, he's talking about toxic shame, the experience of feeling basically unworthy, flawed, imperfect, and inadequate as a human being. Healthy shame encourages acceptance of your limitations and acknowledgment of your imperfections. Toxic shame attacks the core of your identity. If you avoid taking any steps toward recovery because you feel that you don't deserve a better life or it's impossible for you to change, you are succumbing to toxic shame. If you begin recovery but relapse into addictive behavior or a codependent relationship, you may use this to feed your sense of unworthiness. Shame is a feeling like any other. When you begin to experience feelings such as shame and others—as a result of Stage One work—you are actually entering Stage Two and can use the techniques I recommend in that stage to work through your feelings.

In addition to shock and shame, you may feel **angry** as you look at your family of origin and the subtle as well as obvious ways you were emotionally, psychologically, spiritually, and perhaps sexually and physically abused. The purpose of this work is healing, not assigning blame. However, it is often necessary to acknowledge your anger toward your parents and others who mistreated you "for your own good" or because of their disease. Sometimes this means actually confronting them on their behavior. This does not mean they will change or even agree with your interpretation of what happened. You may get guilt-provoking reactions such as "How ungrateful of you after all we did!" or "I did things because I loved you so why are you angry now?" In recovery, you will learn that being angry isn't about judging someone or assigning blame. Being angry is the result of needs not being met. You have a right to be angry at your parents for not meeting your needs as a child and any emotional wounds you suffered growing up. The anger you are feeling is the anger you could never express. Acknowledging the fact that you are angry and have a right to be is an important step you take toward healing and recovery. I spent almost two years being angry at my father for his alcoholism and at my mother for her enabling. My anger was an essential part of my recovery. I had to feel angry before I could shift my focus to forgiving them.

As you explore your past, you may be tempted to rationalize or minimize the trauma you suffered. I often hear my clients make statements like these: "Oh, it wasn't that bad." "My parents did their best." "That was in the past—I can't change it now."

This tendency to minimize the pain of the past is especially likely to occur when you become aware of the losses of childhood. In their book *After the Tears* Lorie Dwinell and Jane Middleton-Moz discuss the need to both acknowledge and grieve the losses of childhood. This is a slow process of dismantling defenses and letting in the truth, feeling sorrow and **grief** over the loss of childhood—and all the losses you have suffered as a result of addictive and codependent behavior.

How Willingness and Awareness Expose Defenses

During Stage One your willingness to examine your life honestly brings greater awareness of the defenses you have used to protect yourself from the pain of growth, as shown in this chart:

Through your willingness to:	You become aware of:
1. recognize your codependence	how you have focused on others for your own sense of self
2. identify your roles and defenses	the stress you have created for yourself

3. identify your belief systems	how you sabotage your own happiness
4. acknowledge your need to control others	how out of touch you are with your needs and feelings
5. explore your family-of-origin interaction patterns, abuse, and emotional oppression	how you learned to survive in your family, the roles you played, and the effect they had on you
6. understand how you deal with emotional pain	your addictive and compulsive behavior
7. surrender control and admit your powerlessness to control others	how out of touch you are with yourself
8. get in touch with your "inner child"	the anger, pain, and fear you are hiding within

As I've said before, in a certain sense, recovery is never over. You will find yourself, as I have numerous times, at Stage One. This means that you are consciously practicing your recovery program and have an opportunity for personal growth. The intensity and amount of work may vary, but the process is still the same.

Tools and Support

In the following sections you will find specific exercises and activities that will help you work through Stage One. These suggestions are organized according to the lines of this book. You will find resources for healing physically, mentally, and spiritually. I encourage you to utilize all the exercises and the tools recommended in this chapter over time. Working with all three dimensions of your being will enhance your recovery.

Healing the Physical Dimension

As you learned in Chapter 5, denying your feelings can cause stress-related illnesses, body armoring, and a frozen, compacted inner feeling space. You become alienated from the wisdom of your body and the sensations of life. Most importantly, you cut off or diminish contact with the core of your being, your inner self.

There are two reasons to focus on improving your physical health during Stage One. The first can be illustrated by a simple action: Right now, clench one fist as tightly as you can. I'll tell you when to unclench it later.

Recovery is a stressful process—and hard work. You need to be in good physical health to benefit from it. Like the hard-driving executive who gets sick on vacation, when you give up the constant tension of codependence, your body must release its pent-up tension in some way. As you work at dismantling the codependent behavior patterns that you've maintained for several years, you may experience minor illnesses, chronic fatigue, muscle aches, and other symptoms of stress. It is essential to establish practices to take care of yourself physically.

Second, you want to improve the ability of your frozen inner feeling space to transmit feelings. This means healing the emotional wounds of the past. As the feeling space is healed, your body will become a more fluid and open vehicle through which to experience and express your true inner self.

The exercises and tools described in this section are directed at these two goals.

Stretching and Exercising

Through the years you've developed chronic patterns of tension and defense. As described in Chapter 5, every time you repress a feeling, your muscles tighten. If you never express those feelings, the tension in your muscles remains.

Are you still clenching your fist? As a result of years of stuffing your feelings, your muscles, especially those in your chest, neck, upper back, and stomach, are tight like your fist. In essence, clenching your fist is the same thing you have been doing with the muscles in your body when you push your feelings away and repress them. Unclench your fist now. Notice how your fist feels as you unclench it. Now gently stretch your hand and fingers and notice how this helps you to release the tightness and loosen up your muscles. Imagine if you had to hold your fist like that for a few hours? A few days? Twenty years? That's what you have been doing to your body by stuffing your feelings—creating tension and tight muscles. That relaxing process is like the first stage of recovery. Physical stretching will help you release tension and loosen up your muscles.

The ability to contain a feeling without being overwhelmed or controlled by it is an important part of recovery. Strong feelings can cause you to constrict your body and tense up. Regular stretching can help you recognize where you are storing your tension in your body and release it. As you release the tension stored in your muscles, you improve your capacity to feel without being overwhelmed by feelings.

You can create your own exercises; just be sure to be gentle with yourself to prevent injury. Follow these three simple guidelines, which you can also use as metaphors for healing from codependence:

1. Stretch gradually and slowly.
2. Be consistent.
3. Aim for stimulation but not exhaustion.

You will also benefit from a balanced, regular program of physical exercise. This will increase your awareness of your body and its sensations. It's also a great demonstration of your self-love. You can undo some of the damage of early neglect by developing and maintaining good physical health. When you take care of your body, you are saying to yourself "I love you and will take good care of you."

Eating Well

In the other-oriented and hectic world of codependence, you may have neglected your nutritional needs. You need fuel for the journey of recovery, and what you eat is that fuel.

During my drinking days I told myself that I ate well, but I was deluding myself. This belief was part of my denial. I see the same denial operating for many of my clients when I ask them about their eating habits.

Do you skip breakfasts or call coffee and a Danish breakfast? Do you skip lunch or grab a candy bar and a soda pop? Do you drink coffee or cola to keep yourself going? Do you get a headache when you don't have your coffee or other form of caffeine? Do you binge on sugary or salty foods?

I was surprised by how changing my eating habits changed my sense of well-being. For many years my eating patterns reflected my life-style—they oscillated wildly. Sometimes I ate well-balanced meals; other times I existed on fast foods and sugar (for instance, snacking on sugary granola bars). I gobbled down my food as if

I was never going to get any more. I changed my habits gradually. Instead of skipping breakfast, I began making it the nutritional foundation of my day. I chose to eliminate red meat from my diet and started drinking more water—my goal is to drink six to eight glasses of water a day. I also started taking mineral and vitamin supplements daily. The pattern of eating I developed was focused on balance and following some simple wisdom about eating natural foods as much as possible and avoid sugar, fats, and processed and refined foods. I often recommend that clients talk to a nutritionist or their doctor about a good diet and the use of vitamin supplements if they are unsure.

These changes have been gradual, and I've had a chance to experiment on myself; for instance, noticing how I feel when I eat sugar. This practice makes me more aware of my body. When I eat what's right for me, I feel centered and grounded. My mood swings taper off. As with exercise and stretching, eating well gives me a sense of taking care of myself, which is an important affirmation of my value.

I encourage you to explore your current eating patterns and try some changes. As a start, you might want to follow my recommendation to my clients and monitor your food intake for a week. Write down everything you eat, when, and under what circumstances.

There are many conflicting suggestions about the healthiest diet. But most experts agree that Americans need to eat more fruits, vegetables, and whole grains (whole-grain cereals, whole-grain breads, and whole grains). Other suggestions that are helpful to most of my clients include eating a nutritional breakfast and cutting down on or eliminating caffeine and sugar.

When one of my clients looked at her eating habits, a clear pattern emerged, a pattern that coincided with her hard-driving rescuer role. Just like me, Ellen snacked on granola bars to keep her energy level up. She also used coffee to sustain her busy life-style. With coffee and sugar as energy sources, she was sometimes able to keep going from 4:00 in the morning until 10:30 at night. Her busy round of family, friends, meetings, work, etc., was fueled by chemicals.

Ellen decided to alter her eating habits and slowly eliminated caffeine and sugar from her diet. At first she was surprised by her fatigue. She started sleeping more, and she wasn't able to take on so many projects. This made her uncomfortable. As she became more accustomed to relying on the natural energy of her body, she was able to make wiser choices about how to use her time. Instead of scattering and fragmenting her energy in several directions, she more often chose what was right for her, what was self-nurturing.

Reflecting on Your Medical History

The following summary sheet is designed to help focus your attention on your own body and your health. Completing it will give you perspective on the stress your body has experienced. Pay particular attention to the diseases and surgeries of childhood. The emotional traumas related to medical problems are still lodged in your body and may be haunting you today.

MY MEDICAL HISTORY

Family History *(check if present)*

__ stroke __ high blood pressure   __ diabetes   __ cancer

__ heart problems   __ mental disorders __ other _____

__ high cholesterol and triglycerides   _____

Personal Habits *(indicate yes or no)*

__ smoking   __ drug use (type   __ sleep problems __ exercise

         and amount ___)   __ alcohol use (amount: _____)

__ coffee & tea __ restricted diet ___

Medications I Take: _____

Accidental Injuries: _____

_____

Allergy History: _____

_____

Diseases/Surgeries of Childhood *(age and circumstances):*

____ _____

____ _____

____ _____

____ _____

____ _____

Operations/Hospitalizations Since Childhood:

_____

_____

_____

_____

Other Personal Health History *(Check if applicable and include your age when the problem first appeared):*

_____ skin problems _____ *(age)*   _____ eating problems _____

_____ diabetes _____   _____ thyroid problems _____

_____ cancer _____   _____ tension headaches _____

_____ kidney problems _____   _____ muscle tension _____

_____ herpes _____   _____ backache _____

_____ leg cramps _____   _____ muscle tremors _____

_____ ulcer _____   _____ nausea _____

_____ diarrhea/irritable bowel _____   _____ gas/indigestion _____

_____ stroke _____   _____ heartburn _____

_____ elevated cholesterol/   _____ high blood pressure _____
triglyceride levels _____   _____ asthma _____

_____ migraine headache _____   _____ mental problems _____

_____ frequent colds/flu _____   _____ depression and mania _____

_____ excessive perspiration _____   _____ anxiety _____

Take time to complete this survey thoroughly. Then take additional time to reflect on what was happening in your life when you experienced various illnesses and surgeries. Have you had any chronic illnesses? You might want to look back at Chapter 5, especially the section on disease and codependence, to see if you can make correlations between the illnesses you've experienced and the circumstances of your life at the time.

Consider your childhood medical history. What was like for you as a child to experience the illnesses, hospitalization, and surgeries you did? If you can't remember, what do you think it was like? If any of these occurred when you were a young child, ask yourself how you could have expressed your fear, anxiety, and pain. The experience of invasive medical procedures can be terrifying to a young child. The isolation of hospitalization can bring up fears of abandonment. The memories of these experiences are recorded in your body in the form of feelings in the same way your body records any abusive experience. As you identify the traumas you experienced as a child, you will get a better sense of the compassion and understanding needed by your inner child.

Giving Up Addictions

Like most codependents, you have probably developed some addictive or compulsive behaviors that you use to help protect yourself from anxiety and pain. In many ways codependence itself in an addiction to a process of control. Like all addictions, it limits your ability to experience your inner self and your feelings. Addictions also provide artificial sensations of life to replace those that have been numbed through repression and denial.

The defenses of denial and addictions are closely intertwined. Addictions are used to deny the pain of a codependent life-style. For instance, you may be addicted to the intense emotional highs and lows of a roller coaster relationship because it helps you feel the intensity of feelings that are missing in what is otherwise an unfulfilling relationship. At the same time you may deny that your turbulent relationship is addictive, believing that the intense emotions you experience represent genuine love.

The questions below will help you discover whether you are using any process or substance in an addictive way. They will also help you begin to examine the situations and feelings that trigger addictive behavior.

AM I ADDICTED?

1. What do I do to alleviate feelings of stress, conflict, anxiety, and depression? Do I use a substance such as food, drugs, nicotine, or alcohol? Or do I use a process such as meditation, exercise, relationships, or sex?

_____

_____

_____

_____

_____

Stage One: Identifying and Dismantling Defenses

2. What happens (or what do I think would happen) if I were not able to alleviate my feelings of stress, conflict, anxiety, and depression using the methods identified in question 1?

_____

_____

_____

_____

_____

3. What happened in the past when my ways of coping with the above feelings were not available?

_____

_____

_____

_____

_____

4. Have I ever felt the need to keep certain activities or behaviors a secret from others? Which behaviors or activities do I want to keep secret?

_____

_____

_____

_____

_____

5. Have I ever resolved to give up or reduce my involvement with something (either a substance, like tobacco, or a process, like a relationship) only to find that I could not maintain my resolve? Which substances or processes have I tried to give up? What happened when I tried to give them up, and what happened when I realized I could not maintain my resolve?

_____

_____

_____

_____

_____

6. Do I find myself preoccupied with planning for a particular activity or making it the major focus of my life? For instance, do I plan my whole day around running or meditating or food? Which activities are a source of major concern for me? How do I feel if I don't fit these activities into my schedule the way I planned?

_____

_____

_____

_____

7. What happens when I take time for myself, alone, to reflect on my life, my activities, my aspirations, and my feelings about myself?

_____

_____

_____

_____

_____

Answering the above questions thoughtfully and honestly will help you identify addictive behaviors that are keeping you out of touch with your feelings and your inner self. You will have to give these up as you proceed through your recovery.

Keep in mind, however, that recovery is a process. You won't give up all of your addictions at once. The process is more like peeling an onion. You may work on some compulsive behavior that really troubles you now, perhaps giving up an addiction to cigarettes or working on a compulsion to eat. Later, after having gone through the cycle of recovery, you may take a new look at your life and realize that you want to work on giving up other addictions, such as perfectionism or intellectualization.

At the beginning I recommend choosing one or two addictive behaviors to work on. If you are addicted to alcohol or drugs, you may want to consult a chemical dependency expert for advice on the best way to proceed. Becoming involved with one or more of the Twelve-Step programs will provide support and encouragement if you are trying to give up alcohol (Alcoholics Anonymous), drugs (Narcotics Anonymous), cigarettes (Smokers Anonymous); or an addiction to sex (Sexaholics Anonymous), food (Overeaters Anonymous), or gambling (Gamblers Anonymous). It's important for you to have a lot of support when you are giving up a defense that has protected you for so long. Don't do this alone. Make sure you have plenty of support and encouragement, whether from a therapist, a group, or caring friends.

Your Inner Child: Healing the Wounds of the Past

Once you begin using any of the tools introduced in this chapter for working through Stage One of the recovery process, you may experience deep, inexplicable, and often overwhelming feelings. Because these exercises help you give up your defenses, they can lift the top off the well of feelings that has been covered for so long. You may only sense these feelings deep within. Or you may actually experience them fleetingly. When you come into contact with them, you may want to retreat into your defensive patterns again. After all, that's why you developed your defenses in the first place—to protect you from the painful feelings you repressed in childhood.

Stage One is the time to lay the groundwork for the deeper healing work of Stage Two by contacting your inner child and reassuring that child of your love and concern. This relationship is vital to your inner child's emotional growth and sense of security and thus is vital to your emotional growth and sense of security. The exercises in this section are designed to help you create safety and security for the emotions of your inner child and thus for yourself.

The first step in contacting your inner child is acknowledging how you treat yourself. During Stage One your willingness to acknowledge your self-abusive behavior is part of the disintegration process and provides energy for moving into Stage Two, accepting yourself and your feelings.

Being Your Own Best Parent

I wish I had followed the advice I gave my friends over the years when they were hurting or in turmoil or feeling frustrated. Because of my codependence, I found it easier to take care of others than to take care of myself. So with my friends I was patient, compassionate, and concerned, while with myself—well, that's a different matter.

If you're like most codependents, you react to yourself, as I did, the same way your parents reacted to you. If they were cold and punitive, you are probably cold and punitive to yourself. If they neglected and ignored you, you probably neglect and ignore your inner child.

Reflect on the way you were treated as a child by reviewing and answering the questions below.

PARENTING MY INNER CHILD

1. How did my parents react to me when I was angry, hurt, afraid, crying, proud, or withdrawn? Did they acknowledge my feelings or tell me to change them? Did they try to comfort me or did they ignore me? Was I told I was bad when I was angry or upset?

   _____

   _____

   _____

   _____

   _____

2. How do I treat myself when I feel the same ways? Do I judge myself harshly and criticize myself, or do I accept what I am feeling?

_____

_____

_____

_____

_____

3. How do I react to my own children (if any) when they are angry, hurt, afraid, crying, needy, or withdrawn? Do I acknowledge their feelings, or dismiss them, or try to change them by offering solutions to problems?

_____

_____

_____

_____

_____

Something to watch out for: your ideals about child rearing may be different from the way you actually behave.

Pictures from the Past

Find several pictures of yourself as a child at various ages. As you look at each picture, think about what was going on in your family at the time it was taken. Put a selection of pictures you have found where you will see them every day, even if it's just a glance.

One of the pictures I chose was a picture of myself when I was four, all dressed up like a 40-year-old man in a topcoat, hat, and tie and with a very sad expression. I didn't know why I chose this picture until about four years later, four years of glancing at it daily. Then I had an opportunity to work on the meaning of the sadness in my own therapy and discovered the memory of an early loss of relationship with my father.

When I was two and three, I used to work with my dad in his workshop in the basement. Although my memory of these times is vague, I do know that they were nurturing for me. Sometime when I was four, the tools were taken away. I can recall the scene vividly. I can still see the tools being loaded into the back of a truck and feel a sense of hurt and confusion. I couldn't understand what was happening, but I felt as if I had lost something. And I had. Only recently did I learn that my father's drinking increased dramatically soon after that and gradually got worse over the next seven years. As a four-year-old, I had experienced a loss that was not resolved in my emotions until my early forties.

GETTING TO KNOW YOUR INNER CHILD THROUGH PICTURES

Use the questions below as a guide to exploring pictures of yourself as a child.

What pictures are available? If there are few or no pictures, what does that mean to you?

_____

_____

_____

_____

_____

How old are you in the pictures?

_____

_____

_____

_____

_____

Stage One: Identifying and Dismantling Defenses

What are you doing in the pictures and what expressions do you have on your face?

_____

_____

_____

_____

_____

What was going on in your family when these pictures were taken?

_____

_____

_____

_____

_____

What would you like to tell the child you see in the pictures?

_____

_____

_____

_____

_____

At different times in your healing process you may find other pictures are more evocative or reveal new aspects of your inner child. Your inner child isn't one-dimensional any more than you are.

Recalling Childhood Memories

You can also learn a lot about your inner child by writing a history of your childhood. List your birth (date, time, place, circumstances, etc.), then list as many experiences as you can recall, including vacations, births, pets, schools, illnesses, family moves, deaths, everything. Include events from your own memory and those that you've been told about by others. I think you may be surprised, like many of my clients, by the number of experiences you can recall from birth to age 10.

As you look over your list, notice any patterns that emerge. When Shelly did this exercise, she wasn't surprised by her memories. As the daughter of a military officer, she vividly recalled the disruption of constant moves from base to base. At one time her family moved four times in two years. However, she was surprised to notice the self-message she had developed as a result: "I can't have a lasting friendship."

At age 29 she had no long-term friendships although she desperately wanted them. Instead, as she said, she "always managed to drive people away by wanting to keep them in my life." Remembering the anxiety she felt as a child about not being able to develop lasting friendships helped her see that she was actually continuing this pattern in her life.

As you work on your recovery, you will undoubtedly recall other experiences that aren't on your original list. You can keep adding to your autobiography as you explore memories and work with feelings throughout recovery.

Blankets and Teddy Bears

When I was young, I had a favorite blanket. For some of you a doll, a teddy bear, or some other stuffed animal might have been your special comfort object. Perhaps you got your comfort from a family pet, such as a cat or a dog.

Whatever it was, it was an important part of your childhood. It helped you get your needs met. You can use the feelings associated with this object in your recovery. If you can remember your childhood comfort object, find something similar and use it whenever you need comforting.

When I was working on healing my inner child, I found a blanket that I used to comfort my inner child. I would wrap the blanket around me and rock back and forth, which is what I used to do in my childhood. It felt soothing, relaxing, and nurturing.

SUMMARY

The following suggestions will enhance your Stage One healing in the physical dimension:

1. Adopt a regular exercise program that includes stretching.
2. Review your eating habits and change them if appropriate.
3. Fill out the brief medical history on pages 154–55 and answer the questions that follow it.
4. Identify any addictions by answering the questions on pages 156–58 and take steps to give them up. If the idea of giving up an addictive substance or process seems overwhelming, enlist the support of a counselor or attend Twelve-Step meetings.
5. Answer the questions on pages 160–61 about how you treat your inner child.
6. Find a childhood picture or pictures to represent your inner child and display them someplace like the bathroom mirror, where you will see them daily.
7. Write out your childhood memories as suggested on page 164.
8. Find a comfort object—ideally like one you used in your childhood, such as a blanket or stuffed animal—to use to comfort your inner child.

• • • • • • •

Healing the Mental Dimension

During Stage One of recovery you begin to dismantle your defenses, the codependent thinking and behavior patterns you've developed. This is the experience of disintegration, like the leaves of autumn falling to the ground. But Stage One doesn't mean completely discarding all those ways of thinking, acting, and reacting, which have served a definite purpose in your life and have a positive side. The functions of your mind can be great allies during recovery, and that is how they are used in this section.

Which Roles Did You Play?

During Stage One you begin to identify your beliefs, self-messages, and roles. Becoming aware of these allows you to understand how you have maintained and repeated self-destructive behavior patterns. Once identified, you can begin to experiment with letting go of these concepts and behaviors, which will open you up to experiencing your buried feelings during Stage Two.

Roles are important defenses used to avoid feelings. In Chapter 3 I described a number of different roles that family therapists and other experts have identified in dysfunctional families. A list of these roles is provided in the following exercise. Check off those roles that you have played at various times in your life.

WHICH ROLES ARE MINE?

__ Hero/Messiah: I maintain self-worth through achievement and responsibility.

__ Caretaker/Enabler: I focus on keeping things going and looking normal.

__ Scapegoat/Black Sheep: I take the blame for things not working and keep the focus off problems.

__ Rescuer: I focus on helping others out of situations as a way of avoiding the discomfort of powerlessness.

__ People Pleaser/Nice Person: I focus on pleasing others and being nice to avoid conflict or tension.

__ Clown/Mascot: I provide comic relief during times of stress, conflict, and tension.

__ Tough Guy or Gal: I maintain an image of strength to avoid helpless feelings and anxiety.

__ Rebel: I go against rules, authority, and structure as a way of coping with powerlessness.

__ Perfectionist: I maintain focus on perfection as a means of controlling stress and anxiety.

__ Victim: I focus on a sense of helplessness.

__ Martyr: I derive a sense of self from giving up my own needs and enduring what others do to me, often in the name of "love."

__ Saint: I focus on being good, righteous, and meek to avoid "bad" feelings.

This list is by no means exhaustive. You may be able to identify other roles you play, or you may use another name to describe any of those in the exercise. I worked with one man who called his nice guy role "wimp." Another man referred to his people-pleasing role as "the robot."

You will have a chance to work with the information you've just gathered in subsequent sections. For right now, identification is the important step.

What Do You Tell Yourself?

Self-messages are those messages you give yourself about your self-worth, your capacities, your skills, and particularly your limits. Looking at your self-messages and taking responsibility for them is usually uncomfortable. Take some time to reflect on the messages you give yourself. They may be different in different circumstances and with different people. What do you tell yourself about your capacity to love and be loved, about your fear of success or failure, about your need to control people and situations?

SELF-MESSAGES

Examples

Some common self-messages are listed below. Look them over and see which ones resonate for you.

"I have to work hard to get anywhere."

"I have to help everybody."

"I have to hide my _____ ."

"If I take care of my own needs, I'm selfish (and that's bad)."

"I have to be perfect."

"I have to be right."

"I can't lose control."

"I have to be the perfect _____ [mother, father, daughter, son, etc.]."

"I don't deserve to be happy."

"It's my fault."

"I am not lovable."

"I better not be too _____ [successful, happy, etc.]."

"I don't count."

"I'm not important."

"I'm a loser."

"I have to stay in control."

My Self-Messages

Try to come up with your other self-messages. Look for statements that start with these phrases:

"I have to _____ ."

"I can't _____ ."

"I am _____ ."

What Do You Believe?

Your self-messages reflect beliefs you have developed about yourself in relation to other people and the world. As you try to identify your beliefs, you may be tempted to write down the beliefs you *wish* you believed. Rigorous honesty is the key to doing this work. You may not like what you find out, but remember, you must identify something before you can change it. Those beliefs that you refuse to acknowledge can continue to haunt you because you can't see them.

BELIEFS

Examples

As with the self-messages that stem from them, many codependents espouse certain common beliefs. These are just a few examples.

Work

"You have to work hard to make it in this world."

"No one appreciates my talents."

Friendship

"Women will always put men before their female friends."

"Your friends will stab you in the back if you do better than them."

Intimacy

"If I reveal my fears, they'll think I'm weak."

"When you're intimate, you lose yourself."

"If I express my real feelings, people will leave me."

People in General

"People are out to 'screw' you."

"You have to watch out for (beautiful; sloppy; foreign) people."

"If you're too powerful, people won't like you."

"People will always let you down."

The World/Life

"Life is a struggle."

"To be really happy, people need (money; a spouse)."

"The world is a dangerous place."

"Never be too happy, because it won't last."

My Beliefs

Now it's your turn. Try to be honest and state what you do believe, not what you *wish* you believed.

Work

What do I believe about work?

Earning a living?

(It may help to review places you have worked, the times you've left jobs, whether you quit or were fired, and what you told yourself about what happened.)

_____

_____

_____

_____

_____

Friendship

What do I believe about friendships with people of the same sex?
Of the opposite sex?

_____

_____

_____

_____

_____

Intimacy

What basic principles inform my intimate relationships?

_____

_____

_____

_____

_____

People in General

What do I believe about people in general?

_____

_____

_____

_____

_____

The World/Life

What are my beliefs about life in general?

_____

_____

_____

_____

_____

Also consider your beliefs about these categories:

Money

_____

_____

_____

_____

_____

Sex and Sexuality

_____

_____

_____

_____

_____

Religion

_____

_____

_____

_____

_____

Success and Failure

_____

_____

_____

_____

_____

Love

_____

_____

_____

_____

_____

Maintaining Control

Think about your current and past relationships. Codependence is marked by a focus on controlling others, which can be subtle or obvious. Consider the questions in the next exercise.

HOW PEOPLE CONTROL OTHERS

Examples

These are examples of how you might try to control others:
- By avoiding telling them your feelings about their behavior
- By trying to make them feel guilty about their behavior
- Through intellectual intimidation
- By acting like a victim, a martyr, a saint, or a rescuer
- By creating either-or situations
- By manipulating other people to see things your way

How I Control Others

1. How have you controlled others?

_____

_____

_____

_____

_____

2. Have you ever tried to control what another person does because you think you know what's best for him or her? Describe the circumstances.

_____

_____

_____

_____

_____

If you answer these questions carefully, you should acquire valuable information about how codependence has affected your relationships with others.

Shaping Your Life Through Fantasy

Fantasy is another powerful defense system employed by codependents to avoid the pain of reality. Your fantasies can tell you a lot about the roles and behavior you've chosen.

LOOKING AT FANTASY

Examples

You believe that you will finally be appreciated when you meet your soul mate.

You believe you will receive recognition for your talents when you get that promotion.

You believe that you will be healed if you take the right workshop or study under the right spiritual leader.

My Fantasies

From time to time, answer these questions again, choosing a new fantasy to examine.

1. Describe one powerful fantasy that feeds into or supports your codependence.

---

2. What effect does this fantasy have on your life?

_____

_____

_____

_____

_____

If you are grieving over the loss of a relationship, take a look at the dreams you had to give up as a result of the end of the relationship. Did you have dreams of living happily ever after, fulfilling the American dream, or being part of a happy family? You may still be looking for the kind of love you didn't get as a child. Sometimes these dreams may keep you in a relationship that has already ended because you don't want to give up on your fantasy.

Childhood fantasies can be revealing, too. My client Susan remembered childhood fantasies of being crippled. While dating her first boyfriend, she also had fantasies of terrible near-fatal accidents that would bring her boyfriend running to the hospital to see her. She noticed that in both of these fantasies her suffering brought love and attention from other people, a fantasy that reinforced her role of martyr. Actually it was only in fantasy that this role brought her the attention and love she craved.

Exploring Your Family of Origin

Exploration of family-of-origin issues often begins as part of the assessment and fact-finding process in formal therapy, although you can do it on your own. It's a logical, intellectual process, requiring fact-finding and data collection.

Family-of-origin work is difficult. Most of my clients would rather do any kind of therapeutic work than work on family-of-origin issues. I don't blame them—it is hard and painful work. I'd like to suggest a playful way of looking at this difficult task by comparing it to being a private investigator.

Maybe you've read novels or seen movies in which the hero is a private investigator. Usually he's good-hearted and ethical but behaves cynically because of some terrible loss he experienced in the past. The plot goes like this: The detective hero takes on a case and solves it by gathering evidence, interviewing people, and following others, often while being threatened and pursued himself. The hero may quickly solve the case at hand yet continue his investigation, drawn into probing into the dark, teeming forces that motivated it, perhaps going into the underworld, meeting with sleazy low-life characters, and delving into the past. Eventually his perseverance uncovers the source from which a distorted web of lies and conspiracies has been spun. Often he has to face a dark secret from his own past.

If you look at this plot as a metaphor, you can apply it to codependence. Your true inner nature, your passionate values and fresh perspective on the world, have been buried beneath codependent behaviors designed to protect you from deep pain due to abuse that you suffered in the past—the denial of your inner self. The case you have been assigned is this: explore your personal past, your family of origin. This involves collecting data, perhaps interviewing people you'd rather not talk to again. You'll be asking yourself and others some tough questions. You'll probably hear the usual evasive or dismissive answers:

"Let bygones be bygones."

"What does it matter what your grandfather did? He's dead now. Let him rest in peace."

"Respect the dead."

"How ungrateful! After all I did for you, why do you want to know what happened when you were a baby?"

The resistance you feel to doing this work isn't surprising. When you start asking questions about your family, you enter a world where silence and denial are the rules. You have to grope for clues. Everyone has some inner pain to protect and conceal.

You are still affected by the way you were cared for in childhood, the way you learned to get your needs met, the messages you received, the models you watched. This does not, however, mean that you are a victim of your past. You can't change what happened back then, but you *can* change the choices you make now. To do so, you have to understand the grounds for those choices. You will have solved your case when you understand the context from which your codependence evolved. Investigating your family of origin provides you with a means for understanding the background for your choices about your identity, your feelings, and your dreams.

Creating a Family Map

Creating a family map is a good way to begin your family-of-origin work. Maps can be very enlightening. Besides providing an overview of the family, they often reveal repeated patterns of behavior that have been adopted within the family system. When you look at a map of your family and see the intergenerational nature of codependence, you get a sense of the importance of the work you are undertaking. In order to recover you have to change the course of history.

I can remember looking at Tony's map with him. I had shown him how to draw a family map and asked him to create one as homework after our fourth session. When he showed me the map he had constructed, I was struck by the dramatic repetition of certain themes—particularly divorce and alcoholism.

"What does this reveal to you?" I asked Tony.

"Look at all the divorces!" he said. "Of my four brothers and sisters, all of us have been divorced at least once. My brother, Nicky, is on his third marriage."

"Any thoughts about that divorce rate?" I asked.

"Well, it's not surprising when you consider the family history," Tony said with excitement. (There can be moments of great elation when you identify the specters that have haunted you since childhood.) "I couldn't get everybody on one page, so I continued on another."

He handed me another sheet of paper that detailed his mother's relatives. His notes indicated that alcoholism was a problem on both sides of his family. When I saw his family map I had a better understanding of why Tony had called me for an assessment. His family map was riddled with the word *alcoholism*. Given this history, his chances of developing an alcohol problem were well above average. In addition, his ability to maintain long-term intimate relationships had been severely hampered by the codependence his family history would inevitably produce.

"I can understand now why I was worried about my drinking," Tony said. "I think practically every man in our family has been alcoholic. I found out while talking to my mom that my grandfather, her father, had a drinking problem."

He paused for a moment and looked at me, wincing as if in pain.

"What was that? You look like you're in pain," I said.

"I'm scared," Tony admitted. "Do I have a chance of overcoming this family history? Jesus, this is unbelievable. My whole family has lived in such pain."

THE FAMILY MAP

Here are some instructions for creating your own family map. The chart below shows some of the symbols you can use to indicate the relationships and dynamics of your family system.

Male with name and birthdate

Female with name and birthdate

Deceased with date and cause

Illnesses indicated

Married and date

Divorce and date

Separation and date

Living together

Children in order of birth

Miscarriage

Divorce/children with mother

Adopted child and date

A Sample Family Map

I'm going to use the example of Belinda's family to show you how to create a family map. Belinda is in her early forties. She has not been married and has had several relationships lasting from two months to four years. For two years she had been living with Jason, who, she suspects, is an alcoholic. She is employed as an office manager for a trucking company.

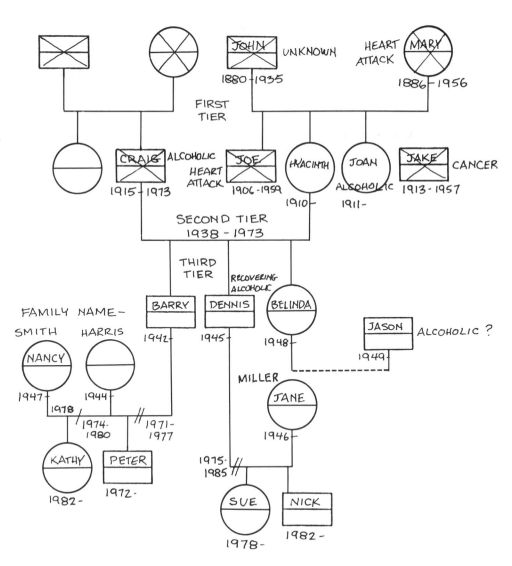

My Family Map

1. Start with your grandparents at the top of the paper. This is a good way to start gathering information about your family. (You'll note that in the example Belinda does not have any information about her paternal grandparents.) Insert names, dates of birth and death as applicable, and cause of death.

2. On the next line, in order of date of birth from oldest to youngest (left to right), place symbols for each of your parents' brothers and sisters. (On Belinda's family map you can see that her father had a sister that no one knows anything about. Her mother had three siblings, two of whom are dead—Joe and Jake. Joan is an alcoholic. Hyacinth, Belinda's mother, married Craig in 1938 and stayed married to him until he died of alcoholism in 1973.)

3. On the third tier of the map, draw your own brothers and sisters, including information about them and their relationships. (On Belinda's map she shows that her brother Barry has been married twice and separated from his second wife, Nancy, between 1979 and 1980. Dennis is a recovering alcoholic who married in 1975 and divorced in 1985. He has two children who are living with his wife, Jane.)

4. Include any relationships in which you are or have been involved. (Belinda indicates that she's living with Jason, who she believes is an alcoholic.)

Having constructed your family picture, what do you do with it? Look for repeated patterns. In Belinda's family certain themes are clear. There's a history of alcoholism, heart problems, and failed marriages. You may also notice certain messages that get passed down from generation to generation. Or you may notice that certain events happen at the same point in people's lives. As you look at your family map, ask yourself "What did I learn from being part of this system?"

You may need help interpreting your family map. That's when it's important to have a therapist who understands family dynamics and codependence and can help you identify the underlying dysfunctions in your family.

It may also help to find pictures of your relatives. One of my friends noticed a certain similar grim countenance that appeared again and again in the couples of her family album. The pictures she had of her parents when they were young showed

Stage One: Identifying and Dismantling Defenses

two radiant and handsome people, but after their marriage both acquired the worried, dissatisfied look of their predecessors. "That's when I was able to identify a certain attitude that I had sensed only dimly before," she said. "My parents had 'settled' for each other, but neither was really happy in the marriage, which is probably why I've been so marriage-shy. You can see the same pattern in my siblings and cousins."

The process of becoming an individual involves separating from your family and differentiating yourself. You *can* behave differently; you *can* change the family history. But first you have to know what it is that you are trying to change.

Writing Your Family's Story

Writing a family autobiography as a story can be a fun way to get a family overview.

MY FAMILY'S STORY

This story will include as characters all the people in your childhood and end with your leaving home. Limit yourself to three pages. Here are some guidelines:

1. The story should begin like so many stories: "Once upon a time . . ."

2. Next describe each of the persons in your family. What were they like? What did they do?

3. Describe the more important family events. Describe the family's struggles and challenges.

4. End with whatever event or act symbolized your leaving the family.

Don't worry if you think no one else in your family would agree with your story. Often this is the most upsetting part of family work. You come up with an important memory of what your childhood was like, only to be told flatly, "You're crazy. That never happened." Or, as one of my clients, Melanie, was told by her mother, "You're just making it up to get sympathy." Melanie wasn't surprised by this reaction from her mother, for she knows that her parents would never let anything destroy their illusion of how wonderful they were as parents. This illusion was part of their focus on social conformity and keeping up a good show for people to admire.

Fortunately Melanie had her perceptions of her childhood confirmed by another source. In a letter to me she described the moment when she realized that her perceptions of her childhood were fundamentally true despite how they differed from her mother's version. What follows is an excerpt from that letter:

The most healing gift I received at Christmas came from my mother—in a backward sort of way. She had converted several old movies into videos. My friend Phil and I watched alone (thank God!). It was all there. I seemed to be continuously on the periphery of the screen. Each "performance" was juxtaposed by one which was "better"—older or simply more skilled. My mother would make a gesture of affection when the camera was on her, but the gesture didn't last, and I stood, always quietly waiting, waiting to be told what to do or where to go, always making sure that my hands were folded, that I was being "good." "Am I measuring up?" I seemed to say.

As we watched, we both wept. And he said quietly, "They didn't celebrate your life. It's as if you didn't exist!" And I was quietly relieved. I was reassured at last that my memory of my childhood was not a fabrication in order to "gain sympathy." What my mother thinks happened in her mind and in my mind *are* different. And although it was truly painful to watch, I can finally rest in knowing where my insecurities began and how and why they were manifested.

Analyzing the Family Drama

Maybe as a result of writing your family's story, you recognized the role you played in your family. That's what I'd like you to consider right now. You identified the roles you played on pages 166–67. Now identify the roles you think the other members of your family played by writing their names next to the roles. Remember that roles are interchangeable and that every family member can play several roles.

WHO PLAYED WHAT ROLE IN MY FAMILY?

Hero/Messiah: _____

Caretaker/Enabler: _____

Scapegoat/Black Sheep: _____

Rescuer: _____

People Pleaser/Nice Person: _____

Clown/Mascot: _____

Tough Guy or Gal: _____

Rebel: _____

Perfectionist: _____

Victim: _____

Martyr: _____

Saint: _____

As you learned in Chapter 3, role playing is a normal part of life. It becomes problematic only when you identify rigidly with certain roles and don't allow yourself the full range of human expression. When roles are parceled out in a family, family members are assigned certain characteristics that go with their roles. Other family members may feel that they can't express those characteristics since they are already "claimed."

ROLES NOT PLAYED

Examples

If your older brother was the family hero and caretaker and you were the rebel and scapegoat, you may believe that you can't be competent and responsible and successful.

If your sister played the role of clown and you were the victim, you may think now that you can't make jokes or laugh too much.

Roles I Didn't Get to Play

What qualities and feelings were not yours because they were "claimed" by other members of your family?

_____

_____

_____

_____

_____

There is another side to this picture too. Each person playing a role provides an outlet for expression of those feelings and qualities for the family as a whole. Again, if you were the black sheep, you may have expressed the anger, unconventionality, and irresponsibility for the whole family.

SWITCHING ROLES

Examples

If you hadn't been the black sheep, maybe your father would have expressed his anger instead of holding it in; maybe he would have played hooky from work occasionally to go hiking in the mountains and taken you with him. Maybe if you hadn't been the caretaker for your mother while your father ignored her, your father would have had to change his behavior.

Switching Roles in My Family

What roles did I play? How might my family—my father, mother, and siblings—have behaved if they had played my roles?

_____

_____

_____

_____

_____

This is not to suggest that you are to blame for playing a particular role. You do not just adopt roles; you are "assigned" them by the system, and the whole family works to keep each member "in character." But this exercise can help you see that all the members of your family, like you, had a full range of feelings and experiences that they were unable to express because of the rigidity of the system.

Figuring Out the Rules

Most dysfunctional families operate under a variety of spoken and unspoken rules. I examined some of these rules under general headings—denial, silence, isolation, and rigidity—in Chapter 4, and you may want to begin thinking about your family's rules by reflecting on these. What topics were forbidden? What kinds of questions were you not allowed to ask? Could you tell your parents when you felt sad, afraid, or upset by their behavior? What were your family's secrets? How did you find out about them?

Your family may have explicit rules that are spoken, such as "We don't talk about what goes on in the family outside of the family." But your family probably also operated by implicit rules that were never spoken but were communicated instead with body language, like a frown or clenched teeth. I worked with a client who could vividly recall her father's stare. "I never knew what I did wrong," she said, still shuddering at the memory. "But I'll never forget those burning eyes." Another client remembered vividly the way her mother winced to indicate her disapproval. These kinds of rules are often denied when they are stated explicitly.

Your family probably had rules for a number of areas: appropriate sex role behavior (what makes a man a man and a woman a woman), attitudes toward money and work, and expression of sexuality. Rules about sex can vary from permissiveness and sexual abuse to strict taboos on the subject. Only by identifying these rules can you escape from their inexorable dominion.

FAMILY RULES

Examples

Spoken

1. "Never bother your father after dinner."

2. "Don't talk back to me."

3. "Always clean your plate."

4. "Do as I say."

5. "Be a good [girl, boy, son, daughter]."

6. "Always say 'please.'"

Unspoken

1. "Don't talk about Dad's drinking" (communicated by silence).

2. "When Dad's drinking, give him the silent treatment."

3. "Don't get angry" (communicated with a stare).

4. "Only sissies cry" (communicated with a frown).

5. "If you loved me, you'd [behave, smile, stop crying]."

6. "Nice boys and girls don't touch themselves there" (communicated with a look of horror or a slap).

My Family's Rules

In the space below, write out your family's spoken rules. Add to this list as you continue your investigations into your family of origin.

Spoken

1. _____

2. _____

3. _____

4. _____

5. _____

Unspoken

1. _____

2. _____

3. _____

4. _____

5. _____

Deciphering Negative Messages

Unlike family rules, negative messages are spoken directly to you as a child. These messages have a damaging effect on your development of a healthy self-image and can be major sources of your feelings of shame and unworthiness.

NEGATIVE MESSAGES

Examples

Here are some examples of negative messages:

"Shame! Shame! You ought to be ashamed of yourself" (usually delivered with one finger wagging in the air).

"You'll be the death of me."

"If only you were like _____."

"If only you were a better _____."

"Either you behave right or I'm leaving."

"How can you be so cruel [selfish, stupid, clumsy]?"

"I know you don't feel that way!"

"Why did you do that? Now look what you've done!"

"If you haven't got anything nice to say, don't say anything."

"You're going to be just like your father [mother, uncle]" (said after a derogatory comment about the other person).

"You shouldn't feel that way!"

My Family's Negative Messages

List the negative messages you heard as a child. Do you recall any that you heard repeatedly from your mother or father?

My mother used to say:

_____

_____

_____

_____

_____

My father used to say:

_____

_____

_____

_____

_____

These remarks may seem silly or patently false when viewed from your rational adult perspective; they were devastating when you were a child.

One of my clients, Vic, who came to see me because he had trouble letting go of relationships that had ended, was describing his family in rather general terms during one session when he recalled one of these early negative messages. This message had been so terrifying for him as a boy that he had developed many defense mechanisms to protect him from remembering the feelings associated with it.

Vic was saying, "I really can't remember much. It's kind of blank. It was the typical stuff that you experience in an alcoholic family. But my mother puzzles me. I always thought the problem was my alcoholic dad, but my mom . . . ," when he suddenly stopped talking and stared off into space for a moment, almost as if he were going into a trance. After a brief pause Vic went on talking for a minute or two about a completely different topic.

I pointed out what had happened and asked Vic what was going on when he mentioned his mother.

"I remembered something she used to tell me all the time," he said hesitantly. He gazed off into space again. "She used to say, 'Either you behave or I'm never coming back.' Then she'd march out the door. I'd cry, and my older sister would comfort me; I guess I was about eight or so. I really believed that she was never coming back. I was always terrified when she did that." He stopped for a moment and returned his gaze to me. "Is that why I hate it when a relationship breaks up? Because I fear I'm going to be abandoned?"

"I don't know, Vic," I replied. Vic had dissociated from his feelings as evidenced by his gazing off into space while he talked. His immediate intellectual assumption ("Is that why I hate it when a relationship breaks up?") was another sign of his discomfort with the feelings evoked by this statement. There were reasons why Vic disassociated from the feelings this experience evoked in him. I'll come back to this session with Vic in Chapter 10 to illustrate what happens in Stage Two, when defenses such as disassociation are dismantled.

Your Family's Beliefs

As you complete these exercises on your family of origin, you will discover a lot about your family. Just as your childhood experiences contributed to the formation of your beliefs, so did the beliefs of your parents.

Your parent's beliefs may not have been communicated directly. These beliefs often show up in your mind's constant chatter. But start paying attention to what you say to yourself about the world in general ("Don't give the other guy an inch or he'll take it"), about work ("A task worth doing is worth doing right"), and about sex roles ("Men are after only one thing"). These could very well be the general operating attitudes your parents conveyed to you.

Sometimes parental beliefs are based on a family image; for instance, "We Smiths never . . ." or "We Smiths always . . ." Think about these sentences, substituting your family name. Did your family have a myth, a motto, a special source of pride, or a family legend? What stories did you hear about your parents when they were young? What stories did you hear about other relatives? Can you identify the beliefs that shaped the identity of your family?

FAMILY BELIEFS

Examples

My mother believed that women should always support their husbands in whatever they decide and that if you are just nice to people and don't get them upset, you'll be okay. My father believed that you had to be tough to make it and that other people were out to get you if you weren't careful.

My Family's Beliefs

Make a list of beliefs your parents maintained, both spoken and unspoken. Consider the following areas: work, friendship, intimacy, people in general, the world/life, money, sex and sexuality, religion, success, love, etc.

My mother believed:

_____

_____

_____

_____

_____

My father believed:

_____

_____

_____

_____

_____

After you've made your list, compare it to the list you made of your own beliefs. To what degree do you hold the same beliefs as your parents? Are these beliefs working for or against your happiness and self-fulfillment? How do you feel about them as you review them? Were any double messages—such as "Always be happy" and "Better be careful if you're feeling happy, because it won't last"—given to you?

For Parents Only

Those of you who are parents may have living reflections of your codependence. You will find your own beliefs mirrored in your children's beliefs about the world. And you can actually hear your own parents' negative messages—such as "If it weren't for you . . ." and "You should have known better . . ."—as they come out of your mouth. If you have older children, you can ask them directly about the rules, both spoken and unspoken, of your family. If you are willing to hear the truth, this kind of dialogue can help lift the veil of secrecy for your family.

When you begin to recognize how you have passed your negative conditioning on to your children, you may become frightened and upset. Don't blame yourself. Codependency is intergenerational. Since you learn about parenting from your parents, it's inevitable that you repeat many of the same patterns. Working on your own codependence is the best thing you can do for your children. As you change, the family system will change. Meanwhile, appreciate your children for showing you so clearly the areas in which you need to grow.

If you're bothered intensely by the way a child acts, ask yourself if you ever behave in a similar way. Usually we find unacceptable in our children feelings and behaviors that we repressed in childhood and that we are still repressing in our inner children. As you learn to accept and cherish your inner child, you will be better able to accept and cherish your own children.

SUMMARY

The following tasks will enhance your healing of the mental dimension during Stage One:
1. Identify the roles you play, as outlined on pages 166–67.
2. Learn to recognize the self-messages you give yourself; some typical self-messages are listed on pages 167–68.
3. Record your beliefs on pages 170–172.
4. Answer the questions about maintaining control in relationships on page 173.

5. Reflect on the role of fantasies in your life, as described on pages 174–75.

6. Make a family map—instructions are on pages 178–80—and interpret it.

7. Write your family's story as suggested on page 181.

8. Examine the way your role meshed with the roles played by the other members of your family by answering the questions on pages 182–85.

9. Make a list of your family's rules, as on page 186.

10. Make a list of the negative messages you heard as a child (pages 187–88). How did they affect you?

11. Make a list of your parents' beliefs (page 190) and think about how they have impacted you.

12. If you have children, start paying attention to what their behavior and attitudes tell you about your codependent issues.

• • • • • • •

Discovering the Spiritual Dimension

Codependence results in and from a loss of your sense of self—the inner self. As you begin to dismantle your defenses, the impact of this loss will become more and more obvious. What is lost can be found in the process of recovery that you are beginning.

During Stage One there are some practices, such as meditating and keeping a journal, that will help you get in touch with your inner self and the spiritual dimension. Working the first three of the Twelve Steps of Alcoholics Anonymous can also help you begin to surrender your illusory control over life to a higher power.

When I use the term "higher power" I am referring to a power that is greater than yourself and your own willpower. This higher power will vary for each person depending on a variety of factors such as cultural heritage and formal religious background. Although there have been names associated with a higher power— God; Great Spirit; Jesus; Nature; Love; Buddha; Yahweh—the name is not as important as what the term implies. For those of us who have spent our lives exercising our willpower to make things happen the way we wanted and trying to control or change people's behavior and thinking, it can be a real challenge to turn our will over to a higher power—a power greater than ourselves. It can be hard to just understand what this means. The crucial factor is your willingness to begin to surrender control to this higher power. If the concept of a higher power is unacceptable to you at this time, then just keep working through the exercises and your recovery.

Meditating and Contemplating

Throughout the years I have occasionally used meditation as a spiritual practice. Like all of the spiritual practices I suggest, it is optional. You will know what is right for you.

There are many different approaches to meditation. Some people think of it as a simple relaxation exercise. Others practice it as a journey along a serious spiritual path, one that brings them strength and peace. I practice a modified form of meditation called *contemplation*.

Meditation is a way to quiet your mind, to put yourself into a state of rest and peace. You can do it by simply focusing on your breathing as you inhale and exhale, or you can use a word such as *love* or *peace* repeated as a mantra. Some people set aside time for meditation at certain times of the day. But you don't have to meditate for a specific period of time or in a specific place. You can just take a few minutes during the day to relax your body and your mind, focusing your awareness on your breathing or some inner sensation or scene.

For me meditation is a brief period—even as little as 30 seconds—of checking in with my self, noticing what I am experiencing and reflecting on the presence of the higher power in my life. You can take these opportunities just to "see" the presence of a higher power around you—children playing, people smiling, clouds in the sky, the people you work with. At the start it helps to set up some sort of cue that will remind you to do this. I wear a prayer ring, a plain band circled with little bumps, to help remind me to practice contemplation. Seeing the ring or feeling it on my hand reminds me to take a few minutes out for contemplation. You can use almost anything as a cue—from a message taped to the steering wheel of your car to a special rock placed on your desk.

Whether you choose meditation or contemplation or some other quieting practice, the point is to place a healthy focus on yourself, your own experience of life, and to open yourself up to feel the presence of a higher power.

Keeping a Journal

I highly recommend writing in a journal as a supportive spiritual practice. Writing in your journal on a regular basis gives you a better sense of your own history and the process that is your life. Journal writing will help you focus, once again, on you and your experiences. As your trust in a higher power grows and your self-honesty likewise increases, your journal can be the means of reflecting on and gaining insight into your growth and struggles.

I've kept a journal throughout my recovery. I've used it in many different ways, sometimes writing a lot, sometimes very little. What has been meaningful is the process of writing, perhaps just twice a week, reflecting on my experiences, my struggles, my hopes, and my pain.

There are many different ways to keep a journal. You can find inspiration and ideas in the many books available on journal keeping. Experiment—eventually you will find the way that feels right for you.

Your journal can be your workbook. It can be the place where you write out and reflect on the answers to the questions in this chapter and the following chapters. You might find it easier to work on a big project—like recording your childhood memories—a little bit at a time in your journal. You can write as much as you want at one time, then make notes to yourself about what you plan to do the next time you have time to work in your journal. Working on examining your past and identifying your current defenses is a little like working on a jigsaw puzzle. You can see the separate pieces, but it's hard to see how they all fit together. Reading through the entries in your journal can help you gather all the individual pieces into one coherent picture.

Your journal can be a place to express your creativity safely. You can compose prayers, poems, or fairy tales.

Your journal can be a motivational boost for your recovery. As you read books and gather information about codependence, write out your insights and thoughts in your journal. Write inspirational poems and quotations into the pages.

You can create dialogues with all kinds of people, real and imaginary, dead and alive. You can use the journal as a way of reaching your inner child by writing out conversations with your inner child. Since it helps to have a clear image of the person you are engaged in dialogue with, you may want to keep a photograph that reminds you of your inner child tucked inside your journal. Beginning with certain questions like "What do you have to tell me?" and "What do you want from me?" helps provoke dialogue. Don't worry about whether or not you are making up the responses. Your inner child is a part of you. If you let yourself write freely, without worrying about the validity of the dialogue, you will be surprised by the information and insight you receive from dialogues.

The dialogue technique can be used in many ways. If someone important to you has died, you can communicate with that person in your journal by imagining his or her responses to you. You can also learn from and have a dialogue with your higher power. Write letters to your higher power. Surrender your pain and acknowledge your joy in these letters.

Working the First Three Steps

For decades the Twelve-Step program of Alcoholics Anonymous has been a source of healing and recovery for millions of alcoholics.* The Twelve Steps are steps that guide the individual forward along the path of recovery. The same Twelve Steps that help the alcoholic have been adapted to help the drug addict, the sex addict, the gambler, the overeater, and the smoker. These steps can also help the codependent. Codependence is very similar to alcoholism. Codependents have difficulty with the same issues that trouble alcoholics, among them control, willpower, denial, and low self-esteem. As you learned in Chapter 2, codependence is the context from which addictions develop, and addictions foster the growth of codependence.

I use the Twelve-Step programs as a key element in my work with clients and in my own healing process. Because many of my clients and participants in my workshops find it difficult to apply the Twelve Steps to codependence, I provide below brief explanations and exercises you can do to enrich your understanding of each of the first three steps. (We'll cover the rest of the steps in Chapters 10–12.)

I recommend attending Twelve-Step meetings, where you will have the benefit of hearing many people share their perceptions about and responses to the Twelve Steps. I also recommend taking each step in turn and reflecting on it for a week or so. You can use the step as the focus of your meditation or contemplation. You can write it out in your journal, then write out the feelings and thoughts that it evokes in you.

---

* A complete list of the Twelve Steps of Alcoholic Anonymous is provided in the appendix. The steps provided in this workbook have been adapted for the book.

Step 1. We admitted we were powerless over alcohol—that our lives had become unmanageable.

In this first and fundamental step you admit and accept that you are powerless to control people or circumstances and that your attempts to do so are stressful and unmanageable. You can substitute a variety of words for the word *alcohol*. The point is to admit your powerlessness.

The task of Step 1—Accepting your powerlessness—is perhaps the most difficult thing you can do during Stage One. I can recall how I would blithely say the words "I am really powerless," but that's all they were—words. I didn't really believe that I was powerless. It took me a long time to be ready to admit this. The following exercise may help you realize your own powerlessness.

ADMITTING POWERLESSNESS

Examples

When someone upsets me, I tell a mutual friend hoping that she will intervene or exert pressure to get the person to change.

Rather than risk a confrontation of a fellow employee who constantly mistreats me, I'll keep quiet and do strenuous exercise to release the anger.

My Powerlessness

1. List all the things you have done to exercise power over yourself and others. You might start with the list of controlling behaviors you made in response to the questions on page 173 and your answers to the questions on addictions on pages 156–58.

_____

_____

_____

_____

_____

2. Now reflect on each of those attempts to exercise power one by one. What were the results? List specific results such as headaches, arguments, confusion, anger, frustration, anxiety, etc.

_____

_____

_____

_____

_____

When one of my clients did this exercise, she realized that all of her attempts to control her boyfriend's late nights out with the boys—her constant calls, checking up on him, and arguments when he got home—had no effect on his staying out late but resulted only in rage and unresolved tension. She had to admit that she was powerless to control him; she couldn't prevent him from staying out late.

Having admitted your powerlessness, you can move on to hope with Step 2.

Step 2. We came to believe that a power greater than ourselves could restore us to sanity.

In this second step you are invited to believe in a power greater than yourself that can restore sanity (peace, health, serenity) to your life. This step is a process of coming into belief.

If you are easily able to believe in a power greater than yourself, that's good. If you have problems with this idea because of your religious background or experiences with religion, that's okay. You don't have to _believe_ in a higher power; just entertain the possibility that there might be a power greater than you.

The other part of this step asks you to reflect on how your life could be saner. The following exercise will help you identify the "insanity" in your present life-style:

THE INSANITY OF CODEPENDENCE

1. Examine the results of the controlling behaviors you listed in the preceding exercise. Do the results indicate a happy, sane, and wise set of behaviors?   Yes _____   No _____

2. Would you be willing to consider the possibility that a power greater than you can restore sanity to your life?   Yes _____   No _____ Maybe _____

Rather than focusing on controlling others and yourself, with Step 3 you can focus on healthier behavior and acknowledge the truth of your powerlessness.

Step 3. We made a decision to turn our will and our lives over to the care of God *as we understood Him.*

In this third step you make a choice to surrender your life and your will to the care of your higher power as you understand it. Notice that you are turning your life and will over to the care of that higher power.

Stage One is marked by disintegration—the breaking down of various habits of thinking and behaving that are not life-giving or self-affirming. The first three steps of the Twelve-Step program contain the essence of what happens in Stage One of the recovery process.

SUMMARY

To begin discovering or deepening your awareness of the spiritual dimension during Stage One:

1. Begin a regular spiritual practice like meditation or contemplation. If you're going to meditate on a regular basis, set aside the time and place for it. If contemplation seems more compatible with your life-style, choose the cue that is going to remind you to focus on yourself and your higher power.

2. Begin keeping a journal. Go out and get a notebook you can write in. Set

aside a time when you're going to write or carry it with you. For suggestions on what to write about, see pages 194–95.

3. Work the first three steps of the Twelve Steps by reflecting on the meaning of the steps, attending Twelve-Step meetings (such as Al-Anon), and doing the exercises on pages 196–98.

• • • • • • •

GENERAL RECOMMENDATIONS

In addition to the exercises in this chapter, the following general recommendations will help you move through Stage One in your recovery:

1. Review the chart at the end of Chapter 2 to assess your own codependence.

2. Investigate the availability of Twelve-Step support groups in your area. Begin attending one (or two).

3. Determine whether you want to work with a therapist.

4. Attend workshops and read books and articles to increase your understanding of the dynamics of codependence.

5. Develop a network of a few supportive, loving friends who understand recovery and are into their own recovery process.

Moving On to Stage Two

The willingness of Stage One becomes acceptance in Stage Two naturally—but not necessarily comfortably.

As you identify and dismantle defenses and acknowledge your inner child, you will feel a growing sense of discomfort. You always have a choice—you can accept reality, or you can deny it again. The former leads to Stage Two. The latter triggers a relapse into codependence and addictions.

As you move from Stage One to Stage Two, you may feel a strong temptation to call a halt to your recovery journey. Do any of these comments sound familiar?

"It wasn't that bad and besides I can't be disloyal to my parents."

"I really have managed very well; I don't need to change much."

"I've worked through all this already."

These statements express the denial discussed earlier. It is at this point that many individuals quit therapy. When I was in therapy during this stage in my recovery, I avoided reality by trying something different, looking for a new, quick, and painless cure.

If you accept the parts of reality you want to deny, you will move gradually into Stage Two. This doesn't mean you'll enjoy the process. You may go into Stage Two kicking and screaming. That's okay. You don't have to like it; just accept it. What's being asked of you is the surrender that leads to acceptance.

Moving into Stage Two isn't something you schedule. I can't suggest a specific amount of time you should spend on Stage One. The recovery process is different for every person and depends, in part, on the amount of work you are willing to do, the amount of support you get, and the depth of the pain within. Don't blame yourself if you think you are moving very slowly; that may be the most gentle and self-respecting pace for you.

One of the first signs of the beginning of Stage Two is the emergence of deep feelings. When you begin to feel intense sadness, grief, inner pain, or abandonment, you are entering Stage Two. That doesn't mean you're finished with Stage One. You will have Stage One work to do as long as you are in recovery.

10
·······

Stage Two: Accepting Yourself and Experiencing Your Feelings

Every bad feeling is potential energy toward a more right way of living if you give it space to move toward its rightness.

EUGENE GENDLIN,
Focusing

E VENTUALLY AUTUMN BE- comes winter. Nature turns inward. The nights are long and dark, and the days are gray and cold. Trees are bare, their branches sharp and skeletal against the steely sky. It seems as if life has stopped, as if nothing is happening, but beneath the snow and frozen ground the seeds of new life are preparing for the flowering of spring.

The second stage of the recovery process is like winter, a time of turning inward, of going deep within. During Stage One you dismantled some of the defenses you've used to avoid uncomfortable feelings and the anxiety of facing reality. This process brings with it a sense of **disorientation**. After all, you founded your self-image on those behaviors and thought patterns. Who are you now that your defenses have been stripped away like the leaves on the trees?

Disorientation

Without your familiar behavior and thought patterns to guide you, you move into the experience of disorientation. You used to know what to do and how to act, but now you don't know. You feel confused because your old ways of coping no longer work but you don't have replacements.

In the Pacific Northwest we have frequent fogs at certain seasons. Winter is one of them. I love walking in the fog, especially at night. Although I know I'm only a few steps away from my front door, familiar landmarks are gone. The glimpses I get of houses and trees shrouded with fog seem strange.

At Stage Two you may feel like you are walking through a fog at night. You've lost your familiar landmarks. You can't see where you're going. Although you may be somewhat encouraged by knowing that the feeling of disorientation is the next stage of recovery, it is usually not a welcome feeling. It can, in fact, be profoundly disturbing.

Remember the experience of my client Vic that I described in Chapter 9. Vic was the man who gazed up into space as he told me about his mother's threat, "Either you behave or I'm never coming back." His upward gaze was a way of disassociating from his feelings. I'd like to continue telling what happened in our session. I asked him if he could repeat his story and look at me as he told it.

Although even thinking about doing this made him uncomfortable, he agreed to try. It took many minutes before Vic could describe a typical incident during which he had received this message from his mother. Tears poured down his cheeks as he spoke, and he had to pause frequently to regain his composure. He found that looking away from me broke his connection with his feelings, but I encouraged him to take these breaks. The experience of these deep emotions, typical of Stage Two of recovery, can be overwhelming. You may choose to use the defenses you developed to protect yourself in childhood to protect yourself during recovery, as long as you do so consciously. Vic was ready to let go of his defenses and experience the feelings behind them.

Most codependents, like me, spent their lives avoiding these feelings. When I thought about giving up control and my self-image, I felt vulnerable. I wanted to preserve the shell I had built to protect myself from all the buried feelings and childhood wounds I carried inside of me. Sometimes that shell cracked, and I experienced a short period of confusion until I rebuilt my defenses. When I finally acknowledged my codependence and recognized my defenses, I realized why maintaining that shell was so important: the pain of disorientation was unlike anything I had experienced. Stripped bare of my protection, I felt alone, lost, and vulnerable. Painful childhood wounds were exposed and started hurting all over again. I felt anger, despair, and sadness about the losses I had known—not the least of which was the loss of so many years of my life. It seemed as if I had wasted 20 to 30 years letting my need to please and be in control of others ruin my life.

During Stage Two the frozen constellation of feelings within begins to thaw. Have you ever been out in weather so cold that your fingers or toes almost froze? Do you remember the pain you felt when you finally got into a warm place and they began to thaw? That's just like the pain of Stage Two. It's a welcome feeling since it means your extremities are returning to normal, but you definitely hurt more than you did when they were frozen. One of my clients put it this way: "It hurts to be feeling all the pain, but it hurts good."

Facing the Darkness

The night of the winter solstice, the date on which winter officially begins, is the longest night of the year. Sometime during Stage Two you may experience the "long dark night of the soul," a time of darkness during which you may feel you will never see the sun again. It's important to realize that this feeling won't last forever. Remember that after the winter solstice the nights grow shorter and the days grow longer. What we mark as the first day of winter is really the first day of the return of the light, which is why this time of year is celebrated with light festivals like Hanukkah and Christmas.

In mythological terms Stage Two is the time when the hero or heroine enters a dark place, often pictured as a descent into Hell or a visit to the Underworld. The entrance is usually guarded by a fierce monster, like Cerberus, the three-headed dog that barred Aeneas from entering Hades. Once inside, there are more ogres and obstacles to confront, like the Minotaur in the center of the labyrinth or the dragon in its lair. What qualities does the hero or heroine need to deal with the dark, the unknown, and the monsters?

The heroes and heroines of myth always got wise advice about what to expect and how to handle certain situations. The Sibyl who conducts Aeneas through the

Underworld silences the dog Cerberus with a cake saturated with poppy juice and honey. In this chapter you'll get information on what to expect and techniques you can use to handle various situations. It's easier to cope with difficult times when you expect them and are prepared for them.

Of course information alone is not enough. You need two qualities to face the dark of Stage Two: **courage** and **compassion.** These two concepts are related. Courage comes from the Latin word for *heart* and compassion means "to feel with"; literally, "to suffer with." The courage required in Stage Two is the courage to feel your feelings. Compassion enables you to accept yourself.

Accepting Yourself

Accepting yourself means accepting the totality of your being: your experiences growing up, your losses, your roles, your mistakes, your illusions, and the fact that you've been wounded. It means accepting your dark, shadowy side. It means accepting yourself as a loving and lovable human being.

Compassion transforms. Your compassion for yourself can transform your most frightening feelings into gifts.

You've probably been avoiding your feelings for so long because they seem overwhelming. Locked in the dark, kept in the dungeon, they've grown into monsters. You believe that you can't survive a confrontation with them. The truth is that you are stronger than they are and they are all part of you. The monsters you've been running from are your own repressed feelings and the dark aspects of yourself.

C. G. Jung, writing about the Shadow, said that it represents all those things you can't bear to see in yourself. Therefore, you project them onto the outside world. If you are unwilling to acknowledge your own anger, then you probably see it all around you in a hostile world. If you can't face your own helplessness, you may surround yourself with helpless people.

Suppose you were raised to believe that anger was wrong, and you learned how to avoid conflict. Now, as you move through Stage Two and begin to feel your own anger and run into more conflicts in the world around you, you may be tempted to turn around and run. But the monsters of anger and conflict aren't new. Your anger has always been with you. It's actually a much more malevolent force when unacknowledged than when felt. And conflict has always existed in the world around you, even though you've pretended it doesn't.

Or suppose you have gone through life needing to be a nice person who pleases others and always does what's right. Now, having looked at some of your defenses during Stage One, you recognize that you are often manipulative and play the role of the martyr, trying to get others to do what you want by suffering conspicuously. Having to face this dark side of yourself may be revolting. You may be tempted to run away.

But don't. Turn around and look at those monsters, those dark sides. Confront them, face them, look them in the eyes. And accept them for what they are. They are all part of you. If you can accept them, embrace them, they will be your allies. If you turn and run from them in terror, they will pursue you.

Compassion is more than just feeling sorry for yourself. Compassion means understanding that you have been doing the best you could. Compassion means loving the wounded inner child who has been hidden within the recesses of your emotional being.

Experiencing Your Feelings

When you let go of your defenses, the repressed feelings of the past will emerge. Letting go is a pivotal part of recovery—not just letting go of others and your need to control them but also letting go of your need to control your feelings and keep them at a distance.

Have you ever stood at the edge of a diving board? Can you recall how you felt standing there, poised at the edge? Do you remember the sensations, the quivering, the anticipation of how the water would feel? During Stage Two you will come up against many such edges.

Edges are the frontiers of your self, the boundaries between who-you-have-been and who-you-think-you-are and who-you-could-be if you follow the road of your recovery to the edge of your known world. The edge is the place of growth.

Letting go is an edge experience. Instead of holding on to outdated beliefs or an old self-concept, you let go and trust the fall. Remember Alice's experience falling through the rabbit hole? As she falls, she tries to orient herself by reciting well-known poems, but nothing comes out right; everything is topsy-turvy. Your old concepts don't work when you've gone off the edge—you're in the upside-down world of disorientation. Growth and change involve going beyond edges.

Letting go is a pivotal part of the process during Stage Two—letting go of denial and control, letting in the truth of your feelings, and letting the natural process of healing take place.

Tools and Resources

Stage Two work is hard. As you'll see in this chapter, I provide a number of exercises and tools to help you work through the disorientation and into integration. When I was writing this chapter, I was surprised by how long it became. Then I realized that it couldn't be any other way. Stage Two is the time of the most extensive, intensive, inward-oriented work.

Healing the Physical Dimension

The major focus of Stage Two work on the physical dimension is on recovering your ability to experience your feelings. Feelings are living realities that want to be acknowledged. Once you acknowledge them, they pass through you like a wave. Sometimes they feel like a tidal wave.

The exercises in this section provide you with skills that will increase your awareness of the wisdom of your body and the varieties of feelings you can experience. You will also learn how to work with strong and intense feelings.

Breathing

Breathing is such a natural process that we tend to take it for granted. Yet most codependents don't breathe properly. We operate most of the time in crisis mode, breathing rapidly and shallowly or even holding our breath. These are appropriate responses to an emergency situation; they seem to hold off pain. They become inappropriate when they are used continually to muffle emotional pain, since they also muffle feelings and prevent relaxation.

When you allow yourself to breathe fully, you get in touch with your body and thus with your feelings. Full and complete breathing is an important foundation for the work you will be doing in Stage Two. It will support you during experiences of intense feelings and calm your agitated body. Deep breathing helps you center and ground yourself in the face of conflict or perceived threats. Because your body associates deep breathing with relaxation and safety, you can calm it down when it goes into crisis mode.

I invite you to become aware of your breathing right now. Just sit back for a moment and notice how you breathe. What parts of your body do you move? Do you tense your jaw, neck, or shoulders? Focus on the exhalation. Are you releasing all of the air within you? Exhalation is letting go, and letting go is essential to this stage of recovery.

The following exercise is provided as a way for you to practice breathing more fully and completely. Try it as you read about it and see how your body responds.

BREATHING

1. Sit or stand in a relaxed but upright position.

2. Breathing through your nostrils, take in a deep breath and imagine it filling up your abdomen. Let your stomach expand as you breathe in. Imagine that it swells like a balloon when you blow it full of air.

3. Continuing to breathe in, imagine filling your midsection with air.

4. As you draw in the end of this long, deep breath, lift your shoulders, push out your chest, and fully expand your lungs with air.

5. Pause for a few seconds, savoring your deep breath.

6. Now exhale fully. Let the balloon that is your stomach shrivel up as the air leaves your abdomen. Let your shoulders droop and your chest contract as the air leaves your midsection and lungs. Let all of the breath go.

Repeat these instructions. I recommend taking at least three full breaths each time you practice this exercise.

At first it may be hard to learn to breathe like this. Most of us were actually taught to breathe wrong. We were told to hold in our stomachs when we take a breath. This is the opposite of natural breathing. Watch a baby if you want to see how to breathe naturally. The baby's stomach rises with each inhalation and subsides with each exhalation. After years of breathing incorrectly, you must make a conscious effort to reverse the process, but I think you will quickly notice the benefits.

This is also an exercise that you can practice almost anywhere—on the bus, in your car while waiting for a green light, when you sit down to work, before you exercise, whenever you feel agitated and upset.

Bodywork

As Ken Dychtwald describes in his book *Bodymind*, the body and the mind are inextricably related. Your body reflects your life experiences. It has its own memory. One of my clients was reading a book on shame in families when she got a "memory feeling"—a feeling she couldn't explain—that she felt in the pit of her stomach. She knew the feeling was important and trusted that with patience and through recovery she would understand its message for her. Another client who was sexually abused as a child recalled how she became sick and nauseated while watching a movie about sexual abuse. She had been avoiding this issue in her own healing and did not want to discuss it. However, seeing the movie released some very powerful feelings that she couldn't deny. The next day she called me and said, "I just want you to know that I'm ready to take some feelings off the shelf." Perhaps you remember my story about the intense stomach pain I felt after watching a film about alcoholism in the family. Shortly afterward, during a massage, powerful images of my childhood were released.

Therapeutic bodywork can enhance your recovery during Stage Two. It is, however, only an adjunct to the recovery process. I have heard people claim they're "cured" after doing intensive bodywork. Too often they feel better for only a short time because the underlying emotional issues have not been addressed.

You don't have to become involved in some specialized form of bodywork to reap the benefits. Dychtwald, in an interview in *Medical Self-Care* magazine, explained that "anything that takes you out of your normal patterns of muscular or sensory activity can be considered valid bodywork. For some people, it may mean sports or massage; for others, sitting quietly in a peaceful place."

Identifying Feelings

In his book *The Betrayal of the Body*, Alexander Lowen points out the importance of truly being in your body:

A person experiences the reality of the world only through his body. The external environment impresses him because it impinges upon his body and affects his senses. In turn, he responds to this stimulation by acting upon the environment.

When I first read Lowen's book, I could understand what he was saying intellectually, but that was all. I knew my experience of the external environment was causing something to occur in my body. I just didn't know that what was occurring was a feeling. I had so little experience in feeling my feelings.

The four steps outlined below will help you get in touch with your feelings.

GETTING IN TOUCH WITH FEELINGS

1. **Acknowledge** that you are feeling something, typically something you want to suppress and deny. A feeling is a sensation in your body. So-called "negative" feelings such as anxiety, gloom, and fury are often experienced as uncomfortable or edgy. "Numb," "dead," "nothing," and "empty" are feelings too!

2. Take a few minutes to allow yourself to **feel** these feelings. It may be painful. You may judge yourself with critical self-talk, admonishing yourself for even feeling what you are feeling. Just feel and breathe.

3. **Name** the feeling. This is a bigger challenge than it seems because most of us know the name of only a few feeling states: sad, angry, or happy. In the process of naming a feeling you can use your intellectual abilities to explore and name various feelings. Once you name a feeling, something very interesting happens. The feeling seems to respond. When I name a new feeling and it's the right name, my body responds with a "yes." An inner alignment seems to occur.

4. Just **sit with** the named feeling as you continue to breathe. Get to know the feeling so that you'll recognize it the next time.

Shades of Feeling

There are shades to all the major feelings, just as there are shades to colors. Do you feel sad? Or do you feel lamentable, miserable, pathetic, pitiful, unfortunate, woeful, or wretched? Or perhaps you feel grim, serious, sour, or stern? Or maudlin or sentimental? Or bleak, blue, cheerless, dejected, dismal, forlorn, melancholy, moody, somber, or unhappy?

Use a thesaurus to help you identify the possibilities. You might even want to post a list of possible feelings somewhere to use as a reference. I've provided such a list on the next pages. It doesn't represent all the feelings you may experience in your life, but it will help you get started.

You may also find it helpful to look up the derivation of the word you've chosen in a dictionary. This may help you understand some of the difficult aspects of your feeling. "Sorrowful" when turned into "full of sorrow" helps give you a sense of the feeling and an image.

I get very excited when I experience and name a new feeling. My life becomes more alive, vibrant. Writing this book has given me many opportunities to experience different feelings, from gutless to zealous, from thrilled to mixed up. I can recall one instance when naming a feeling provided me with a great healing lesson. It was a Sunday evening, the close of a relaxing and fruitful weekend. Chapter 6 of this book was completed, and my first feeling was one of satisfaction. But this was quickly followed by a new feeling. At first I thought it felt like shame, but I realized it was different, deeper and bigger. I used the focusing technique that I'll describe in the next section and felt a deep part of me that felt ill at ease. As I explored it more, I encountered a new aspect of my inner child, a frightened little boy who seemed to be cowering in a corner of the room. As I sat with the feeling, it changed from ill at ease to petrified. I had never experienced this feeling before, or if I had, I hadn't named it. But that's exactly how I felt—petrified. What if people don't like what I've written? What if I get a lot of criticism? For the next hour I worked with and felt the petrified part of me that was scared of you, the reader. As I acknowledged my feeling and reassured the petrified inner child, the feeling changed again. My inner child is still scared, but both of us are learning to trust in the power of our strength and conviction.

Shades of Feeling

Sad—choked up, dreary, heavyhearted, in the dumps, lamentable, low, miserable, out of sorts, pathetic, pitiful, unfortunate, woeful, wretched. Grim, serious, sour, stern. Maudlin, sentimental, pitiable. Blah, bleak, blue, cheerless, concerned, dejected, depressed, desperate, despondent, disappointed, discontented, discouraged, disheartened, dismal, distressed, down, dreadful, dull, flat, forlorn, gloomy, hopeless, ill at ease, joyless, lonely, melancholy, moody, mournful, oppressed, quiet, somber, sorrowful, sorry, sullen, sulky, unhappy. Sympathetic, compassionate.

Humiliated—ashamed, embarrassed, chagrined, abashed, mortified, shamed, useless, worthless.

Happy—blithe, cheerful, cheery, festive, gay, glad. Contented, relaxed, calm, complacent, satisfied, comfortable, serene, peaceful. Bright, radiant, rejoicing, ebullient, ecstatic, elated, encouraged, enthusiastic, excited, exuberant, hopeful, inspired, optimistic, positive. Confident, pleased, grateful, merry, sunny. Lighthearted, buoyant, carefree. Surprised, brisk, spirited, sparkling, vivacious. Hilarious, exhilarated, jolly, jovial, joyful, playful, jubilant, mirthful, thrilled, upbeat.

Eager—keen, earnest, intent, zealous. Ardent, avid, anxious, enthusiastic, desirous, excited, proud, thrilled. Breathless, impatient, impetuous, impulsive, passionate, raring. Covetous, craving, greedy, hungry, longing, yearning.

Hurt—injured, isolated, offended, distressed. Pained, suffering, afflicted, worried, crushed, heartbroken, despairing, tortured, tragic, lonely, pathetic, cold, upset. Aching, wounded, strained, devastated, lost, burned, heartsick, sore.

Angry—resentful, irked, irritated, annoyed. Aggravated, hot, incensed, irritable, mad, pissed off, teed off, upset. Boiling, enraged, ferocious, fierce, furious, fuming, heated, inflamed, infuriated, indignant, intense, irate, wrathful. Awkward, bewildered, confused. Provoked, offended. Savage, severe, terrible, vehement, vicious, violent. Bellicose, belligerent, combative, contentious, hostile, militant, pugnacious, quarrelsome. Cranky, cross, feisty, grouchy, grumpy, hot-tempered, irascible, ireful, peppery, short-fused, sulky, sullen, testy, touchy. Alienated, bitter, emotional, envious, frustrated, hurt, jealous.

Brave—audacious, bold, courageous, daring, dauntless, determined, encouraged, fearless, gallant, game, gutsy, hardy, heroic, independent, intrepid, loyal, proud, reassured, secure, stalwart, unafraid, undaunted, valiant, valorous.

Interested—absorbed, curious, drawn, engrossed, excited, fascinated, inquisitive, intrigued, involved. Committed, concerned, creative, dedicated, sincere.

Doubtful—dubious, equivocal, evasive, incoherent, indecisive, muddled, muffled, murky, perplexed, precarious, questionable, shaky, suspicious, unbelieving, uncertain, unclear, uneasy, unsure, vague, wary, wavering, wishy-washy. Cynical, distrustful, helpless, hesitant, incredulous, leery, pessimistic, questioning, shy, skeptical, skittish. Defeated, helpless, hopeless, powerless.

Physical—taut, uptight, tense, stretched. Immobilized, paralyzed. Sluggish, tired, weary. Empty, hollow, weak. Breathless, nauseated, shaky, sweaty. Alive, restless, vital. Strong, alert.

Loving—affectionate, amorous, caring, close, devoted, enamored, fond, passionate, romantic, seductive, tender. Compassionate, considerate, empathic, gentle, kind, kindhearted, responsive, softhearted, sympathetic, warm, warmhearted.

Afraid—anxious, cowardly, dependent, dismayed, doubtful, gutless, hesitant, impatient, insecure, nervous, recalcitrant, reluctant, shy, timid, unwilling. Aghast, alarmed, appalled, apprehensive, awed, concerned, fearful, fidgety, frightened, horrified, hysterical, nervous, panicky, paralyzed, paranoid, petrified, pressured, scared, shaky, shocked, suspicious, threatened, terrified, worried.

Miscellaneous—bored, cooperative, cruel, distant, envious, hypocritical, humble, mixed up, preoccupied, phony, torn up, two-faced.

Giving Feelings Substance

I know how deep and overwhelming feelings can be. You can experience rage and anger powerful enough to destroy a house, sadness that throws you into a pit of despair, joy so great your body can't contain it, an abyss of abandonment that threatens to swallow you up, a torment of shame.

I believe feelings want to come out of their hiding places, those caves within us where we have buried them. Finding safe and effective ways to do this is part of the healing process. It's both a challenge and a responsibility.

Talking about feelings is only one way to express feelings. And many codependents become experts at talking about feelings without really feeling them.

For those of you who are having trouble experiencing and expressing feelings, I encourage you to follow the suggestions below. These methods will help you externalize and concretize feelings, giving them flesh. Pick whichever seems easiest and most natural to you; then try one that seems more challenging and pushes you to one of your edges.

EXPRESSING FEELINGS

Work with Clay.

Use your hands to work the clay into an expression of your feeling.

Drawing.

Use whatever medium you like (crayon, ink, chalk, etc.) to draw your feeling. Create images of the different feelings you experience.

Writing.

Write about your feeling. Imagine you can talk to your feelings and they can talk back. Have a dialogue with them. You can even take one of your drawings of a feeling, set it on a chair, and have a dialogue with it by asking questions and listening for the answers.

Focused Catharsis.

You can pound pillows and chop wood to release energy, particularly angry energy. One of my clients uses a rubber hose and bundles of newspapers. Without a focus, the release has only a minimal effect. Allow yourself to see the person you are angry at and focus on that image.

Movement.

This is one of my favorite ways of working with feelings. Begin by moving one part of your body as if it were a feeling. For instance, you can move your hand in grief, anger, or fear. Or move your arm in a gesture of love. Or sway your head with sadness. Just allow yourself to move and feel. Allow yourself to move more and more of your body as it feels right.

I usually find that a five- to 15-minute period provides a release of tension and facilitates the expression of the feeling for me. How long you move is your choice.

When I first started to use movement as part of my healing process, I felt silly and embarrassed. Now it's an important part of my life. I use movement when I feel uncomfortable facing a blank page in my writing. I look forward to it with eagerness.

Drumming and Chanting.

Drumming and chanting have been used for centuries in many cultures to aid expression of feelings. I include them here because I've found them useful.

You may feel hesitant or shy about this concept. Here's a simple way to try it. Get a cardboard box and a stick. When you are feeling disturbed, upset, or even happy about something, start tapping on the box with the stick and allow some sounds to come from your throat. If this appeals to you, you may want to obtain a drum for your use.

Be careful not to hurt your vocal cords. I once chanted for so long and so loudly that I could barely talk for a few days. If you need to really let loose, use the box and the stick, not your voice.

Focusing.

Focusing is a simple process developed by Eugene Gendlin and described in his book *Focusing*. I use focusing to explore my feelings. It takes practice and is often easier when done with the assistance of a friend. Focusing helps heighten your awareness of the wisdom of the body. You will find a summary of the focusing process in the box.

FOCUSING—SHORT FORM

1. Clear a Space

How are you? What comes between you and feeling fine?

Don't answer; let what comes into your body do the answering.

Greet each concern that comes. Put each aside for a while, next to you. You can use helpful images such as putting your concerns into a cupboard and closing the door or watching them drift past you like clouds or birds.

Except for that, are you fine?

2. Felt Sense

Pick one problem to focus on.

Don't start exploring the problem.

What do you sense in your body when you recall the whole of that problem?

Sense all of that, the sense of the whole thing, the murky discomfort or the unclear body sense of it.

3. Get a Handle

What is the quality of the felt sense?

What one word, phrase, or image comes out of this felt sense?

What word would best describe this quality?

4. Resonate

Go back and forth between word (or image) and the felt sense. Do they match? If so, experience the sensation of matching several times.

If the felt sense changes, follow it with your attention.

When you get a perfect match, the words or images that are just right for this feeling, let yourself feel that for a minute.

---

5. Ask "What is it about the whole problem that makes me so _____?"

When stuck, ask questions:
  What is the worst of this feeling?
  What's really so bad about this?
  What does it need?
  What should happen?

Don't answer; wait for the feeling to stir and give you an answer.

What would it feel like if it was all okay?

Let the body answer: What is in the way of that?

6. Receive

Welcome what came. Be glad it spoke.

It is only one step toward resolving this problem, not the last.

Now that you know where it is, you can leave it and come back to it later.

Protect it from critical voices that interrupt.

Does your body want another round of focusing, or is this a good stopping place?

All of the methods described above have two purposes. They will help you express blocked energy, thus enhancing the healing of the emotional wounds of your past. And they will enable you to become more aware of your inner feelings.

Once you learn the art of experiencing strong feelings, pleasant or unpleasant, your confidence will increase and you will develop a sense of healthy self-control. You will gradually be able to endure intense feelings without fear of falling apart. More importantly, as you let yourself feel more and more of your repressed feelings, there will be less for you to fear and repress.

I have experienced this in my own recovery and observed it in the experiences of my clients. As I feel feelings that were denied, I experience less emotional frigidity. I have a wider range of emotions to draw on in my life. I can more easily identify my feelings, and I experience less pain.

The Inner Child Emerges

During Stage Two you will experience many deep feelings. Whether they are painful or joyful, they are often associated with your inner child discussed in Chapter 3. You may be striving, as I did, to conjure up an image of your inner child as a child at a certain age. This isn't always what happens. Sometimes the inner child emerges as just strong feelings, other times as inner symbols or a strong physical sensation in your body. One of my clients calls her inner child "Knot" to describe the constricted feeling she gets in her stomach that she associates with the wounds of her inner child. Other clients have used the names of colors or shapes. You can develop an intimate relationship with your inner child and help this child to emerge out of the fearful place that he or she has endured for so long. A way to do this is presented in the exercise below.

HELPING YOUR INNER CHILD TO EMERGE

Three personal interactions that I avoid as much as possible are:

_____

_____

_____

Which of these three interactions do I most avoid?

Now think about that interaction. Notice how your body feels as you think about it.

Write down any feelings or physical sensations you are having. If you feel scared, write that down. If your chest feels tight, write that down.

_____

_____

_____

_____

_____

What you are experiencing are the feelings of your inner child, feelings that you want to avoid. As you dismantle the defenses you have used to avoid your feelings and enter Stage Two of recovery, you will experience the feelings of the inner child that you have avoided.

Comforting the Inner Child

We often mimic the attitudes our parents modeled for us when we were children. If your parents felt threatened and got angry whenever you expressed anger as a child, you're likely to respond the same way, bullying your inner child. If your parents were judgmental and critical, you may treat your inner child with cold contempt.

You *can* make the choice to change. You don't have to treat your inner child the way you were treated. Accepting the feelings of your inner child is a key part of the work of Stage Two. You can treat your inner child with compassion by providing the nurturance and comfort that were probably missing in your childhood.

There are many ways you can reassure your inner child. You can talk to him or her directly or in your journal. You can comfort your child using a comfort object, like the way I described using a blanket in the previous chapter. You can also use physical touch or caresses to soothe your inner child. I recommend to my clients that they touch the place on their body where they tend to feel the most uncomfortable or painful sensations when these feelings are happening. I have noticed that often they do this type of gesture without being consciously aware of it. I am suggesting that you do it consciously and use this as an easy and personal way to nurture your inner child.

Expressing Anger

Anger is a natural outcome of moving from Stage One to Stage Two. As you allow yourself to take the lid off your feelings, anger will be one of the strongest feelings to emerge.

You have a right to be angry about the abuse you suffered. Anger also plays an important role in helping you set your boundaries, a subject I will address later.

Feeling and expressing anger are difficult for my clients and the people I see in groups. It's difficult because it has the quality of losing control.

SUMMARY

Following these suggestions will help heal your physical dimension:

1. Practice deep breathing (page 207) on a regular basis; use deep breathing for relaxation during times of stress and fear.
2. Consider bodywork—massage, movement therapy, etc.—as an enhancement to your recovery.
3. Identify your feelings, following the suggestions on page 209.
4. Become aware of the variety of possible feelings; use the chart on pages 210–12 as a starting point.
5. Work with your feelings using the following techniques, described in more detail on pages 213–16:
   a. working with clay
   b. drawing
   c. writing
   d. focused catharsis
   e. movement
   f. drumming and chanting
   g. focusing
6. Feel the feelings of your inner child.
7. Comfort your inner child; you'll find suggestions on how to do this on page 218.
8. Explore your anger by writing a statement about it.

• • • • • • •

Healing the Mental Dimension

I can recall when I treated my mind with disdain—I couldn't stand all the chatter and constant frustration that it created in its constant debates about how to please people, control situations, and look good. As much as my mind helped me to survive childhood, it was doing me little good as an adult. I had to learn to reorient my thinking processes. I became more conscious of my mental messages and my fear-based thinking. Gradually I enlisted my mind as an ally in my healing.

The following exercises and suggestions will provide you with ways to use your mind as an ally in your recovery. They show you how to use your mental functions—your intellect, your imagination—in ways that are healing.

The Four Questions

The primary purpose of your intellect is to help you reason and understand. Obviously your intellect can be an important part of your recovery. But, like me and many of my clients, you may be stuck in *analysis paralysis*, which is what happens when your intellect gets stuck trying to answer the question "Why?"

If you're like many codependents, you will recognize this train of thought. Something happens, and you immediately begin asking yourself questions. "Why did I do that?" "Why did they do that?" "Why did my parents do that?" "Why didn't I do something else?" "Why didn't I think of that?" "Why can't I change that?"

There are too many variables in any human interaction to answer the question "Why?" However, there are four other questions you can ask that will be much more conducive to your healing process and give your intellect something to chew on: "How?" "What?" "Where?" "When?"

How?

It's important to be aware of *how* you experience situations, circumstances, and encounters with people, and how these experiences feel in your body. You can gather valuable information about internal states of being by asking yourself "How?"

"How do I feel about this?"

"How do I experience anger [or any other feeling]?"

"How do I cut myself off from feeling?"

As illustrated in many of the case histories in this book, I frequently ask my clients to describe how they are experiencing something or how they know something. This question helps them get down to a concrete and tangible level. For example, if a client says "I tend to withdraw from conflict," the question "How?" helps clarify how the withdrawal occurs—is it through internal numbing (dissociation) or through escape into fantasy?

What?

Use "What?" to get information about situations and your behavior. Asking this question increases your awareness of your reactions to various circumstances. For instance:

"What do I do when faced with confronting someone?"

"What do I think will happen?"

"What am I afraid of?"

Sometimes our unexamined fears seem less frightening when they're out in the open.

You can also ask this question to get at some root issues. Just keep asking yourself "What?" The exchange below, which is typical of similar interactions I've had with clients, shows how this works:

"If I tell my friend how I feel, he'll be mad at me."

"What would happen then?"

"He'd either stalk off or start yelling at me."

"What would happen then?"

"I'd feel rejected."

"What would happen then?"

"I'd withdraw. I'd feel alone. After a while I'd come back to him and say I was sorry, and we would make up."

By following through on the question "What?" you can become aware of how you react to situations in which you normally remain unaware.

"What?" is also good for uncovering the circumstances that provoke your reaction. For instance, I'd continue exploring the situation above by asking what preceded the feeling. When I did this recently with one client, Clark, he realized that he reacted strongly when his girlfriend pointed her finger at him accusingly. As we worked with this finger-pointing image, he recalled that his mother had done the same thing. Given this information, Clark could look for other ways of responding, including telling his girlfriend that this gesture bothered him.

"What?" questions are particularly good to ask yourself if you're distressed about how you acted in a certain situation. You can sit down and ponder your reactions in depth. If you write them down on paper, you'll be able to do a better job of assessing them.

Where?

The answer to this question is not an external location, but rather an internal one. Ask yourself where you experience your feelings and where you feel the sensations associated with them.

"Where is that feeling in my body?"

"Where do I feel the sensations associated with it?"

"Where do I experience, anger, grief, or shame?"

The answers to these questions will help put you in touch with your feelings.

When?

The answer to this question will help you link the present with the past. This question helps elicit information about the past from your memory banks. Use questions like these:

"When do I feel like this?"

"When have I felt this way before?"

"When did I first feel this feeling?"

The following exercise lists all of the questions and shows some possible responses to them so you'll have a better idea of how to use them.

ASKING THE FOUR QUESTIONS

Examples

Awareness of a feeling state or physical experience you want to know more about	Fear or Anger

Questions to Ask Yourself

Answers

How are you experiencing the feeling state?	Tightened chest Tight jaw Shallow breathing Tense neck and arms Discomfort in stomach

Stage Two: Accepting Yourself and Experiencing Your Feelings

What did you observe, hear, think, smell, or feel that preceded the feeling?	People shouting Boss frowned Friend got angry
What did you do?	Left the room Made a critical remark
What thoughts occurred?	"She's mad at me." "He disapproves of me."
Where are you feeling the emotions?	Chest Jaw Stomach Neck and arms Eyes
When have you felt this before?	Whenever I get scared Whenever I get angry When I try to avoid getting upset
When did you first feel this feeling?	When my dad screamed at me When my mom made me feel guilty When my dad came home drunk

Asking Myself the Four Questions

Now choose one feeling you want to know more about and ask yourself the four questions.

Awareness of a feeling state or physical experience I want to know more about _____

How am I experiencing the feeling state? _____

What did I observe, hear, think, smell, or feel that preceded the feeling? _____

What did I do? _____

What thoughts occurred? _____

Where am I feeling the emotions?

_____

_____

_____

When have I felt this before?

_____

_____

_____

When did I first feel this feeling?

_____

_____

_____

Ask yourself the four questions whenever you need to center yourself, when you feel scattered, when you want a tool for examining the patterns you employ in different situations and with different people. The more you practice answering these questions, the easier it will become. Using this tool will enhance your own awareness of the way in which you keep yourself locked in self-defeating behavior patterns.

Using Your Imagination Effectively

Earlier in this chapter I described several ways you can use your imagination to express feelings, including artwork, movement, and focusing. Now we will explore the use of imagination as a resource.

You can use your imagination to face the challenges of recovery. For example, one of my clients, Carl, who was in Stage Two of his recovery, was angry a lot. He was changing, and his friends were upset with him. He wasn't playing the old games and had altered the equilibrium of the system. When I asked him how he saw himself, he came up with two images of himself: a bull in a china shop and a little boy. We talked about ways to work with these two powerful images, such as embodying them, writing about them, and exploring them through movement. All of this work involves imagination in a creative, life-giving way.

Imagination provides an effective way to work through conflicts or deal with problems. I encourage my clients to close their eyes and imagine the struggle they are in and what they are struggling with. Then I suggest that they imagine the struggle being resolved and the changes they need to make to resolve it. I *don't* suggest that they imagine the other person or situation changing.

Wayne's struggle with his boss provides a good example of how this works. Wayne is a service repairman for an appliance company. For several months Wayne had been feeling angry that Tom, his boss, hadn't acknowledged the good work he had been doing. Wayne's way of finally dealing with this situation and his feelings was to ignore Tom and just do his job, which wasn't working. As an exercise I suggested that he create mental images of the struggle he was having with Tom.

After almost a minute had elapsed Wayne said, "I see two pictures. In one I'm beating him up and in the other I'm on my knees begging him for something."

Wayne explored these two images and realized that Tom's opinion of his work was important. Wayne wanted more feedback but his way of getting it wasn't working at all. Wayne then focused on ways he could resolve this problem for himself.

"I want Tom to change but he may not. I've been trying to get him to say what good work I have done by dropping hints. I could tell him I need more feedback from him. I could ask for it. That's seems simple yet feels difficult. He could say he doesn't have time or doesn't want to. But at least I'll have asked and I'll know his answer."

The steps you can follow in using this problem-solving technique are outlined below.

USING YOUR IMAGINATION TO RESOLVE A CONFLICT FOR YOURSELF

Create a mental image of the struggle or conflict.

_____

_____

_____

_____

_____

What do I want from the other person that I am not getting?

_____

_____

_____

_____

_____

What can I change to resolve the struggle or conflict? What can I do to change myself in this situation? Resolution means you are going to feel less upset and controlled by the struggle. It doesn't mean you are going to get what you want from the other person.

_____

_____

_____

_____

_____

Create an image with the change made. How does this change the original image I had?

_____

_____

_____

_____

_____

What will I do if I don't get what I want? Will I continue to try to get the other person to change?

_____

_____

_____

_____

_____

If I decide not to make a change, what stands in my way?

_____

_____

_____

_____

_____

This process takes practice at first because we are so used to focusing on changing things outside of us.

When using your imagination as a recovery resource, watch out for unhealthy fantasy. Unhealthy fantasy is another way to deny or avoid feelings and reality. Healthy use of fantasy supports you in recovery. You can tell the difference between the two by looking at this comparison.

Unhealthy Fantasy	**Healthy Fantasy**
Focuses on changes that other people have to make.	Focuses on changes you can make.
Is oriented on the future.	Is oriented on what is happening today that will affect the future.
Is used as an escape from current problems.	Is used as way to create solutions to current problems.

I often teach my clients a technique for using healthy fantasy to help them release tension from their bodies and relax. I recommend that they develop an image of a place that is very relaxing, a place to which they can mentally go to get away from the stress of current problems and challenges and recharge their energy. You can do the same for yourself following the steps outlined below. However, if you slip away to this place every time you feel some negative feeling such as sad, depressed, or frustrated, you are probably using this exercise as a way of avoiding your feelings and reality.

CREATING A RELAXING PLACE IN YOUR IMAGINATION

1. Sitting comfortably, allow your body to relax and your eyes to close.
2. Take some deep long breaths, allowing any tension to flow out of you with each exhalation.
3. Imagine the image of a place that is very relaxing to you. It might be a meadow, by the sea, or in your own home.
4. Imagine yourself in that place. Allow your body to relax even more as you picture yourself there. If disturbing images or thoughts enter the scene, gently bring yourself back to your special place.
5. Continue to breathe deeply and relax for a few minutes.
6. Gradually bring your awareness back to your body and its present posture. Feel your hands and arms in whatever position they are in. Become aware of any sounds around you and gradually open your eyes.
7. Stretch your body at this point.

Making Affirmations Work

I've worked with several individuals who have abused the concept of affirmations. I've done this myself. Still I believe that affirmations can be a useful tool for recovery. An affirmation is a positive statement that is used repetitiously to replace negative thoughts and ideas. Affirmations can be very helpful, but only if they are based on a realistic assessment of the truth of your life.

I thought affirmations would be a shortcut for me on the road to recovery, so I developed ones like this:

"I am healed perfectly in body, mind, and spirit."

"I am a perfect human being."

"My life is wonderful at all times."

Well, the truth was that the more I said these to myself, the more dissatisfied I became, because they weren't coming true. I finally realized that I needed to have more realistic expectations and use affirmations that described the process, not the end goals. For example, I now use simple affirmations like these:

"As I love myself more, I can love others more."

"I, Brian, am developing the patience and discipline to write a book."

"I am a healthy person and getting healthier."

"I am growing in courage to be myself fully."

Affirmations are always written in the present tense and describe your desires as if they are being fulfilled right now. When you try to create an affirmation, you may encounter a lot of resistance. You might hear negative self-talk like "Oh, sure you're healthy. You don't exercise at all." This is one of the gifts of the process. Grab a pen and write down all these negative messages. Get them out into the open so you can look at what you are really saying to yourself. Don't fight these negative messages. Just accept them as part of the house-cleaning you are doing in recovery.

I discourage affirmations about receiving material things, such as a Mercedes-Benz or a good relationship. Asking for things outside of yourself for validation simply perpetuates codependence. If you affirm yourself and your recovery, you will draw to yourself what you need to live your life fully.

CREATING HEALING AFFIRMATIONS

Create three healing affirmations for yourself that will assist you in your recovery. I have provided some suggestions as examples.

I (your name) am growing in my ability to recognize and express my feelings.

As I heal the pain from my past, I grow stronger for the future.

My higher power guides me as I allow myself to be guided.

Your affirmations:

_____

_____

_____

Remembering Childhood

Remembering the past is a major part of the work of Stage Two. By recalling and reexperiencing painful memories you can release yourself from their tight grip. The energy you have been using to repress and protect the memories will be available for your creative use. You won't have to fight with yourself so much.

You have already learned several exercises that are likely to evoke memories from childhood, including:

- Recording your childhood memories
- Recalling childhood illnesses
- Looking at old photographs
- Making a family map
- Writing your family's story
- Analyzing the family drama
- Identifying family rules
- Recalling negative messages
- Listing your parents' beliefs

In the section that follows you will learn another way to evoke memories: inventorying "hot buttons."

Inventorying Hot Buttons

"Hot buttons" were introduced in Chapter 5. In the following exercise exploring your hot buttons will help you call up some memories you may not currently be conscious of.

INVENTORYING MY HOT BUTTONS

Identifying My Hot Buttons

Examples:

1. Someone ignores me when I am talking.

2. People who interfere in conversations I am having.

Hot buttons I can identify are:

1. _____

2. _____

3. _____

4. _____

5. _____

My Responses to My Hot Buttons

Examples:

1. A surge of anger and I want to shake the person and let him know I am here.

2. Frustrated and I want to turn my back on the person who interferes.

When these hot buttons are touched I feel _____ and I want to _____ .

1. _____

2. _____

3. _____

4. _____

5. _____

My Family and My Hot Buttons

Examples:

1. My father always ignored my mother when she was talking.

2. Whenever I spoke at supper my brother would start talking and I'd never get a chance to talk.

My hot buttons relate to my family experiences in this way:

1. _____

2. _____

3. _____

4. _____

5. _____

As you identify and work through your hot buttons, you will open yourself up to healing some old painful memories.

The healing potential of exploring hot buttons was demonstrated to me during a session with Arlene. Arlene had been married for eight years and divorced for four years when she started seeing me. For about three months Arlene had been working on the anger and jealousy she felt in her current relationship. She felt ignored, frustrated, and upset by her partner's lack of responsiveness: "I feel like Jack just turns his back on me, and then I have to work to get his attention. It's always my fault, because I need his attention so much."

"Arlene," I asked, "what's it like when someone turns his back on you?"

"It really gets to me," Arlene confessed. "I don't know why, but I just can't stand it."

I asked Arlene if she was willing to explore this further, and when she agreed, I got up and turned my back to her, standing about five feet away from her chair.

Within minutes I heard faint sobs, followed shortly by angry words. "Why did you ignore me? You told me I had to do things right and then just walked away. You turned your back on me."

When I asked Arlene whom I represented, she said quickly, "My dad. He always ignored me."

I asked Arlene if she could take the place of her father, sensing that it was time for her to switch roles. She stood with her back to me and, taking on the role of her father, spoke in a firm voice: "I did what I did to make you strong. You see, I'm not always going to be with you, and I want you to be able to take care of yourself."

This was the start of a 20-minute dialogue during which Arlene and her father figure talked intimately about what happened to her as a child and how she felt about it. At the end, drenched with sweat and puffy-eyed from her tears, Arlene ended by hugging a pillow that she used to represent her father.

As the session came to a close, Arlene reflected on this experience: "I think I understand now what I want from Jack. But I also see that he may not be capable of giving it to me. I feel relieved, like settled inside. And I sure understand my dad more." She shed a few tears. "I really want to forgive him and heal myself, and I think it's started."

During the following months, Arlene developed new ways to get the attention she craved instead of demanding it from Jack. She explored new friendships at her church and decided to take some night classes in drama that she had been interested in but had set aside to spend time with Jack. She began to recognize and accept the fact that Jack was never going to be the affectionate and demonstrative partner she wanted. Most importantly, she knew the positive benefit of recalling and reexperiencing old and painful memories. She learned to trust the recovery process.

Assessing the Benefits of Your Roles

During Stage One you assessed your family and its roles and dynamics and the ways this environment may have affected you. When you are playing your role, you are meeting the needs of your family. At the same time, you are getting some of your needs met. This exercise involves taking an honest look at the benefits you derived as a child from the roles you played.

Sometimes clients are surprised when I ask them about the benefits of their roles. But there are benefits to you that are part of each role. For example, one client realized that being the scapegoat meant he could act out and misbehave, which increased his opportunities for having fun in his rigid, puritanical family. I was the family hero; in that role I was encouraged to strive and achieve. I got social status and recognition as a result. Some people's roles were the only way they could survive threats of physical or emotional abuse.

BENEFITS OF FAMILY ROLES

Examples

Roles

Scapegoat

Benefits

Got to have fun
Lots of attention
Felt unique and different

Martyr

Got to be right(eous)
Didn't have to ask directly for what I
    wanted
Got attention and sympathy

Benefits of My Family Roles

Write your roles and the benefits you derived from them below. Remember, most people play more than one role.

Roles

Benefits

_____

_____
_____
_____
_____
_____

_____

_____
_____
_____
_____
_____

_____

_____
_____
_____
_____
_____

After you've considered the benefits you gained from your roles in your family, consider the benefits you continue to acquire while continuing to play the same roles in your relationships, at work, and in other areas of your life. Here's an example of the next step in this analysis:

CURRENT BENEFITS OF ROLES

Examples

Role: Scapegoat

Circumstances	Benefits
At work	Less responsibility
	Attention
In relationships	Feel less vulnerable
	Take fewer risks (don't get hurt)
	Less responsibility
In groups	Focus of attention
	Less responsibility

Current Benefits of My Roles

Role:_____

Circumstances	Benefits
At work	_____
	_____
	_____
	_____
	_____
In relationships	_____
	_____
	_____
	_____
	_____

In groups

_____

The benefits you derive from your roles are valid. If you are going to give up your roles, you are still going to have to find some way to meet these needs. Continue this exercise by coming up with alternative ways to acquire the benefits you listed above. Create five alternatives for each benefit above. Stretching yourself to think of five forces you to get beyond the obvious and into some creative possibilities. Later you can come back and try to double and triple your prospects. As thoughts come to you, note them on the side as shown in the example.

ALTERNATIVES TO BENEFITS

Example

Benefit

Attention

What kind of attention do I want anyway? Respect? or outrage?

For who I am.

Alternatives

1. Change my hairstyle
2. Write a letter to the editor
3. Say something true in every conversation
4. Paint designs on my car
5. Paint a picture expressing my self

My Alternatives

Benefit

_____

What kind of

_____ do I

want anyway?

_____

_____

_____

_____

Alternatives

1. _____

2. _____

3. _____

4. _____

5. _____

Some of you were raised in families where anger was used as a weapon of control. The thought of allowing yourself to be angry may carry with it grim images of terror. Some of you have never seen explosive anger; you only felt the steely cold oppressiveness of rules that prohibited any expression of anger. Few of us have effective role models for expressing anger.

During Stage Two much of the anger you feel is a natural and direct response to your growing understanding of how you were abused as a child and how you have continued to deny your self. This is the anger that Carol Tavris in her book *Anger* describes as the anger of despair. The phrase "anger of despair" comes from the work of Dr. John Bowlby, a pioneer in the study of attachment and separation in infants. Bowlby found that rage is the natural response of an infant whose mother leaves. This rage is followed by apathy if the mother doesn't return quickly or if she leaves repeatedly. It's almost as if the anger of red-hot rage freezes into the anger of cold despair. I believe that the anger of Stage Two is the anger of despair.

You are not being disloyal if you are angry at the abusive behavior of your parents. In fact you are experiencing the honest feelings that you could not feel or express as a child. Although you may feel like blasting your parents or other family members for their behavior toward you when you were a child, I don't recommend it. However, confrontation is appropriate if abusive behavior still occurs. If you decide to confront your family members on their behavior, be clear about your intent. If you expect an apology or any change from them, you may be disappointed. I recommend confronting them after you have identified the specific behaviors about which you are angry and how these behaviors affected you as a child. Tell them about what you are angry about and what you are going to do to take care of yourself as result.

In recovery you are challenged to find healthy ways to express your anger. I recommend that you use the exercises suggested in the earlier sections on identifying feelings and working with feelings to feel and express your anger. However, the deep feelings and energy that come with the "anger of despair" may seem overwhelming. Answering the following questions will help you see it in perspective.

WORKING WITH ATTITUDES TOWARD ANGER

Example

1. Write down all the messages you are telling yourself about your anger.

"My anger is too much to express."
"If I get angry, I'll explode."
"I'm afraid I'll hurt someone if I really let go."

2. Create a new message that affirms your anger and then describe the situation or behavior that angers you.

"I am angry about the way my father broke promises he made to me."

3. Add to this message a statement about what you want to do with your anger.

"Write in my journal."
"Work on it in therapy."
"Spend 15 minutes a day taking care of my hurt and angry inner child."

Working with My Attitudes Toward Anger

1. Write down all the messages you are telling yourself about your anger.

_____

_____

_____

_____

_____

_____

_____

_____

2. Create a new message that affirms your anger and then describe the situation or behavior that angers you.

I am angry about _____

_____

_____

_____

_____

There is another kind of anger—corrosive and lethal—that you may encounter: anger at yourself. As you work through Stage Two, you may get angry at yourself for allowing others to control your life, for being dishonest, or for the hundred other little sins of omission and commission that are a part of your codependence. Some of you may even get angry at yourselves for not being able to express your anger.

Let your self-directed anger point the way to developing a sense of your own values and needs. You may have been taught that anger was bad, wrong, or destructive. But anger is a useful emotion. It tells you when your values are being violated or when you are being abused. Welcome your anger as a friend and ally on the road to recovery.

SUMMARY

The following exercises will promote your recovery, enlisting your mental abilities as allies in your healing:
1. Ask yourself the four questions described on pages 222–24.
2. Use your imagination in the following ways:
    a. to develop images that help your recovery
    b. to visualize the resolution of challenges and conflicts
    c. to create a relaxing place for yourself
3. Work with affirmations in a positive way, as explained on pages 229–30.
4. Continue the process of evoking childhood memories, using the techniques mentioned on page 230.

5. Inventory your hot buttons; see pages 231–32 for more on this.
6. Assess the benefits of the roles you played in your family, as described on pages 234–37.

• • • • • • •

Experiencing the Spiritual Dimension

The experiences of Stage Two call you to a deeper trust and surrender to a higher power. Through this process you will experience the grace-filled healing love of your higher power. This love will heal the wounds of your inner child and strengthen you to continue your process of recovery.

The exercises described in this section on the spiritual dimension are intended to support you in that process.

Prayer

My own recovery has taught me an important lesson about prayer. For years I thought prayer was something to do in church or on my knees in a quiet place and time. There was always something formal about it. I now know that prayer has very little to do with posture, words, or location. I believe this book is a form of prayer, particularly the act of writing it.

Prayer is a recognition of the presence of a higher power and a willingness to come into union with that power. Prayer is our response to our higher power's communication of acceptance and love. During the difficulties and struggles inherent in Stage Two, prayer can be a source of healing and nurturing grace.

Prayer is a unique communication between you and your higher power. It can be anything that works for you. I describe it as "an action of the heart." I often pray by making a simple statement or a simple request of my higher power, saying something like this: "God, teach me of love and compassion for myself and others."

Right now, reflect on your own prayer life. What can you do to communicate with your higher power? Make some sort of prayer a part of your daily life.

Nature Walks

Taking a walk through nature can be a form of prayer. Nature provides many metaphors for healing and subjects for reflection. Go for a walk in the woods or the desert, a hike in the mountains, or a stroll along the beach. Or just walk around the block.

In my walks through the woods around Seattle I see the harmony of nature. Yes, there is decay and death and the cycle of life. Vibrant ferns grow out of rotting tree stumps. Drops of rain splash into streams, which merge, forming rivers, which flow to the sea. This is nature's cycle of growth and change. The same force that moves the seasons and the streams will also heal you if you let it.

I encourage you to go for a walk whenever you are faced with the difficulties and challenges that recovery brings. Look for answers in nature's ways. Allow your eyes to be open to suggestions and solutions. If possible, find a quiet, natural place where you can be alone and meditate on whatever nature presents to you there.

I was told about the experience of a woman who went for a solitary walk in the woods during a time when she was feeling bad about herself. As she looked for a place to sit down, she realized, too late, that she had blundered through a spider's web and destroyed it. This confirmed her feeling that she ruined everything she touched. But as she sat there, near tears, she saw that the spider was already beginning to repair the web. Fifteen or 20 minutes later, when she left, the web was almost back to its original dimensions. She felt that she had learned something about patience and persistence. The spider didn't waste time bemoaning what had been lost but simply did the best with the given circumstances.

You are part of nature and also called by the same force to yield to the development of your own unique pattern and process.

Writing a Spiritual History

During my childhood I thought of God as a distant father figure. Raised as a Catholic, I believed that I was tainted by original sin and that I would go to Hell if I committed any sins. As my life progressed, I didn't have to worry about going to Hell. I managed to create it in my own life.

My image of my higher power and my understanding of my relationship with my higher power have changed a great deal. My image of a distant, punishing, and powerful Father has been transformed into an embracing, forgiving, inexhaustibly loving force in my life. I believe my higher power hurts when I hurt, laughs when I laugh, and cries when I cry. My higher power is both Father and Mother. My higher power does not just dwell in Heaven, but also on Earth. My higher power, whom I call God, is in me and in everybody else.

I encourage you to write your own spiritual history. This will help you get an overview of the beliefs that have shaped you and will probably surprise you with the depth of spiritual experience you have already known. We tend not to talk about spiritual experiences because they are so personal and intimate. Then, because we don't process them with the intellect, we forget what we've felt. Your description of your spiritual past may help clarify the direction in which you are now moving.

Here are some suggestions to help you in your writing.

MY SPIRITUAL HISTORY

Make a list of your beliefs. Start with beliefs from your childhood and work your way up to the things you believe now. What do you believe about a higher power? About good and evil? About the meaning of life?

_____

_____

_____

_____

_____

_____

Describe the important spiritual experiences of your life.

_____

_____

_____

_____

_____

Which religious values were you taught in childhood? How have they changed? What are your values now?

_____

_____

_____

_____

_____

What spiritual practices have you followed? How have they worked in terms of enhancing love and solidity in your life?

_____

_____

_____

_____

_____

What is your understanding of the meaning of life? How do you know that? Has your understanding changed over time?

_____

_____

_____

_____

_____

Describe those times you recognized the intervention of a higher power in your life.

_____

_____

_____

_____

_____

How has your image of a higher power changed? How has your relationship with a higher power changed? How do you feel about your relationship with this power? How do you want to change it.

_____

_____

_____

_____

_____

_____

_____

Writing your spiritual history helps give you a sense of yourself as a person with a rich spiritual background. As your relationship with your higher power develops, you will have much to add to your spiritual history.

Making a Moral Inventory

I recommend working on the fourth, fifth, sixth, and seventh of the Twelve Steps during Stage Two because these steps help you accept yourself. The exercises that follow will help you work these steps.

Step 4. We made a searching and fearless moral inventory of ourselves.

In the fourth step you look at and accept the things you don't like about yourself. I recommend starting with a list of your controlling behaviors. I used a chart like the one in the next exercise to do one of my inventories.

The Twelve Steps aren't over when you do them once. Just like the four stages of recovery, you will find yourself returning to them again and again for deeper work. The next time you do the fourth step you will probably find yourself focusing on something different, perhaps resentment ("Whom do I resent?") or dishonesty ("Whom have I been dishonest with?")

MORAL INVENTORY

Examples

Whom Do I Want to Control?	What Is My Need to Control About?	How Does My Behavior Affect Me?	What Am I Denying About Myself?
God	Doesn't tell me how to do things Won't give me what I want	Makes me angry Cuts me off from source of inner strength	impatience, fear, self-pity, lack of trust in God
My wife	Thinking I know what's best for her Fear of confrontation	I withdraw Causes anxiety Makes me rigid	pride, fear of the unknown, difficulty trusting others, demanding

My Moral Inventory

Whom Do I Want to Control?	What Is My Need to Control About?	How Does My Behavior Affect Me?	What Am I Denying About Myself?

When I first started doing my step work, I understood the value of the fourth and fifth steps from my experiences with confession in the Catholic Church. It was and still is a great relief to me to "lay my burden down" when I do a fourth and fifth step.

Step 5. We admitted to God, to ourselves, and to another human being the exact nature of our wrongs.

In Step 5 you take your fourth step work and share it with another person. You do this for yourself so that you can get rid of all the little secrets, the things about yourself that you believe you must hide. This can be an important part of your recovery process as it helps you accept yourself.

Don't go to just anyone. Making your fifth step disclosure makes you vulnerable. Choose someone that you can trust. I often suggest sharing with a minister or rabbi or priest, especially one who understands the Twelve-Step process, not someone who will seize the opportunity to preach to you or shame you. Therapists and counselors can also be valuable listeners, as can close friends. I don't recommend sharing with your wife, lover, parents, other family members, or anyone else with whom you are in an intimate relationship. Respect others' boundaries as you respect your own.

Step 6. We were entirely ready to have God remove all these defects of character.

Can you imagine what life would be like if all the negative, self-defeating character traits you listed as part of your fourth step were removed? Hard to imagine, isn't it? You've become quite attached to these qualities; they've been an important part of your self-image and your life for years. In Step 6 you become ready to let go of them. This is a process. I've learned from my own Twelve-Step work and from talking with others that you need to keep working on being ready. There may be some character traits that you don't want to give up. At this point, ask yourself "Which of these character traits am I really ready to have a higher power remove?"

Step 7. We humbly asked Him to remove our faults.

Notice that the process of letting go of your faults happens in two parts. First you become willing, then, in the Step 7, you ask your higher power to remove your faults. This doesn't mean abdicating your own responsibility for yourself. Take some time to list the steps you can undertake to help in the process. When I looked at my fourth step work, shown in the exercise above, I came up with the following things I could do to help let go of my desire to control my higher power:

1. Pray for understanding of the will of my higher power for me
2. Seek spiritual direction when I am struggling with anger toward my higher power
3. Continue working the Twelve Steps, particularly Steps 1, 2, and 3

When I'm doing seventh step work, I ask my higher power to remove my shortcomings, and I participate in that process by working on those things I can.

Letting Go

Letting go is a fairly popular term right now. "Let go and let God" is one of the aphorisms associated with AA. What is meant by "letting go"?

Codependents tend to cling tightly to the illusion of being in control. They believe they can have everything they want by exerting pure willpower. There is only one way I know to use willpower in a creative, life-giving way—through surrender to the will of a higher power.

When I say this, I often hear "I did that already! Do I have to keep doing it?" Other people ask, "How do I do that? I don't even know what it means." My answer to that question is "I'm still finding out myself."

When I undertake a project or an activity, I always ask myself this question: "Whose will is my willpower serving?" Sometimes I don't like the answer I get. Sometimes I get mixed messages and have to keep asking. For example, I hope and believe that this book is the product of my cooperation with the will of my higher power. But at times I wonder and question my motivation. Am I doing this for recognition? Do I still want to take care of people? Am I after the money? Well, I'm motivated by all of these things but also by something much greater. I believe that when I am truly co-creating with my higher power my efforts flow naturally. I may still experience resistance. But it won't be the sort of resistance that I feel compelled to fight against. I can just surrender, trust, and keep on working.

This book began in 1984 as some scribbled notes about my ideas and experiences. During my relapse in 1985 I completely put aside any idea of writing. I was involved in surviving. By the following year my interest in the book resurfaced, and I wrote a 50-page summary. In the spring of the following year I produced a workbook. In the middle of that summer I sent out query letters to publishers and got back several encouraging responses. This inspired me to begin the writing, but it was a slow and painful process. By fall I had completed a rough draft of the first three chapters and realized that at the rate I was working it would take me three years to finish the book. I felt overwhelmed, so I turned it over to my higher power, saying something like "If you want me to write this book, then you might as well know I can't do it alone."

Within one month I was introduced to an excellent writer and editor, Waverly Fitzgerald. Soon the process of writing was less intimidating. Waverly and I developed a working relationship that flows with a productive rhythm. Her enthusiastic response to the ideas in the book, the interest of publishers, and the support of friends have encouraged me. The writing process has been time-consuming, and it has required discipline. Yet it has given so much to me. I have grown as a result. I have learned the wisdom of "letting go and letting God."

I also ask my clients "Whose will is your willpower serving?" when they're enmeshed in relationship struggles and operating out of highly focused willpower. Often this type of willpower shows up as control and enabling behavior. Rather than allowing the natural consequences of events or other people's actions to occur, they try to "keep things together." When clients tell me they're doing all the work in a relationship, that's often a clue that codependence is active and that sheer willpower is maintaining the relationship.

What does letting go really mean? The reflections below might help give you some ideas:

What Is Letting Go?

Letting go . . .

is not taking responsibility for others. It is taking responsibility for yourself.

is not enabling another person in denial. It is allowing others to learn from natural consequences.

is not controlling others. It is admitting your own powerlessness.

is not trying to change or blame others. It is making the most out of what life offers.

is not caretaking. It is caring about.

is not fixing others. It is supporting them in their growth.

is not being in the middle, rescuing others. It's being on the sidelines, cheering and encouraging.

is not protecting others from reality. It is allowing others to have their reality.

is not holding in your feelings out of concern for others. It is expressing your feelings.

is not denying reality. It is accepting reality.

is not insisting on being right. It is being open to new information and change.

is not scolding, nagging, or arguing. It is identifying your own shortcomings and correcting them.

is not defending your behavior and ignoring its effects on others. It is accepting the feedback of others and honestly assessing your behavior's validity.

is not trying to adjust things to your desire but taking every day as it comes and accepting yourself in it.

is not judging and criticizing others. It is being all you can become.

is not holding on to the past. It is living now and growing for the future.

is not withdrawing. It is taking care of yourself.

is fearing less and loving more.

Embracing the Shadow

John Giannini, writing an article entitled "Into the Shadowy Place" for *Creation* magazine, says that the deep pain felt by your wounded child becomes part of the dark side of yourself, the shadow side that you try to avoid. The inner child represents all those feelings that were "not okay" during your childhood, all those feelings you had to deny to be acceptable.

As Giannini describes:

This depressed, sorrowing child . . . cannot be tolerated and so we cover up our hurts with the above noted activities [i.e., addiction, codependence]; and even worse, we convert that inner hurt into a contemptuous put-down of our own children as well as spouses and peers.

This is one explanation for the child abuse and violence that are rampart in our society.

At the core of the wounded inner child is the disabling and corrosive sense of not being worthy. It's a feeling of shame that, like a dark filter, distorts your perception of yourself so you see yourself as a failure, completely inadequate, a phony, incompetent, helpless, and unworthy of help. Going into this shame and feeling it is like walking in the dark. It's one of the uncomfortable experiences of Stage Two of recovery.

Shame—that sense of your own unworthiness—is deeply rooted. Recovery means uncovering that feeling and replacing it with the truth: you deserve to experience the joy and abundance of life and your unique value as a person.

The prayer that follows can help you heal your wounded inner child, the child who has been shamed into feeling and thinking he or she is unworthy.

Put it somewhere where you will notice it and recite it to your inner child. Or record it on a tape and play it back to yourself. Imagine your higher power is reading it to you. I read this little prayer to myself whenever I feel the feeling that I recognize as shame. I also use it when thoughts of scarcity invade my mind—those thoughts that tell you you'll never have enough money, you'll never have a good relationship, you'll never be recognized, and so on. When I pray this prayer, I let the words sink into my heart and let my higher power do the work.

Prayer to Heal the Wounded Inner Child

Oh, how I love you! I long to draw you closer to myself. Lay your life before me and trust me, for I will not forsake you. I know your heart. I am close to those whose hearts are breaking. Will you not trust me? I will heal you. Bring everything to me, for I love you. You are my precious child. Can you not see my hand in your life? See how gently I have guided your steps. My Presence is here for you. I am the Great Spirit you seek. Reach out. Reach out and I will meet your needs. I am your Mother and your Father. You are my Child. I long for a beautiful relationship with you. I love you so. Draw close to me. I wait in love, my child.

I also recommend using this meditation as part of an exercise. I use it this way in my spirituality and recovery workshops, and it always evokes deep healing experiences for the participants.

Choose one of your friends with whom you feel supported and loved and ask him or her to join you in this exercise. Find a relaxing, private, safe environment where you won't be interrupted or distracted; a dimly lit, quiet room is ideal. Stand facing your friend and close your eyes. Your friend places his or her hands on your shoulders and walks you backward very slowly, counting down from your current age to some age in your childhood at which you've earlier agreed to stop. Pick the age that seems right to you. You can pick 16, 14, 8, three, one, or the time of your birth. Your friend then reads the above meditation to you. Breathe slowly and absorb the words.

You may experience feelings of deep warmth and release. You may cry or feel the pain of your inner child. Spend a few minutes after your friend is finished reciting just feeling the sensations of your body and your feelings. Close the experience with a hug or some other acknowledgment that you are finished and count your way back up to your current age.

Learning to Love the Dark

Like the winter, Stage Two is a time of darkness. Many of us are afraid of the dark. We're afraid of the darkness of the pain and hurt we've been avoiding for so long. And we've been taught that evil lurks in the dark, all those desires and feelings that we suppressed because they were "bad." Stage Two is a time of learning to be in the dark and move through it.

It's a challenge to learn to love yourself, especially those behaviors that you've despised. But this is what recovery requires: learning to love yourself.

Here's an exercise that will help you develop a sense of compassion for yourself and acceptance of your dark side.

EMBRACING THE DARKNESS

1. List all of the things you know or are discovering about yourself that you don't like, those things that embarrass you or that you consider petty and weak. Consider roles, behaviors, feelings, and attitudes.
2. Beside each, describe what it is you don't like about it.

What I Don't Like About Myself

1. _____

2. _____

3. _____

4. _____

5. _____

What I Don't Like About This

_____

_____

_____

_____

_____

3. Now imagine that a young child came to you describing the same things and giving the same reasons for not liking them. Reflect on what you would do. Would you scold and judge? Would you explore the child's feelings and fears? Most likely you would treat the child with compassion and understanding.

4. Allow yourself to accept the various aspects and traits you don't like in yourself. Relax, breathe deeply, and let it be okay that you are a fallible and imperfect human being.

As you embrace the darkness and learn to accept your wounded inner child, you will experience profound healing.

Example

What I Don't Like About Myself

1. I've been dishonest about my feelings.

2. I've emotionally abused partners in relationships.

3. I've acted like a rescuer and then a victim in relationships.

What I Don't Like About This

Being dishonest is manipulative and I hate to think of myself that way.

This is selfish and I knew I was doing it.

It was foolish of me to be so immature.

Having Compassion for Yourself

One of my clients, Bonnie, in the midst of some very difficult work, wrote the following description of her experience:

---

21 July 1988 Thursday

I cry even now. The sorrow is so unbelievably deep—like the endless darkness I envision so often. I know Daddy forgives me . . . if only I could forgive myself.

I wished so much to be dead today . . . to stop the endless pain and grief I feel. Endless yards of pain strewn across the vastness of forever to the neverending darkness that encompasses all sparing nothing leaving raw and vulnerable flesh that stings and shrieks with the raging of the wind. Hiding is impossible, and what is left in the way is shreds of a body bleeding and crying in its dust.

Quiet and peace at last as slivers of my being crawl together for comfort and warmth.

I just tried to draw what I was feeling. Not satisfied with the work. Maybe if I move, dance to the pain. I dance with Little Bonnie; for the first time I notice that she does not smile. I pick her up and she melts into me. She seems worried about me since I am crying. I talk with her about being whole and complete. She does not understand.

Dancing in agony to "Somewhere in Time" and healing with hope and love to "On Golden Pond," I dance my feelings. At the end remains Bonnie with a sparkle in her eye and hope in her heart and thanksgiving to God, dear God, for her life.

When Bonnie gave me this passage from her journal to read, I saw in her what I have seen in many individuals who are committed to their recovery: a growing sense of compassion for herself.

When you have compassion for yourself, you understand that although you may have acted in self-defeating ways, you were struggling to get love, acceptance, and recognition. These are natural and very human desires.

When you have compassion for yourself, you have a passionate, loving involvement in your own life. Such loving acceptance of yourself is one of the most unselfish attitudes you can adopt, for through your understanding and acceptance of yourself you will be more accepting and understanding of others.

To help develop compassion for yourself, reflect on the following questions.

DEVELOPING COMPASSION

1. What is in the way of your loving acceptance of yourself?

_____

_____

_____

_____

_____

2. If you were to present yourself before the most loving force you can imagine (perhaps your higher power), what would that force tell you about your struggle to be loved?

_____

_____

_____

_____

_____

3. Can you accept that your codependence is based on your basic human need to be loved? If not, what thoughts get in the way?

_____

_____

_____

_____

_____

When I find that I am judging or criticizing myself harshly, I move into a space of compassion by taking a deep breath and saying as I exhale, "Ah! That's me: imperfect, fallible, human, loving—that's me."

Dignity: Acknowledging Your Own Worth

An increasing sense of dignity is also a manifestation of Stage Two of recovery. Dignity is the opposite of the toxic shame that attacks your inherent worthiness. In fact, the word *dignity* derives from the Latin word for "worthy." When you have dignity, you are open to your humanness, your imperfections, imbalances, and limitations. Dignity is the result of letting go of control and trusting in the loving acceptance of your higher power.

As a child of a higher power you have a right to affirm your dignity. It can be a simple affirmation such as "I am growing in worthiness to experience the grace of my higher power" or "I am worthy of being loved and I am growing in love of myself." The statement that works for me when I doubt my worth is "I stand as a man in the presence of my God." You might want to make a creative statement of your value. Draw a picture, write a poem, or dance a dance that affirms your value. Take a few minutes now to create a statement that affirms your emerging sense of dignity and value.

AN AFFIRMATION OF MY DIGNITY AND VALUE

Write down an affirmation of your dignity, worthiness, and value as a person.

_____

_____

_____

SUMMARY

The following exercises will help deepen your experience of the spiritual dimension:

1. Develop a prayer you can use on a daily basis.
2. Get into the habit of going for walks and observing nature.
3. Write your spiritual history, on pages 243–45.
4. Work the fourth, fifth, sixth, and seventh steps of the Twelve Steps, using the suggestions on pages 245–48.
5. Practice letting go, using the suggestions on pages 249–50.
6. Say the Prayer to Heal the Wounded Inner Child found on page 251 to yourself or have a friend read it to you.
7. Embrace your shadow side, doing the exercise on pages 250–51.
8. List ways you treat yourself with compassion; answer the questions on page 255.
9. Make a statement that affirms your worth as a person.

• • • • • • •

GENERAL RECOMMENDATIONS

You can probably tell by reading through the description and the exercises contained in this chapter that working through Stage Two can be difficult and painful. Being disoriented, experiencing repressed feelings, and letting go will take you into uncharted waters. The exercises I've described are designed to support you during this stage. In addition, here are a few general recommendations:

1. If you discover or even have a vague sense that you were sexually or physically abused, I urge you to contact a knowledgeable therapist to work on these issues.

2. It's not unusual for individuals to have thoughts about suicide or experience depression during Stage Two work. Once again, if these conditions persist, seek the help of a professional.

3. Continue your work with Twelve-Step support groups. If you are not already involved in counseling, you might want to consider individual or group therapy at this time.

4. Utilize any of the exercises from Stage One that seem useful to you.

5. Nurture yourself by nurturing others who are already in recovery. Maintain your support network.

6. Take time to have fun.

Moving on to Stage Three

Slowly the fog will begin to lift. The experience of disorientation that is prominent in Stage Two will gradually give way to an emerging sense of self-awareness and strength. You will still feel discomfort and pain, but they won't be so extreme. The snow and frost of denial have melted, and the rivers of feeling are running again. The wounds of the inner child, exposed to the light, are beginning to heal. You have learned to face the monsters and move through the darkness. A light is beginning to glow at the end of the tunnel. You gradually trust your ability to take care of yourself.

Stage Three usually begins in small ways, just like spring. One day there's frost on the ground; a few days later the green shoots of crocuses appear. The seeds and bulbs that have matured during the winter burst into growth, propelling themselves up toward the sun.

You'll notice that you take increasing responsibility for yourself and your feelings. This is more than just saying "I know it's my stuff." You make a commitment to act differently in situations or with people that were disempowering before. You become aware of feelings and values that you denied before. You begin to see that you have choices about how you respond to your feelings and thoughts. All of these are signs of the beginning of Stage Three.

A client who has been working on her recovery for four years described the differences between Stage Two and Stage Three in this way. During Stage Two she felt the fear and panic of her inner child. During Stage Three she could feel the fear and panic and respond as a healthy, centered adult. Now she says she can be "authentically nice," not "controlling nice."

You will find, as I and so many others I know have, that you'll be ready to move to Stage Three in some areas of your life and not others. For example, you may be ready to take responsibility for yourself and your feelings in some friendships but not in more intimate relationships. I encourage you to move into Stage Three when you are ready and in whatever little ways seem appropriate.

11

· · · · · · ·

Stage Three: Taking Responsibility for Yourself and Your Feelings

Experience is not what happens to you but what you make of what happens to you.

ALDOUS HUXLEY

ALTHOUGH SPRING SEEMS like a brand-new start, it isn't, of course. It's simply another part of the cycle. The leaves that fell off the trees in autumn became compost, enriching and nourishing the soil. The cold and dark of winter provided the right conditions for the germination of seeds and bulbs in the spring. The understanding gained during the first two stages of recovery becomes the foundation for new behavior and ways of relating.

Spurred by the cycle of growth, bulbs and seeds crack open. Life energy urges them on. The growth of spring is the result of action. The tiny shoots of plants and flowers push up and through the soil. It's as if they are taking responsibility for their own lives by reaching for the light.

259

Taking Responsibility

Stage Three is a time for the development of responsibility. When I was asked at a recent workshop what I meant by responsibility, I wrote this definition on the blackboard:

Responsibility = response-ability

During Stage Three you will increase your ability to implement life-giving and self-affirming responses in your life—in relationships, at work, and with friends. Most of the work of Stage Two was inner-directed; Stage Three is a time for outer-directed action. After a necessary period of hibernation you're ready to try your new insights in relationships.

As you take greater responsibility for yourself, your sense of self will grow clearer. As you become more familiar with yourself, you will find it easier to make choices, take action, and express yourself.

At the same time, you will gradually realize that you alone are responsible for your experiences.

During Stage Three your relationship with your higher power will also deepen. Your earlier work has opened a lot of the channels that were blocked. Now you can respond to and receive the blessings of your higher power more easily.

The process of taking responsibility for yourself and your feelings means:

1. acknowledging and accepting your limitations
2. creating choices for yourself about your responses to people and situations
3. defining your personal boundaries
4. acting on your trust in your higher power
5. making changes in your life that reflect your own responsibility for meeting your needs in healthy ways
6. intervening in the cycle of codependence and redirecting it into a cycle of growth.

Stage Three is a time of growth through action. But it isn't all flowers and promise. You will have setbacks as you integrate new behaviors and beliefs into your life. You might think of these as the windstorms and rains of spring. They are mini-cycles of growth and change. Some of your new behavior won't survive, some of your relationships will be altered, but the general direction of the force of life in spring is forward and upward and outward.

Just as the sun becomes brighter and the days longer, so will your self-confidence and self-esteem flourish. Instead of coaxing yourself through the dark places, you will be stepping forth into the light.

Integrity and Integration

Stage Three is a time of **integration**. Integration means taking various parts and combining them into a harmonious whole. As a result of codependence you have denied or repressed certain aspects and qualities. Having learned to accept these formerly unacceptable parts of your self during Stage Two, you can now blend them together as part of your unique self.

Integrity is the key quality of Stage Three. Integration and integrity are related words, both deriving from a Latin word meaning "whole." During recovery, as you bring together the fragmented parts of yourself, you develop a sense of wholeness. You feel an inner alignment that helps you determine your values and your desires. You act out of your integrity, out of your awareness of your self and your inner truth. Your growing ability to try new things and take responsibility for yourself comes from this growing sense of integrity.

Tools and Support

The exercises and recommendations in this chapter are intended to enhance your response-ability in your life. You will notice that I don't offer as many specific exercises for Stage Three work as I did for the previous stages. That's partly because you'll be continuing the exercises from Stages One and Two as the necessary foundation of your recovery. When you feel a strong emotion or a sense of discomfort, you can use the techniques you've already learned for working with feelings. You can continue using deep breathing to relax, body- work to promote the healing of your body, and a regular exercise program and healthy diet to provide a necessary foundation for your recovery. You can use the methods you've already learned—including prayer, nature walks, and keeping a journal—to deepen your relationship with your higher power.

In some ways Stage Three is quite different in focus from Stages One and Two. The previous exercises were geared toward healing the impact of codependence on your physical and mental dimensions to clear the way for a growing sense of Self.

The challenge of Stage Three is to *act* out of that sense of self. You will be standing up for your own values and expressing your own needs. At the same time, you will be interacting with other people. Instead of acting out of the rigid roles of the past, you will be responding with more spontaneity. I can't offer specific guidelines for behavior, because every situation is different, but I can suggest certain exercises that will enhance your response-ability.

Healing the Physical Dimension

Throughout Stages One and Two you've become more aware of your body and feelings. By allowing your feelings to surface and expressing them, you've started healing the wounded inner feeling space. And you've developed ways of honoring your inner child. It's essential to continue these practices. They are the basis of your recovery program.

Before starting recovery, most of your responses were automatic, the results of defenses you developed during years of codependence. During Stage Three you actively change these reactions, giving yourself a broader array of responses.

Paying Attention to Yourself

Recovery is a process of expanding your awareness of yourself. This exercise will help you maintain your awareness. I recommend doing brief "inner assessments" throughout the day by asking yourself the following questions.

CHECKING IN

1. How am I breathing right now?

_____

_____

2. Am I tense in my back, shoulders, neck, face, etc.?

_____

_____

3. Can I relax my body for a few minutes and focus on my bodily sensation?

_____

_____

4. Is my jaw tight or loose?

_____

_____

Until this practice becomes habitual, you might want to set up a way to remind yourself. You could paste a note that says "Check In" someplace where you will glance at it frequently, perhaps on your computer terminal, your bathroom mirror, or a kitchen cupboard.

This simple process will help you stay in touch with your body and how it's feeling. It will also help you stay centered and grounded during times of stress. This practice was helpful as I wrote this book. I just checked in and found myself with a tight jaw and tight shoulders and breathing shallowly. After checking in, I reminded myself to open up my body, sit up straight, breathe deeply, and relax.

As a codependent you have probably spent most of your time focusing on others. This exercise will bring the focus of attention back to where it belongs—on _your_ feelings and thoughts.

Becoming Grounded

When you are grounded, you have a sense of solidity and contact with your self. You feel rooted in the reality of the world around you just as a plant is rooted in the ground. The plant needs to be in contact with the earth for both support and nourishment. Grounding can provide you with both a sense of strength and a sense of connection.

You will not be grounded if you rely on something outside yourself to hold you up. You're probably very familiar with the spaciness of codependence, a life-style in which you're buffeted by insecurity because the input you're getting from others changes all the time.

The feeling of being grounded comes from within. It's a natural by-product of the recovery process. As you get more in touch with your feelings and develop a relationship with your higher power, you will feel more grounded.

This exercise will help you feel grounded, feel your own center and your strength. It is also useful, like deep breathing, during times of stress.

BECOMING GROUNDED

1. Breathe deeply and become aware of your feet on the ground.
2. Continuing to breathe deeply, notice how your legs are connected to your feet.
3. Bring your awareness up to your hips, remaining aware of how they are connected to your legs and your feet.
4. Continue breathing deeply and slowly, moving your awareness up your body until you have reached your head.
5. Feel the presence of your body balanced on your feet.

I have found this simple process very useful when facing difficult situations or when I want to strengthen my sense of presence. Often between appointments I will do this exercise to ground my awareness. It's something you can do at work, while standing in a line, or while waiting for someone.

Caring for Your Inner Child

Some clients I work with think that uncomfortable feelings will go away as a result of working through Stage Two of recovery. They don't. You will still feel fear and apprehension about expressing yourself and your feelings. But at Stage Three there is a difference in the way you relate to your feelings. Because you trust your growing ability to take care of yourself, you don't have to avoid powerful feelings or the people or situations that evoke them. You can respond to your feelings as a mature, healthy adult, choosing to express them in self-affirming ways. You can treat your inner child the same way—allowing your inner child to express his or her feelings, then responding in ways that both honor and reassure the inner child.

I mentioned earlier that one of my clients had named her inner child "Knot." Debra associated intense feelings of anxiety in her stomach with her inner child. Before recovery, she had tried to ignore this feeling or stifle it with food. By this stage in her recovery Debra understood that this was the way her inner child communicated with her. When she felt "Knot," she recognized that something in the situation was threatening or anxiety-producing. For instance, Debra frequently felt the "Knot" in her stomach when around her mother, a recovering alcoholic who often tried to hook Debra into taking care of her, a role Debra had played in the past. She would then check in with her self using a brief form of the four questions described in Stage Two. Once she identified the thoughts and self-messages that were causing her anxiety, she could choose to respond in a healthy way.

Debra also found the messages she received from her inner child useful in her relationship with her boyfriend. She made an inventory of all the times she felt "Knot" with her boyfriend and realized that she had trouble telling him she didn't want to see him. Her pattern was either to say no and torment herself with guilt or to see him and feel anxious and resentful the whole time. She also recognized that her boyfriend tried to control her by making her feel guilty about not seeing him. Once she understood this, Debra was able to tell him quite clearly that she would not respond to his behavior. She was acknowledging the feelings of her inner child and showing her respect for them by acting on them.

Parents honor their children by listening to and acknowledging their fears and feelings. Parents reassure their children by providing safety and a sense of security. But parents must also help their children become self-confident and take risks. Sometimes they must challenge their children—for instance, saying "Yes, I know you're afraid, but go ahead and try this new thing anyway." Sometimes parents must set limits for their children: "Yes, I know you're angry, but you can't throw things." During Stage Three you will find that you are providing structure and setting limits for your inner child more than ever before.

SUMMARY

The following exercises will help you heal the physical dimension:
1. Get in the habit of conducting a physical assessment (as described on pages 262–63) several times a day.

2. Use the grounding exercise given on page 264 to calm yourself in times of stress.
3. Continue to care for your inner child by using the exercises from Stage Two and acknowledging your feelings.

● ● ● ● ● ● ●

Healing the Mental Dimension

During Stage Three the world becomes a laboratory in which you can experiment as you learn how to express your truth in interactions with others. Most of the exercises I suggest for the mental dimension teach you communication skills that will make it easier for you to acknowledge your feelings and needs in relationships. You'll learn how to develop new choices about your responses to various situations and new ways to make decisions.

Intervening in the Cycle of Codependence

During Stage Two you released some of the pain of the past and learned to nurture your wounded inner child. You have greater trust in your ability to handle intense and painful feelings. During Stage Three all of this comes together as you intervene in the cycle of codependence by trying new behaviors and developing new self-messages and beliefs based on your experiences.

This is not always an easy process. Like learning to ride a bike or to roller-skate, there will be times when you stumble, fall down, and scrape your knees.

With each intervention the cycle turns in a new, life-giving way. It's risky and uncomfortable. Like the seeds and bulbs that must struggle to sprout, you'll push against forces that may hold you back—in this case, your old roles, messages, and fears.

As you take responsibility for yourself and your feelings, you will change your beliefs and self-messages. The following exercise will help you become aware of those changes. I encourage you to take the time to list your old beliefs and the new ones you are developing in recovery, as shown in the example below:

CHANGING BELIEF SYSTEMS

Examples

Old Beliefs

1. People will reject me if I tell them I am upset or angry.

2. Making a mistake means something bad will happen.

New Beliefs

1. People may reject or accept me when I tell them I feel angry or upset.

2. Mistakes happen.

My Changing Belief Systems

Look back at the beliefs you listed on pages 169–72. How have they changed now that you're at Stage Three?

My Old Beliefs

1. _____

_____

2. _____

_____

3. _____

_____

4. _____

_____

5. _____

_____

My New Beliefs

1. _____

_____

2. _____

_____

3. _____

_____

4. _____

_____

5. _____

_____

Do the same thing with your self-messages, as suggested in the next exercise. Notice that your old self-messages probably began with phrases like "I can't," "I am not," "I should," and "I must." Your new self-messages will usually begin with "I can," "I will," and "I am able."

CHANGING SELF-MESSAGES

Examples

Old Self-Messages

1. "I'm always going to be rejected when I tell someone I am upset."

2. "I'm never going to be accepted for who I am."

3. "I can't let anyone know when I make a mistake."

New Self-Messages

1. "I can tell someone when I am upset and can take care of myself regardless of that person's reaction."

2. "I can develop relationships with people who will accept me as I accept myself."

3. "I can learn from my mistakes even though it's uncomfortable."

My Changing Self-Messages

Look back at the self-messages you listed on pages 167–68. How have they changed now that you're at Stage Three?

My Old Self-Messages

1. _____

_____

2. _____

_____

3. _____

_____

My New Self-Messages

1. _____

_____

2. _____

_____

3. _____

_____

Sometimes experiences with others will help stimulate new messages. Other times you will develop new beliefs and then find they are confirmed by your experiences. The important thing is that you have an opportunity to break the cycle of codependence by doing this work.

Of course writing down new beliefs and messages doesn't mean change has actually occurred. Again, Stage Three is a time for growth through action. You've got to take little steps, trying out new behavior and breaking old patterns.

Using I

During Stage Three you take response-ability for your life, and that means being intimate with yourself, knowing how you are feeling, and honoring your feelings. Being intimate with yourself is a basic skill needed for recovery.

There is one technique I've found invaluable in helping people learn how to honor their feelings. It's very simple. It's the word *I*.

You may already be aware of this technique for clarifying communication. Sometimes it's called "giving I-messages." What it means is that you begin your sentences with *I*. You were probably taught not to be selfish or self-centered, so the idea of starting sentences with the word *I* might seem arrogant. But this practice helps take responsibility for your own experience. Intimacy—with yourself and with others—begins with the letter *I*.

It's typical for codependents—people who have always focused on others—to begin sentences with *You*: "You're not paying any attention to me," "It's your fault I don't have time to go for a walk," and "You're behaving like a spoiled brat." Look at the differences in these sentences when they're rephrased using *I*: "I'm feeling sad and lonely," "I need to be alone for a while; I'm going for a walk," and "I want to hear what you have to say, but I won't allow you to talk to me that way."

GIVING I-MESSAGES

Start beginning your sentences with these phrases:

"I feel _____."

"I see _____."

"I need _____."

"I want _____ ."

"I think _____ ."

Believe me, this is not a superficial change. When you consciously check in with how you're feeling and what you want when you're speaking, you will truly connect with your own experience.

Asserting Yourself

Have you ever been "prematurely assertive"? Before I started on my recovery, I took a variety of courses, including several assertiveness training classes, that I thought would help me overcome my "nice guy" syndrome. After the first course I figured I could now go ahead and tell people how I felt. I was angry at a co-worker who had been talking about me behind my back. So I practiced telling him how I felt; then, one day when we were together, I blurted out my assertive statement. I can still recall how nervous and shaky I felt. Now I know it was the little kid inside of me who was scared to death of an angry response. And that's what I got. When my co-worker said, "What the hell are you talking about?" I crumpled inside. My worst fears had been confirmed.

That event took place 10 years ago. Now I know that it is one thing to think assertively and another actually to be assertive. I didn't have a solid foundation in myself to support my assertive efforts.

During Stage Three you will be exercising your "assertiveness muscles." I want to recommend a simple technique that has been useful for me to clarify what's going on. Use this whenever you are confused or upset by someone else's behavior. You can use it to tell the other person how you feel or just for yourself. For example, my client Marianna was in a relationship in which she usually had to make all the social arrangements. She had dropped a lot of hints about how she would like her boyfriend to make plans some of the time. His response was that he was too busy and thought she should do it. She sensed that she was holding the relationship together by all her planning. As a recovering codependent, she knew that she couldn't make or expect him to change; but she could tell him about the effect his behavior had on her and see if it made a difference to him. She also knew she had to be prepared to take care of herself if her boyfriend continued his behavior. Marianna decided that it was not healthy for her to continue in the relationship if a change on his part did not occur. Before she confronted him, she had worked through the four parts of this exercise in her mind. Her message to him, "Wes, when we get together I find myself feeling resentful that I am the one who makes the plans. As a result, I feel like withdrawing from you when we are out. I'd like to talk about it." Despite talking about it, Wes did not change his behavior and Marianna ended the relationship.

GIVING ASSERTIVE MESSAGES

Examples

1. Describe the other person's behavior in concrete and nonjudgmental terms. For instance, say "when we're talking and your voice starts getting very loud" rather than "when you yell at me."
2. Make a statement about your feelings. Begin with "I feel. . . ."
3. Describe the effect the other person's behavior has on you. Don't preach; just state your feelings.
4. Consider your options. Be clear with yourself about what you will do if the other person's behavior doesn't change. You can include this in your message to that person if you want.

My Assertive Messages

Choose a particular behavior of another person that bothers you and complete the exercise.

1. Describe the other person's behavior in concrete and nonjudgmental terms.

_____

_____

2. State your feelings.

I feel _____

_____ .

3. Describe the effect the other person's behavior has on you, without preaching.

_____

_____

4. Decide for yourself what you will do if the person's behavior doesn't change. Remember, you can't change another person. You can tell a person how his or her behavior affects you. It is their choice to change. If you decide to tell the person what you will do, then I recommend telling them what your reasons are.

Here are some other examples. From a client whose boyfriend acted loud and obnoxious at parties: "Bob, when we are at parties and your voice is loud and you tell off-color, sexist jokes, I feel upset and angry because I lose my desire to be with you." From a client whose friend kept borrowing money without paying it back: "Jane, when you borrow money and tell me you will pay it back and don't, I feel angry and sad. As a result I don't know if I want to spend time with you even though I enjoy your company."

I frequently counsel couples who are locked in dysfunctional communication patterns in which each points the finger of blame at the other, using statements like "You are so cold" and "You make me feel crazy." It's hard to change this pattern. Learning how to describe the effect another person's behavior has on you takes practice and inner awareness, but the result is empowering. There's a big difference between "You make me mad" and "When you arrive late for our appointment, I have to wait for you. I feel angry because my time is precious to me and I don't like waiting." The first statement gives the other person all of your power. The second gives him or her information and doesn't disempower you.

The fourth step of the process is also valuable because realizing your options is an important part of Stage Three work. You might want to do something for yourself; for example, taking a book with you when you're waiting for your habitually late friend. Or you might want to ask your friend to do something different—"Please call me if you're going to be more than 10 minutes late in the future." Or you might want to let the person know what you'll do: "I'm willing to wait for you for only 15 minutes. If you haven't arrived by then, I'll leave." Or you may decide, as Marianna did, to end the relationship if no change occurs.

My client, Debra, used this technique to talk to her supervisor, Ted. Debra was frustrated because Ted had given her some new tasks to do without any clear directions. In the past she would have hidden her uneasiness, but this time she decided to try something new. She acknowledged her fears of rejection and role-played the interaction with me. Here is the message she developed:

"Ted, when you tell me about the new work without giving me instructions, I feel upset and confused because I want to do a good job and I don't have enough information."

When Debra delivered this message to Ted, she was pleasantly surprised by his supportive and appreciative response and has been practicing this technique ever since. A key part of Debra's success has been her conscious awareness of her feelings and her ability to take care of the part of her that "knots up" with terror inside. When she feels anxious about delivering an assertive message, she acknowledges this feeling, takes a deep breath, and affirms the validity of her needs.

You won't always get a positive response when you use this communication technique. Sometimes the person you are talking to will feel attacked and become defensive. When this happens, focus on your own inner feelings and find ways to take care of yourself.

Speaking Your Truth

You can make a simple resolution that will change your life radically. It is this:

Speak your truth at least once every day.

As you learn to recognize your own feelings, honor your own values, and acknowledge your own needs, you may be surprised by how seldom you express them. Deciding to speak your truth at least once a day is a step in the right direction. The level of pretense and deception in your life may shock you.

Reviewing Old Decisions

When your decision-making process has been distorted by codependence, you habitually make choices based on avoiding the pain of growth and maintaining control. Probably you tend to choose short-term gratification and relief from discomfort instead of long-term growth.

It's difficult to change decision-making habits, especially when family and friends reinforce the old behaviors. Yet this change is an essential part of the healing process.

You may find it helpful to begin by reviewing the way you've made decisions in the past. I know that when I did this I was surprised—stunned, really—by my crisis-oriented decision-making style. It was as if I had to create a crisis to make a decision, and then I very seldom made effective, responsible decisions. When I understood how I made decisions (compulsively) and why (to extricate myself from crisis or the results of the last poor decision), I saw that continuing in this way would only produce the same results.

I recommend that you complete a history of the decisions you have made in the last five to 15 years or longer. Give yourself a long enough time span to see trends.

DECISION-MAKING HISTORY

Examples

Decision	What Influenced It	How I Feel About It	What I Honestly Hoped To Accomplish
To move	Job opportunity	Happy	Career success
To buy something	It was the thing to do	Sad	Impress people
To marry	I was lonely	Regretful	Not sure

Other possibilities:

Decision	What Influenced It	How I Feel About It	What I Honestly Hoped To Accomplish
To divorce	_____	_____	_____
To end a relation-ship	_____	_____	_____
To change jobs	_____	_____	_____
To go to school	_____	_____	_____

To leave school   _____   _____   _____

To take up a new
hobby   _____   _____   _____

My Decision-Making History

Decision	What Influenced It	How I Feel About It	What I Honestly Hoped to Accomplish
To _____	_____	_____	_____
	_____	_____	_____
To _____	_____	_____	_____
	_____	_____	_____
To _____	_____	_____	_____
	_____	_____	_____
To _____	_____	_____	_____
	_____	_____	_____
To _____	_____	_____	_____
	_____	_____	_____

Once you've reviewed your past decisions, you'll have a wealth of information about your decision-making habits. In what situations do you make quick decisions? How do you make them? Is this working for you? Once you become consciously aware of how you make decisions, it's easier to change them.

After reviewing the history of his decision-making, Mike realized he made most of the major decisions in his life—his marriage, buying a house, and buying a business—to avoid displeasing other people. In the case of the house and the business he didn't want to tell the sellers that he thought they were being dishonest.

Even though his gut sense told him that things didn't feel right, he ignored it because otherwise he would have to say something that might offend these people.

Alice made her decisions by default. She frequently found herself in situations where she had to do something because she had delayed her decision making for so long that the other options were no longer available. She realized that she preferred being forced to do something rather than risk choosing the wrong option and feeling embarrassed.

Empowering Yourself

There's a communication skill that can help you empower yourself. It seems simple but it will have a dramatic effect on you. Try substituting the verb *will* for *can* and *won't* for *can't*.

FROM *CAN* TO *WILL*

Examples

1. "I *can't* ask my boss for a raise."
2. "I'm afraid he'll say no."
3. "I *won't* ask my boss for a raise because I'm afraid he'll say no."

Using *Will* Instead of *Can*

1. Think of something you have been thinking that you *can't* do.

"I *can't* _____ ."

2. Now think about how you feel. What it is that makes you feel you can't do it? Are you afraid? What are your concerns?

_____

_____

3. Then change *can't* to *won't* and state why not.

"I *won't* _____

because _____ ."

Can you feel the difference between the two statements? When you substitute *will* for *can*, you take responsibility for your own choice. You become empowered. You discover your ability to make choices.

When I suggested to my client Dan that he try this in his relationship with his wife, he balked.

"It feels really uncomfortable telling Sue I won't go with her because I want to work," Dan said. "I'd rather tell her I *can't* go because I have to work. It gets me off the hook."

I asked Dan to think about how that felt for a moment.

"It makes me feel like a wimp," he said promptly. "I feel like that a lot."

For the next several sessions Dan and I explored his "wimpy" feeling and discovered a very frightened little boy inside. If Dan had simply agreed to make the change from *can* to *will* without acknowledging his underlying feelings, he wouldn't have gotten very far. The change would have been only superficial. But thinking about this choice helped Dan get in touch with his "wimpy" feeling and his frightened inner child. Later he was able to change his language.

When Dan told his wife he would rather work than be going out with her, she responded with anger. When Dan changed the way he related to his wife—a change that altered the codependence that had stifled their marriage—conflict ensued. As Dan worked on his recovery, conflicts about his choices increased. Eventually they chose to do some marriage counseling, which was a positive experience in learning to negotiate how the needs of both could be met.

Setting Limits

Taking responsibility for yourself and your feelings means taking steps to maintain your personal resources—emotionally, physically, and mentally—by setting limits.

Setting limits is difficult for many of us who have spent our lives as codependents. It means saying no to people and opportunities and activities. Saying no can be very uncomfortable and can elicit old messages like "Shame on you for being so selfish." Or you may have to acknowledge your own limitations—you can't do everything you think you can do, creating feelings of sadness or anxiety. One of the reasons you have avoided setting limits has been to avoid these feelings in the first place. Setting limits will help you get in touch with some important previously repressed feelings and the beliefs associated with them.

When you set limits for yourself, you clarify the extent to which you can get involved in other activities. To do so you must take into account your own needs, inner resources, and other commitments. If you're like most codependents, you have an inflated sense of what you can accomplish.

When you're faced with making commitments or feel drawn to take on new projects or activities, try asking yourself the questions in the following exercise. As you review them now, think about the commitments you made today.

ASSESSING MY LIMITS

1. How will my personal needs be met by this project or activity?

   _____

   _____

2. How much time, energy, and resources will it take me to follow through on this commitment?

   _____

   _____

3. What aspects of myself will be developed or nurtured by this activity?

   _____

   _____

4. What must I give up in order to take on another commitment?

_____

_____

5. How will this activity or project affect my recovery program?

_____

_____

6. Do I have the time and energy to complete this project or activity?

_____

_____

7. Am I setting myself up for failure or shame if I later have to drop out or fail to complete this project or activity?

_____

_____

Establishing Your Boundaries

Codependence is marked by a high degree of tolerance for inappropriate behavior from others. This is usually the result of a lack of boundaries. In a dysfunctional family the members are often enmeshed. There are no clear boundaries between individuals. We become used to having our personal space infringed on by others.

Many of us have tolerated serious emotional abuse in chaotic and addictive relationships because we had no boundaries. Without boundaries you can't tell someone "No, you can't do that to me." Without boundaries you can't say "I need this time for myself." As a result you are violated over and over again.

Establishing and protecting your personal boundaries is an essential part of taking responsibility for yourself. Take some time to ask yourself the following questions. They will help you identify situations in which your boundaries have been violated.

ESTABLISHING BOUNDARIES

1. In what circumstances and situations do I feel attacked or threatened by another person's behavior? What do I do?

_____

_____

_____

_____

_____

2. Do I find myself doing things that feel uncomfortable or violate my values because I'm afraid of being rejected? What are these things?

_____

_____

_____

_____

3. When I am being ridiculed or shamed, how do I respond? Do I tell the other person how I feel, or do I retreat into a protective role and ignore my feelings?

_____

_____

_____

_____

_____

4. What kinds of inappropriate behavior have I tolerated in intimate relationships?

_____

_____

_____

_____

_____

5. What kinds of inappropriate behavior have I tolerated on the job?

_____

_____

_____

_____

_____

6. What kinds of inappropriate behavior have I tolerated from friends?

_____

_____

_____

_____

_____

You can't protect yourself from abuse until you can identify when someone has crossed the line between what is acceptable to you and what is not. Anger will help you feel your boundaries. As you develop a stronger sense of self and get in closer touch with your feelings, you will know you are being abused by the way that feels.

You can start to establish boundaries in areas where you can most clearly identify abuse. Many of my clients begin by setting boundaries with their family, because the abusive patterns have become apparent through the recovery process. Here are some of the boundaries they have established:

- Not taking responsibility for a parent's disappointment in their choices
- Not participating in family gossip
- Not going to family gatherings at which alcohol is consumed at intoxicating levels
- Not being alone with a parent or other relative who is overly critical or violently angry
- Indicating what they will do if they are judged or their life-style is criticized
- Clarifying any attempts to induce guilt or shame by pointing them out
- Acknowledging that they are abstaining from family events because they feel uncomfortable with the behavior of others.

Of course establishing boundaries extends to others besides your family. In your personal relationships, in your friendships, at work, and in groups you have the right to set boundaries. This means not allowing others to abuse you in any way.

For example, I often see couples who have a problem with anger because each expresses or experiences it in a different way. Jan and David had this problem. When she was angry, Jan would shout and rant and rave. This petrified David, and he would feel immobilized. Jan, who came from a verbally loud family, considered her behavior normal. To David, who was from a physically abusive home, it was threatening. His response was to withdraw in silence until he exploded.

During recovery David experimented with establishing boundaries with Jan about what he could handle. When the intensity of her loud and angry words became too strong, he would tell her how it was affecting him and then take steps to take care of himself, such as going out or calling a friend. When Jan continued to behave in the same way, David chose to leave the relationship rather than stay in a situation that he experienced as abusive and threatening.

When you establish and maintain your boundaries, you are not telling the other person how to behave or judging his or her behavior. You are simply informing that person of the impact of his or her behavior on you and stating clearly what you will do to take care of yourself. You take responsibility for yourself and your feelings.

When I am in a situation where I feel that my boundaries are being violated, I look at the communication that has been directed at me. Did the other person use the word *you* in a discrediting, abusive, or disrespectful way? For example, I have been in situations and relationships in which I was told, "You're so weak," "Can't you see what you are doing to me? Are you blind?" and "You are so out of touch with reality." At the time these statements were made to me, I was dumbfounded and unable to respond. I had no response-ability. I usually felt guilty and ashamed of myself but often didn't know what I had done to deserve such statements. My codependent tendency was to assume that I was wrong or bad.

In the same situation today I have a healthier response. For example, if someone were to tell me, "You are so out of touch with reality" in the same put-down tone that I had heard in the past, I would ask for clarification. As you will experience in recovery, getting feedback from others, although potentially uncomfortable, can be good information for personal growth. In this case I might ask the person, "Tell me what it is about me that makes you think I am out of touch with reality." However, I will not subject myself to the verbal abuse of others as I have in the past. If the person can't communicate with me in a clarifying and respectful manner, I end the interaction.

Recovery involves establishing and maintaining boundaries, but it also means expanding them. When you define your rights and defend them, you will have more personal space and a greater sense of freedom.

A Closing Ritual

Many times during recovery you will experience loss. As you retrieve memories of your past, you may grieve over the losses of the past. You may be called by your recovery to give up people and activities that are important to you now. You may have to end an important friendship or relationship. You may have to give up a cherished self-image and the activities you associated with it.

It's important to honor your losses. I recommend creating a ceremony that will help give you a sense of closure and a chance to express your grief.

I learned the value of this process during my own recovery. For several years I worked as a hospital administrator and consultant. Those were painful years of full-blown codependence. My career gave me the opportunity to indulge all the willpower and control associated with the hero role. In 1985 I realized that I could not go back to that work again. Somehow I knew, and could finally admit, that those years had been years of pain and fear.

At the suggestion of the therapist with whom I was working at the time, I created a ritual to symbolize my end of this phase of my life. I took the big, shiny brass B (for Brian) that I had used as a paperweight during my executive years, some candles, a pen, and a piece of paper and headed for Puget Sound. There I wrote a good-bye letter to my past and wrapped it around the B with rubber bands. Then I threw the B into the ocean. When it hit the water with a big splash, I felt a great wave of tears rising up inside of me, which came pouring out. It seemed as if years of grief left me in a matter of 15 minutes. I lit two small candles, attached them to a piece of driftwood, and pushed the driftwood out into the waves to float away, carrying the candles, my emblems of hope for a better future.

When clients tell me about important neighbors, friends, and pets from the past whose presence they still mourn, I recommend writing a letter or somehow honoring the relationship in words or a ritual. You can use the same idea to honor your inner child by writing your child a letter. For one client who still missed a treasured cat that her mother had taken to the pound, I recommended writing a letter of farewell to the cat as if she were the young child. Once your letter is written, you can burn it or bury it to symbolize closure.

A CEREMONY OF CLOSURE

1. Identify the loss. What is it that you are missing or mourning? What symbols can you use to represent that loss? You might want to take some time gathering together the things you can use in your ceremony.

2. Find a place and set a time for your ceremony. You may want to be alone, or you may want to invite friends to participate. You may want to be at home, or you may want to be outdoors in a natural setting. You may want to choose a significant time or place.

3. Express your feelings about the loss through a letter or by drawing a picture or by creating a dance. You can prepare this ahead of time or do it at the time of your ceremony.

4. Celebrate your ceremony. Have your intention clearly in mind. Take your letter or picture and let go of it symbolically, perhaps by burning it, burying it, or throwing it into a lake or the ocean. Allow yourself time to feel the feelings associated with your loss.

5. Give yourself time afterward to feel the feelings that come up. You may want to write about this experience in your journal.

SUMMARY

Tasks that will support your Stage Three healing in the mental dimension:

1. Intervene in the cycle of codependence by developing new self-messages and beliefs as described on pages 267–68.
2. Use I-messages, as described on pages 269–70 for clear communication of your needs and feelings.
3. Practice true assertiveness using the four-part structure suggested on pages 271–72.
4. Speak your truth at least once a day.
5. Review past decisions, looking for patterns, as on pages 274–75.
6. Substitute the word *will* for *can* (pages 276–77) to emphasize the element of personal choice you exercise.
7. Set limits using the questions on pages 278–79 to help you evaluate your time and resources.
8. Protect your boundaries; use the questions on pages 280–81 to help you identify situations in which you are at risk.
9. Perform a closing ceremony using the suggestions from page 284 to acknowledge formally and mourn your losses and the things you have given up.

• • • • • • •

Healing the Spiritual Dimension

The work of Stage Three may seem contradictory: you're supposed to be taking responsibility for yourself and your feelings at the same time as you surrender control of your life to your higher power. This is one of those paradoxes of recovery that is highlighted in the work you will do in the spiritual dimension.

Frankly, I wouldn't be working on a recovery program if I weren't receiving benefits. During Stage Three you will begin to reap some of those benefits, particularly in the spiritual dimension. Every person will experience these blessings differently, yet certain similarities exist. At this point in recovery you are likely to have experiences of inner strength, peace, grace, and intimacy.

The exercises in this section will help you taste the fruits of your work. At times they may seem bittersweet, but at other times they will be truly life-enhancing and empowering.

Practicing an Attitude of Gratitude

During the early years of my recovery I didn't feel gratitude for my childhood—and I didn't want to. I was angry and felt cheated when I thought of it.

Gradually, as I felt the emergence of strength and courage inside of me, as I experienced more of the depths of the spiritual dimension, a sense of gratitude grew in me. This is another of the paradoxes of recovery: becoming grateful for the pain of the past. The gratitude I began to feel was an experience of grace. It seemed to be given to me as a gift, yet I had to be open to receiving it.

You can practice an attitude of gratitude by acknowledging the little changes that you make and the growth you experience. Take some time now to focus on those things for which you can be grateful.

Here are some of the things on my list: I've acquired a passion for life and a growing ability to express myself. I've "learned" a lot about love, intimacy, and conscious contact with a higher power. I'm in touch with the joy and wonder of the magical child within me. Perhaps these blessings would have come to me even if I hadn't been born into a dysfunctional, alcoholic family and hadn't been struggling through a recovery program. But I believe that those "hardships" provided the motivation for me to seek out my own magical inner child and the grace of my higher power.

Using the exercise that follows, take some time to contemplate the gifts you have received and the ways you can express your gratitude for them:

PRACTICING AN ATTITUDE OF GRATITUDE

Examples

1. As a result of your recovery program, what gifts have you received?

An ability to love others honestly

The strength to go to school and pursue your heart's career

An inner awareness of God within you

The ability to trust yourself

Self-esteem

Discovering play

The gift of feelings

Compassion for others

2. How can you or do you express your gratitude?

Prayer

Tending your garden

Being honest

Writing poetry

Volunteering

Tithing to charities

My Gifts and Means of Expression

1. As a result of my recovery program, what gifts have I received?

_____

_____

_____

_____

_____

2. How can I or do I express my gratitude?

_____

_____

_____

_____

_____

I often feel incapable of expressing my gratitude to my higher power for my life because I feel I can't do enough. I've found that I can best do this by practicing the Twelve Steps, maintaining my recovery, living as honestly as possible, and learning and living the will of my higher power for me.

Forgiving Yourself

Taking responsibility for yourself also means forgiving yourself. At one point in my recovery I could feel God's forgiveness, but I couldn't forgive myself for some of the things I had done. I was talking to a priest friend about this, and he said something that shocked me: "Brian, isn't it interesting that you think you are more powerful and important than God?"

I realized that he was right. By refusing to forgive myself when I knew that God forgave me, I was actually putting myself above God.

Of course forgiveness is easy to talk about but often hard to do. In our focus on perfection we can be very hard on ourselves. And during recovery you will discover many ways you have injured yourself and others. If you hold on to your guilt and shame, if you resent yourself for what you have done, you will hurt yourself further. Recovery means accepting and forgiving yourself.

Use the prayer that follows to ask your higher power to hold and heal your own wounds and the wounds you have inflicted on others. Address your higher power directly at the start of each line in whatever words make you feel most comfortable.

PRAYER FOR HEALING LIFE'S HURTS*

_____ , hold and heal the hurts that happened before I was born: the conflicts, the pain that surrounded my conception and formation, the labor of my birth.

_____ , hold and heal the hurts of my helplessness: my defenselessness and vulnerability as a child, the ways that I feel weak and unable to help myself, the pain of the things I cannot change.

_____ , hold and heal the hurts of my limitations: all the ways I think I should be or wish I could do more than I can do, all the times I've been too tired, too slow, too pressed for time, too poor, too young, too old, too simply human.

_____ , hold and heal the hurts of my differentness: all the times it has been painful for me to be unlike others, to stand out and be apart because of my body, my mind, my feelings, my ways, my beliefs.

_____ , hold and heal the hurts of my failures: all the ways I seem to disappoint myself and others and you, all the things I have failed to do or say, all the ways I have not lived up to expectations.

_____ , hold and heal the hurts of my brokenness: all the things I have broken or that have been broken in my life, especially the relationships that have shattered.

_____ , hold and heal the hurts of indifference: all the ways people have not cared when I wanted them to, all the relationships that have simply withered, all the joy and possibilities that have disappeared because I didn't care.

_____ , hold and heal the hurts of lack of love: all the times when others have been unwilling or unable to love me as I wished, the pain of people around me hurting each other, my own inability to reach out in love and accept myself.

_____ , hold and heal the hurts I have suffered because of the society in which I live: its hurry, chaos, impersonality, and desire for instant

*adapted from the work of the Linn brothers

accomplishments; its stereotypes, exploitation, and oppression; its violence shadowing my future.

_____ , hold and heal the hurt of my losses, all that I have lost in my life: precious possessions, places, ideas, pets, self-image, people.

_____ , hold and heal the hurt of my transience: all the times I have had to move on when I would rather have stayed, the sense of being a sojourner on this earth, the sometimes painful knowledge of how little time I have.

_____ , hold and heal the hurts of my fears: all that restricts me and holds me back, all the ways I am afraid of being hurt again, afraid to embrace life.

_____ , hold and heal my hurts: all that has wounded me, made me feel unwhole, unwanted, unloved; all the ways I have wounded others, intentionally and by accident.

_____ , hold and heal me.

_____ , help me hold and heal.

Forgiving Your Family

During Stages One and Two you investigated your family of origin, identifying roles, rules, and the patterns of relationships that existed in the past. You're learning how to untangle the knots and cut the ties that bind you to the dysfunctional system of your family of origin. You're becoming your own person, differentiated from your family, capable of making clear and conscious choices for yourself.

The family work appropriate for Stage Three of recovery is work on the spiritual dimension: practicing forgiveness, gratitude, and compassion. Those of you who were physically or sexually abused, even those who experienced serious emotional oppression in your childhood, may find it extremely difficult to imagine feeling forgiveness or compassion for your families. Forgiving your family does not mean condoning or agreeing with abuse. It doesn't mean being in contact with them if you choose not to do so. As long as you are angry with someone, some of your focus is on him and what he did. In recovery the focus is on you and what you need to do to take care of yourself.

The process of forgiving your family may take years. I wasn't ready to forgive my father until I was six years into my recovery. It was a gradual process of letting go of my anger, healing the hurts of my inner child, and developing new and healthy patterns of living.

For Corinne the process of forgiveness began during a visit home. She had been working hard on her recovery for about two years, through therapy, group work, Al-Anon meetings, and a spiritual program. She hadn't seen her parents for about 10 months when she went home for the Thanksgiving holiday. In her alcoholic family there had never been room for Corinne; she was the lost child.

On Thanksgiving Day everything went smoothly. But the next day Corinne's parents began giving her one of their "We know what's best for you" lectures, and she felt a familiar quivering. "Anger welled up in me and I wanted to scream," she reported to me later. "Instead I took a few deep breaths and told them I heard their concern but I didn't like the way they were talking to me. I told them that I wouldn't listen to that sort of conversation. And then I just got up and left the room and went for a walk."

Corinne told me that she didn't feel angry; in fact she felt a sense of peace and forgiveness. She understood her parents weren't going to change and that she could love and forgive them despite their rigid and oppressive behavior. Understanding of this nature comes about as a result of recovery. Corinne experienced a sense of freedom in that her parents' behavior could no longer make her feel upset and thus control her life.

"I'm still learning to forgive them, but at least I don't have to let them make me miserable and unhappy again."

Working Steps 8, 9, and 10

Much of the work you are doing at Stage Three is on relationships: working on communicating clearly with others, fostering a relationship with a higher power, forgiving your family. Steps 8 and 9 from the Twelve Steps involve healing relationships.

Step 8. We made a list of all persons we had harmed and became willing to make amends to them all.

In this step you take responsibility for any harm your behavior and codependence have inflicted on others. This was a tough step for me. I used the argument that other people were responsible for their choices, so even if I had tried to control them, they had agreed to participate. Yet the truth was that my own dishonesty, my need to control, and my fear of being myself did hurt others. Some of the ways others are hurt by your codependence include: being in a relationship with someone that you really don't want to be with; encouraging someone to make plans based on what you say and you don't follow through because you didn't want to do it in the first place; supporting someone's addiction by doing things that enable it.

WORKING STEP 8

Make a list of the people who have been harmed by your codependence. Don't forget to include yourself.

_____	_____
_____	_____
_____	_____
_____	_____
_____	_____

Step 9. We made direct amends to such people wherever possible, except when to do so would injure them or others.

This step doesn't ask you to go running off to everyone on your list to beg forgiveness; it asks you to take care of yourself in a very intentional way. After all, you're doing these steps for you.

The amends you make will be different for each person on your list. They might be financial; they might be emotional. It's critical that you avoid causing further harm to others. If you think that your attempt to make amends might cause more damage, make amends to your higher power on behalf of the person you've hurt.

For example, when I thought it might be disruptive to meet with someone personally—a former girlfriend who was now married—I used the Prayer for Healing Life's Hurts on pages 289–90 and asked my higher power to accept my amends. I also wrote a letter, which I did not send but burned after it was written.

Stage Three: Taking Responsibility for Yourself and Your Feelings

When I was doing Step 9, I met with various people—former business associates and friends—and told them what I had done to control them. I got a lot of mixed reactions. A few people expressed anger at first, usually followed by appreciation. Most of the people with whom I met were grateful for the chance to talk about what happened in our relationship. One person even said that now she didn't have to avoid me anymore. You may get the same mixed reactions from people. Just accept whatever comes. You can't change what they think of you but you can change what you think about yourself. This is an important step in freeing yourself from and healing your past. You are doing this for you.

Step 10. We continued to take personal inventory and when we were wrong promptly admitted it.

Step 10 is something you can do daily. Just as you check in with your body periodically, following this step will help you check in with your relationships. When you're reflecting on Step 10, try substituting the word *controlling* or *dishonest* for the word *wrong*, and you will get a sense of what Step 10 is all about: being true to yourself.

When you do a quick personal inventory, ask yourself the following questions.

STEP 10 CHECK-IN

1. When I am focusing on the behavior of others and feel like I need to control them, I am avoiding something and not taking responsibility for my feelings. What am I avoiding?

   _____

   _____

2. Do my actions or the actions I want to take affirm and empower me? How can I take responsibility for my feelings?

   _____

   _____

Contacting Your Higher Power

All of the exercises I have suggested in this section help you develop and maintain contact with your higher power. Surrender is the best way to achieve this contact.

I want to recommend an exercise that I have found useful for deepening my relationship with my higher power. This exercise comes from the book *Wellsprings* by Anthony de Mello. This wonderful book is full of spiritual exercises that I recommend for those in recovery.

THE SURRENDER

Begin by seeking silence.

For this, come home to yourself.
Come to the present.
Ask yourself: Where am I right now?
What am I doing?
What am I thinking?
What am I sensing in my body?
What is the quality of my breathing?

Silence cannot be induced or sought directly.
Just seek awareness—and silence will appear.

If you now wish to communicate with God
within this silence
imagine that you surrender, let go,
each time you breathe out
—that each exhalation
is your way of saying yes to God.
Yes to what you are today
—to the kind of person God has made you,
the kind of person you have become.
Yes to the whole of your past.
Yes to what lies in store for you in future.

Let go each time you breathe out
with the awareness that all will be well.
Let all anxieties cease,
and let peace take over,
for in his hands, in his will
is our peace.

SUMMARY

These exercises will aid your Stage 3 healing in the spiritual dimension:
1. Practice an attitude of gratitude using the suggestions on pages 286–88.
2. Say the Prayer for Healing Life's Hurts found on pages 289–90 to help you forgive yourself and others.
3. Work Steps 8, 9, and 10 of the Twelve Steps, using the exercises found on pages 291–93.
4. Surrender to your higher power; using the exercise on pages 294–95 may help.

• • • • • • •

GENERAL RECOMMENDATIONS

The following general recommendations will support your healing during Stage Three:

1. Continue nurturing yourself with life-giving, supportive relationships.
2. Attend Twelve-Step meetings.
3. Maintain your physical self-care program.
4. Laugh. Find the humor in life and let yourself feel the freedom and joy of recovery.
5. Continue to use those exercises from Stage One and Stage Two that are helpful.

Moving On to Stage Four

When I first began to observe and research the recovery process, I became aware of a reality within myself and others that seems to bloom during recovery. A new person is being born. The potential that was lost is recovered and flourishes.

When you feel this sense of a new identity, you will be moving into Stage Four. You will begin to look at life and situations through different eyes. Your compassion for others and your ability to support them without needing to control them will grow. You may look the same, but you will feel different. You will begin to feel an emerging strength and the uniqueness of your being.

The process of movement between Stage Three and Stage Four is primarily one of spiritual deepening. It's hard to describe it in words; it's much more easily communicated in metaphors, as in this poem from a Christmas card:

> *Within each one of us*
> *There is a desert to travel,*
> *A star to be born*
> *And a being to be*
> *Brought to Life.*

12
· · · · · · · ·

Stage Four:
Affirming and
Expressing Yourself

I think what we're seeking is an experience of being alive, so that our experiences on the purely physical plane will have resonances within our own innermost being and reality, so that we feel the rapture of being alive.

JOSEPH CAMPBELL
The Power of Myth

S UMMER IS THE SEASON of fullness and completion. Under the warmth of the sun flowers burst into full bloom in a panorama of colors. In the orchards trees that were fragrant with flowers in the spring are now laden with fruits so ripe that they drop from the branches.

Stage Four is also a time of fullness and fruition. The insights you have gained and the changes you have made now become part of you. The seeds that were planted in the spring bear fruit.

During Stage Four you express and affirm yourself as a creative, loving, autonomous, and unique individual. This is the essence of recovery. Your sense of self won't come from cognitive awareness or fantasy; you will actually feel the presence of your own personhood within you.

As you work on your recovery, passing through the four stages (many times), your inner self will emerge more and more clearly. You will feel a stronger desire to express yourself as the unique person you were meant to be. Your self-esteem will grow as you live out of the realities of your inner self. Within the inner self are the gifts of deep self-esteem, self-appreciation, and healthy self-love that will nurture you.

During Stage Four you will be affirming and expressing yourself in a variety of ways:

- co-creating with your higher power
- following the principle of "live and let live" in everyday life
- living one day at a time
- developing life-giving ways of responding to external events
- deepening your spiritual program of surrender
- assuming greater responsibility for expressing your gifts and abilities
- experiencing the awakening of your inner self.

Although summer seems idyllic, it has its hazards. Too much of a good thing—the blazing sun—can cause droughts and heat waves. Stage Four has pitfalls, too. The energy you have freed up for yourself will seek a creative outlet, and you may want to change the world. If you attempt to do so, you may lose track of your responsibility for yourself. Or you may begin to see the wounded child in all the people around you and be tempted to help heal those hurts. But you can do nothing to heal the deep pain of others; you can only be honest and change yourself.

Reorientation

During Stage Four you will look in new ways at your relationships, family, friends, and work. Through recovery you have become a new person. You will understand that your most important life task is to be yourself and you will see how in doing so, you will create the opportunity for others to be themselves. You will realize you are a creator of your life instead of a reactor to your experiences of life. The stage of reorientation is one in which you affirm and express the unabridged version of who you are as an individual.

Have you ever hiked to the top of a mountain? As you are climbing to the top, you can see the details that surround you—the plants, bushes, trees, and perhaps birds and small animals. Although you may occasionally turn a bend and come upon a vista, most of the time you are focused on the path. You become intimately aware of its composition—the pine needles or rocks or soil underfoot—and every slight incline or decline, switchback or creek that must be crossed. But when you get to the top, your perspective changes. Suddenly you can see for miles, and your view of the terrain through which you were just traveling is totally different.

This is like recovery. While you are working your way through the early stages of recovery, your main focus is on the path. You are intensely aware of the effort you are making and what you have to do to stay on the path. You may sometimes enjoy the scenery around you. You may sometimes catch a glimpse of the progress you have made. But when you reach Stage Four, your perspective will change as dramatically as if you had reached the top of a mountain. You will see things from a different and a wider perspective.

Creativity

Just as the trees yield their fruit and the flowers offer the sweetness of their nectar in summer, so you will be moved to express your talents and skills during Stage Four. **Creativity** is the key element in Stage Four, a creativity that is expressed in co-creation with your higher power.

This creativity is not necessarily artistic creativity. You don't have to write a best-selling novel or begin painting pictures to be creative. I'm referring to the kind of creativity that urges you to express your love in your relationships, your activities, and your life.

Goethe once said:

Until one is committed, there is hesitancy, the chance to draw back, always ineffectiveness concerning all acts of initiative [and creation]. There is one elementary truth the ignorance of which kills countless ideas and splendid plans: that the moment one definitely commits oneself then Providence moves too. All sorts of things occur to help one that would never otherwise have occurred. A whole stream of events issues from the decision, raising in one's favor all manner of unforeseen incidents, meetings and material assistance which no man could have dreamed would have come his way. Whatever you can do or dream you can do, begin it. Boldness has genius, power and magic in it. Begin it now.

When you allow your higher power to work through you, Providence provides the means to achieve your dreams.

Tools and Support

The exercises you will find in this chapter have two orientations: internal (maintaining contact with your inner self) and external (expressing your self).

It was difficult for me to divide the exercises for Stage Four into the three dimensions. That's because Stage Four is a time when the divisions between these dimensions break down. Through your recovery program you will remove the barriers that have prevented the dimensions of your being from existing as a harmonious whole. All of the exercises will enhance the integrity of being that you are beginning to sense.

Healing the Physical Dimension

During Stage Four it is important to maintain your physical and emotional health. By now you know the importance of assessing your energy level so as not to deplete your resources. You are eating nutritious meals and following an exercise program. The exercises recommended below will deepen your love for your body and your appreciation for your feelings.

Starting an Energy Conservation Program

There's an acronym used in AA to help people recognize the symptoms of relapse. It is *HALT*, which stands for *hungry, angry, lonely,* and *tired*. I recommend that you keep this acronym in mind. If you find yourself feeling hungry, angry, lonely, and tired, take steps to nurture and take care of yourself.

Now that you're no longer using your energy to defend yourself from inner pain, you will probably feel like you have more energy than you used to have. You can use this energy creatively and productively. At the same time, be sure to conserve your energy so that it's available when you need it.

During the last few weeks of writing this book I was driving hard, "pedal to the metal." I also had other commitments—to work, my marriage, school, etc. Some things had to be set aside temporarily, but my physical care program of rest, exercise, laughter, and nutrition was not one of these. I knew that if I stopped taking care of myself, I would burn out and be incapable of doing my best work.

Use the following questions to assess your energy level when you are considering taking on a new project or commitment:

ASSESSING MY ENERGY

1. Have I balanced my activities with a program of physical self-care? Does this need improvement?

_____

_____

_____

2. If I take on something new, will I be pushing my energy resources to the limit? Will I have energy left for important activities such as work, relationships, and hobbies?

_____

_____

_____

3. How do I conserve my energy during the day?

_____

_____

_____

Your body is like a thermostat. It can give you feedback about your stress and activity levels. Your energy resources are limited, so use them wisely.

Embracing the Wounded Inner Child

The process of healing your wounded inner child is, like recovery, a lifelong process. The work gets less intense, but it never goes away entirely. Don't neglect your wounded inner child. Use all the approaches you used during the earlier stages—acknowledgment and recognition, nurturing and providing safety, acceptance and unconditional love—to deepen your relationship with your inner child.

Stage Four is a time for self-expression, and when you begin putting yourself forward and affirming your unique self, your inner child may respond with panic. While writing this book, especially as it got closer to publication, I noticed a strong feeling of fear that I described in Chapter 10: the little boy within me was terrified of the judgments of certain authority figures, professionals who might disagree with what I have to say. Even writing about this is going over an edge for me.

When I feel this feeling, I reassure the frightened little boy within and tell him that we can take care of whatever happens and that I will not abandon him. I also use the techniques described in Stages Two and Three for working with feelings and the beliefs associated with these feelings. I remind myself that this book is based on my observation and experience and in that sense has strength and validity. I also call to mind all the people who have been helped by the concepts I use to talk about and work with codependence and recovery. The little boy is still scared, but I'm not immobilized.

As you develop ways to affirm and express yourself, your inner child may react with fear and anxiety. Acknowledge and work with the feelings that come up and challenge the beliefs that stand in your way.

Playing with the Magical Child

Most of us associate our inner children with pain and sadness because those are the feelings we fear and those are likely to be the first feelings we experience during recovery. But other feelings were buried along with those painful ones: feelings of humor, wonder, curiosity, and joy. These are the signs of the magical, mystical child within.

During recovery you learn to know and feel your magical, mystical child within. As the *Desiderata* says: "You are a child of the universe. You have a right to be here." Your mystical child knows this feeling. Your magical child knows the love of a higher power and knows that that higher power wants you to experience the fullness of creation.

John Giannini, writing on "The Dynamics of the Wounded Child" for *Creation* magazine, has this to say about the magical child: "In the higher consciousness of the Divine Child we embrace all being and enter co-creatively into every moment of life as the intelligent unifying force." He goes on to say that the wounded child can be healed through "heart-felt love and gut-felt love" and that creative play will help bring out the New Child and then the Divine Child.

Stage Four: Affirming and Expressing Yourself

Play, in its wide variety of forms, is a vehicle for creative expression. Since learning about the importance of play, I have chosen some ways to express my playful side. One of my current favorite forms of play is gardening. In the past I treated gardening as serious business and never did too well at it. When I allowed it to be play, when I approached it with awe and curiosity about how things grew, my garden took off. I actually produced vegetables and delighted in eating them and sharing them with others. I've also discovered the playfulness of spontaneous humor, watercolors, and exploring on the beach.

Consider the ways that you play. What brings you an internal sense of mirth and joy? As you feel your way back in touch with your playful child, you'll discover the healing grace of a higher power that is playing through and with you.

The exercise below is designed to help you consider the ways you can play and the things that make you laugh.

EXPERIENCING THE MAGIC OF PLAY AND LAUGHTER

What activities or experiences bring me an internal sense of joy and spontaneous excitement? Examples—playing in the waves of the ocean; sitting around with friends roasting marshmallows at a campfire; making ice cream; playing games with my nephews and nieces; playing board games such as Monopoly or action games like Charades.

_____

_____

_____

How can I create more playful opportunities for myself?
Examples—have friends over for dinner more often and play games; join an organization that offers opportunities to participate in playful activities such as volleyball, baseball, water sports, etc.

_____

_____

_____

What makes me laugh? How can I create more opportunities for laughter to happen?
Example—Joke books and silly greeting cards make me laugh. I can go to the bookstore or card shop occasionally just for fun.

_____

_____

_____

SUMMARY

The following tasks will help your recovery on the physical dimension during Stage Four:

1. Use the questions on page 301 to assess your energy and help you conserve it for what's most important.
2. Continue to care for your wounded inner child.
3. Find ways to play and express your magical, mystical child. Do the exercise on pages 303–304.

• • • • • • •

Healing the Mental Dimension

During Stage Four you might find yourself exploring new avenues of creative expression. As you channel your mental resources in a co-creative way with a higher power's will, you'll be less exhausted and have more mental energy for completing projects. You can use your mental functions to affirm and express yourself.

Accepting Praise, Appreciation, and Gratitude

How do you feel when someone pays you a compliment about your work, your appearance, or even the warmth you may share? Do you find yourself conducting an internal debate about its validity? Perhaps you feel embarrassed or undeserving.

I believe one of the ways you can assess recovery is by your reaction to praise, appreciation, and gratitude. As you affirm and express yourself and reclaim the gifts of your inner self, you will become more loving and accepting. Your strength, understanding, and love will be more noticeable to others.

When you are complimented, will you denigrate yourself to make sure others don't think you are too proud? Or will you graciously accept the gift that has been given you, take it into your heart, and give it back with loving acceptance?

A genuine compliment is truly a gift. Receiving a compliment graciously is a gift in return. When you accept a compliment, without explanations or minimizing, you are affirming yourself and expressing your gratitude to the other person. Thus you are also affirming that person.

Use the exercise below to reflect on how your recovery has affected your ability to accept compliments.

MY ABILITY TO ACCEPT COMPLIMENTS

How comfortable am I acknowledging and accepting compliments?

_____

_____

If I tend to minimize compliments made to me, what beliefs or self-messages stand in my way of accepting them?

_____

_____

What recovery steps can I take to enhance my ability to accept compliments?

_____

_____

Frank Lloyd Wright, the famous architect, once said, "Early in life I had to choose between honest arrogance and hypocritical humility. I chose honest arrogance." Your inner child has this innocent and honest arrogance, too. You are wonderful. You deserve the best. Recovery is about being able to acknowledge this.

Becoming an Individual

During recovery you differentiate yourself from your family and distinguish yourself as a separate and unique individual. Howard Halpern in the last two paragraphs of his book about coming to terms with your parents, *Cutting Loose*, describes the terrors and rewards of this process:

> You may have been rooted in muck all this time, but it was familiar muck. Who you were, what was expected of you, and what limitations you had to accept were all clearly marked. Breaking with all this means facing the unknown and, by yourself, without the aid of your old and timeless fixed stars, using only your own feelings and judgment, daring to navigate through terrifying, uncharted and unpredictable space. Being able means severing the vestigial ties that lead you to the past, and standing upright, knowing your ultimate aloneness, knowing your weaknesses and your strengths, daring to turn your wishes and your potentials toward untried risks. If that isn't alarming, what is?
>
> Most of the time you can open up this alarming possibility not through ending the relationship with your parents, but by stopping the old songs and dances. Each has its own risks, and requires courage, determination and compassion. But whether the freedom of your choices and the actualization of your energies are achieved through ending the songs and dances or, if need be, through severing the parental tie, it is a matter of doing ultimate justice to yourself. And that's worth it all.

Stage Four: Affirming and Expressing Yourself

Claiming your independence, your adulthood, can be frightening. I can recall when I did this with my mother. I had just moved into a new house, and she came to visit for a week to help me set things up. After two days during which she took over, folding my sheets neatly and arranging my socks in perfect rows, I felt invaded. I knew I had to ask her to leave, but the specter of facing her tears, her hurt, and her anger was terrifying. Despite my anxiety, I told her that she would have to go back home.

Although it took some time to heal the breach in our relationship, this was a breakthrough for me. This was my declaration of independence.

By cutting the ties that bind you to the past, you can set your own course through honest and sincere self-determination. Ask yourself the questions that follow to help you reflect on this process.

DIFFERENTIATING FROM FAMILY

1. In what healthy ways have I begun to differentiate myself from my family?

_____

_____

_____

_____

_____

2. What boundaries have I established with my family?

_____

_____

_____

_____

_____

3. How do I feel about family members who may still be angry with me about my choice to change and recover?

_____

_____

_____

_____

_____

4. How do I feel about the growth I have experienced and the ties I have broken with my family of origin?

_____

_____

_____

_____

_____

Examples

1. I no longer get to take sides in family arguments. Even when one of my family members tells me how bad another member is, I am able to listen and acknowledge that the situation seems real uncomfortable without trying to fix it.

2. I will no longer stay at my family gatherings when people start getting loud and drunk.

3. I feel sad that they are angry with me and I told them that but it is their choice to be angry. I can't change them.

4. It has been hard, especially since I choose not to visit my parents. But it's the best thing for me right now. I'm glad that my life is becoming my own.

Is Your Workplace Hazardous to Your Recovery?

You may face the greatest challenges to your recovery in the context of your workplace. Although seldom acknowledged, the workplace is a system just like the family. Many workplaces feature the same symptoms as dysfunctional families, including secrets, rigid roles, covert and overt rules, triangles, and double messages. In addition, the American work ethic stresses willpower and achievement and frowns on open display of feelings and honest communication. No wonder you may find going to work hazardous to your recovery.

Ask yourself the following questions to help you reflect on workplace issues that might affect your recovery:

CODEPENDENCE IN THE WORKPLACE

1. What roles do I play at work?

_____

_____

_____

_____

_____

2. What coping strategies did I use as a child—for instance, withdrawing, rebelling, achieving? What coping strategies do I use on the job?

_____

_____

_____

_____

_____

3. Do I have difficulty setting limits at work? Do I have reasonable expectations for my productivity? What about the expectations of others? What could I do to more effectively set limits?

_____

_____

_____

_____

_____

4. Do I ever feel abused or violated on the job? What boundaries could I establish to prevent this?

_____

_____

_____

_____

_____

5. Do I want to change, control, or avoid any of the people with whom I work?

_____

_____

_____

_____

_____

Stage Four: Affirming and Expressing Yourself

6. Can I express my values in my job? If not, what are the challenges I face in doing this?

_____

_____

_____

_____

_____

Examples

1. The victim and the hero.

2. As a child I either complained or worked hard in school. I do the same things at work. I complain when things don't go my way and I also try to do things so I get lots of recognition.

3. I work extra hours to be on top of things and have to be ready for criticism. I let people tell me what I should be doing even though it's not my job. I guess I'm also a people pleaser. I'm also hard on others, expecting them to be perfect. I could ease up on myself and them.

4. I feel abused by one other worker who is always putting me down in front of others. I could confront him about his behavior using an assertive message.

5. I want to avoid the guy who puts me down. I want to change the whole company and its policies. I want to change the way my boss deals with conflict between the workers. Right now, he ignores it.

6. I express my values in my close relationships on the job. If I did express my values, I would disagree with my boss and might lose my job. He expects everybody to put work as the number-one priority of their life.

The questions above are designed to help you reflect on your work and how it interrelates with your recovery. I'm not recommending that you implement drastic changes in your behavior at work based on the knowledge you gain unless you're willing to take the chance of losing your job. You've heard the expression "Don't rock the boat!" Most workplaces are very rigid systems.

If your workplace challenges your recovery, welcome the opportunity to learn more about your codependence. You can work on your recovery program in the workplace by being aware of your feelings, taking care of yourself, knowing and respecting your limits, and protecting your boundaries. As I suggested in Stage Three, I also recommend courses in assertiveness and communication skills to strengthen your ability to affirm and express yourself. Above all, remember that you are powerless to change others. Attempting to change your workplace will only stress you out and jeopardize your recovery.

SUMMARY

The following tasks will further your recovery on the mental dimension during Stage Four:
1. Learn to accept praise and gratitude from others; the questions on pages 305–306 can help you think about how well you do this now.
2. Consider how you are differentiating yourself from your family using the questions on pages 307–308.
3. Answer the questions found on pages 310–12 to assess how your workplace affects your recovery.

• • • • • • •

Manifesting Contact with the Spiritual Dimension

Stage Four is the time for affirming and expressing yourself. The self you will be affirming and expressing is your inner self—the essence of who you were created to be. Your growing sense of solidity as a person will form the affirming ground from which you can express yourself. This is a time of co-creation with the will of your higher power.

You will begin to experience the paradoxes of recovery, not with your intellect but through an inner knowing that may be accompanied by a wide inner smile or laughter. You will sense within your self the mystery of love and a desire to express gratuitous love for others.

The exercises in this section will help you get in touch and stay in touch with your higher power, your growing capacity for gratuitous love, your awareness of your co-creative responsibility with your higher power, and the dignity of your existence.

Affirming Your Dignity

Thomas Merton, one of the major spiritual teachers of this century, wrote in his book *The Hidden Ground of Love*, "Identify with the ground and you won't worry about the weeds. The ground doesn't." You have the ground within you, the ground on which you can stand and be rooted. The ground is your inner self. The weeds are those parts of yourself about which you feel shame—the shame of not being worthy, not being good enough, not being okay, etc. If you identify with the ground, you can minimize your worries about your imperfections, your mistakes, your humanness.

Take some time to reflect on your life and the journey you have traveled using the following questions. I find these questions, particularly the last one, helpful during a weekly self-reflection or when I feel ashamed of myself.

AFFIRMING DIGNITY

1. In what ways do I identify with the ground within me? Through prayer? Meditation? Journal keeping?

_____

_____

_____

_____

_____

2. What parts of my life are still too shameful to accept? If there are any, how can I forgive and heal them?

_____

_____

_____

_____

_____

3. Am I harboring any resentments? What would I have to do to release them? A fourth and fifth step?

_____

_____

_____

_____

_____

4. What gets in the way of my experiencing the dignity of my own life? How can I remove these barriers?

_____

_____

_____

_____

_____

Examples

1. Regular walks in nature help me to identify with my inner self.
2. I am still ashamed of some of my dishonest behavior, particularly when I was drinking.
3. I still resent myself for staying stuck in a dead relationship so long. I need to work on forgiving myself. Maybe my minister could help me.
4. Resenting myself for being codependent and still believing I'm unworthy of good things are my biggest barriers now. I can keep on acknowledging myself and also work on healing the part of me that feels unworthy.

Tapping the Resources Within You

Codependence muddies your perceptions. While struggling to get acceptance, recognition, and love, you probably gave up on finding meaningful and fulfilling ways to express yourself. The clarity that emerges in Stage Four allows you to look at your activities and interests with a new vision.

Have you occasionally felt a strong attraction to a project or an activity? This feeling may indicate the existence of an inner untapped resource. Perhaps a part of you wanted to be actualized. Thomas Merton says, "If our desires reach out for the things that we were created to have and to make and to be then we will develop into what we were truly meant to be."

By this stage of recovery you know the wisdom of following the will of your higher power. Co-creation with your higher power means paying attention to and acting on your talents and resources. Joseph Campbell calls this "following your bliss." You can trust your higher power to help you become aware of those things that need expression through you.

This exercise will help you identify the internal resources that you may have devalued, ignored, or forgotten as you mired yourself in codependence.

THE EMERGING SELF

List below the things you would do if you were free to undertake any project or activity you want. Then list the traits or aspects of yourself that would be actualized by this activity as well as the resources you bring to it.

After you've made your lists, take a look at them. What wants to emerge in you?

Example

Here's a list I made in 1982:

Project/Activity	Aspects to Be Actualized
1. Write fairy tales and tell stories.	Creativity, playfulness, intelligence, spiritual, fantasy, teacher, artist, dreamer
2. Counseling	Compassion, sensitivity, intelligence, teacher, initiative, resourceful, intuitive, risk taker, alcoholic family

My Emerging Self

Project/Activity	Aspects to Be Actualized
1. _____	_____
	_____
	_____
2. _____	_____
	_____
	_____
3. _____	_____
	_____
	_____

My list contained other activities, but these two illustrate the process. When I look at the list, I see that a creative, compassionate side of me wants to express itself. I haven't written any fairy tales, but I do write poetry. As for counseling, that activity has become very important to me.

I often do a similar exercise with any new projects or activities I undertake. This helps me to get a sense of what aspects of myself I am drawn to express through a particular activity and to set priorities. Given that I have limited time and resources, this process can help me select projects that are truly in line with my growth. Through recovery you will develop a sense of intention in your life. This exercise can support you in setting your intentions by helping to define the growth potential of your interests and activities.

The Fruits of Your Decisions

On pages 274–75 you made a list of past decisions to help you review your decision-making process. The following exercise will help you explore those decisions more deeply, in order to learn about your motivations—both positive and negative.

VALUES IN ACTION

Write the decisions from pages 274–75 below. Then write down what aspects of yourself were seeking to emerge through each decision. Review your answers. What are the common threads or themes that are interwoven into your decisions?

Example

Her are my notes from my 1983 journal when I used this process to examine some important decisions:

Decisions	What Is Seeking to Be Actualized
To leave my job	Freedom to explore creativity, independence, self-expression
To buy a sailboat	Freedom, face fears, seek peace
To marry	Express my love
To divorce	Freedom, expressing myself, independence
To seek counseling	Explore inner self, heal, risk taking, seeking truth

My Values in Action

Decisions

What Is Seeking to Be Actualized

To _____   _____

                                        _____

                                        _____

To _____   _____

                                        _____

                                        _____

To _____   _____

                                        _____

                                        _____

To _____   _____

                                        _____

                                        _____

To _____   _____

                                        _____

                                        _____

When I created this chart I could see that freedom, independence, and self-expression were common threads underlying my decisions. Now I am aware that my codependence blocked and distorted any real expression of these values. Until I started into recovery, I did not have the internal strength to live and acknowledge my values.

After you have identified some major themes that run through your decisions, reflect on how your own codependence has distorted your ability to fully express these values. Those values are still a part of you seeking expression.

It's Like Falling off a Log

Here's another way to find out more about your inner self. What activities have you experienced as natural and easy for you to do? By *easy*, I don't mean it won't take practice, work, or discipline. I mean something that feels as if it fits you, that you enjoy doing.

For instance, writing feels natural to me. In the mid-seventies I wrote several professional articles that were published. Although I'd never taken a writing course, I felt comfortable with the process of writing. On the other hand, repairing a car doesn't feel natural to me. Many years ago I bought a sports car and a manual so I could work on it myself. I knew—but didn't want to admit it to myself—that I felt no real inclination for auto mechanics. My real motivation was to influence others to think of me as a "well-rounded man." I never opened the manual and ended up selling the car for a substantial loss just to get rid of it. In this case I was following a "fantasy" and not "following my bliss."

When you do what is natural, there's a flow of energy that carries you along. The activity doesn't seem taxing, although it may require commitment and persistence. It may be something you haven't done for years—an old hobby or a career you left. The exercise below will help you reflect on what comes naturally to you.

WHAT COMES NATURALLY TO ME

Example

What Activities Give Me Energy or Feel Natural to Me?	How Do I Use This Natural Aptitude in My Life?
1. Translating complex ideas into drawings	To make drawings of concepts I don't understand so I can understand them
2. Woodworking	To build things around the house
3. Teaching	To give workshops
4. Astronomy	To watch the stars

What Comes Naturally To Me

What Activities Give Me Energy or Feel Natural To Me?

How Do I Use This Natural Aptitude in My Life?

_____   _____

_____   _____

_____   _____

_____   _____

_____   _____

_____   _____

In the Tough Times

In your life you have endured many difficulties and learned to survive. The resources you drew on and developed to get through these experiences are still within you. They are aspects of your inner self.

INNER RESOURCES

List below any severe hardships or difficulties you have experienced. Next, list the corresponding inner resources you needed to come through these.

Use your list to assess the inner resources you developed to help you survive the trials of your life.

Examples

Here's an excerpt from my journal.

Difficulties/Hardships

Father was an alcoholic

Resources I Used to Survive

Will to survive, sense of my own destiny apart from my family

Separation and divorce	Willingness to be vulnerable and grow, religious beliefs, inner knowing that I would make it through
Loneliness of my late teens and early twenties	Ambition, determination
My dad telling me just before he died that if he could live his life over he wouldn't marry and have kids	Determination, acceptance

My Inner Resources

Difficulties/Hardships	Resources I Used to Survive
_____	_____
	_____
	_____
_____	_____
	_____
	_____
_____	_____
	_____
	_____
_____	_____
	_____
	_____
_____	_____
	_____

When I reviewed my list, I saw that my determination and willpower were significant resources. They helped me to get three master's degrees. Although my original motivation for getting these degrees was codependent—I was desperately seeking recognition and acceptance—I'm glad I have the experience and knowledge I acquired during my academic studies.

Imagination has also been an important resource for me. In the past I used it to escape reality. Now I am learning to use my imagination to express myself and my ideas through writing and counseling.

Often when I asked my clients to do these exercises, I hear responses like this: "I don't have any resources," "I don't feel like there's anything inside me trying to be actualized," and "I have no trust that my inner self exists." Sometimes it's difficult to see the positive aspects of yourself, especially when your life has been difficult or you are in a lot of pain. Yet I know from my own experience and from my work with clients that there is always something positive buried within what appears to be negative.

When I asked one of my clients, Roger, to list his internal resources, he said bluntly, "Look at my life, Brian! It's a mess! And you want me to list resources that I have or qualities I'm trying to express! I'm 34, and I have nothing! And I can't imagine my life changing either."

"If you don't see your life changing," I asked, "then why are you here talking with me?"

Roger thought about that for a minute. "I'm looking for answers," he said. "I just can't give up."

"Well, what internal resources are influencing you to keep on looking for answers?"

Roger looked at me thoughtfully. "Hmmm," he said, "I guess determination, and hope, and faith. There's something else too, a feeling I can't quite explain—I don't know what it is."

As Roger discovered with a little bit of coaxing, he did have internal resources he was using, even in the midst of crisis. In the same way, you have internal resources, innate abilities, and inner strength that have supported you throughout your life.

Affirming Yourself

I'd like to suggest a concluding exercise to tie together all the information that has surfaced during the last four exercises.

AFFIRMING YOURSELF

Look back over your answers to the last four exercises. Then write a statement affirming your many resources and talents.

Example

I am a person of diverse talents and strong inner resources that I utilize to express myself in loving and creative ways.

Affirming Myself

_____

_____

_____

_____

_____

Your inner self has a life force, an energy that will never quit. It will call you and impel you throughout your life to become who you were created to be.

Developing Your Capacity for Gratuitous Love

You're probably familiar with the term *unconditional love*. Some of you may have stayed in difficult relationships because you thought you could learn about unconditional love by accepting someone who violated your boundaries or was emotionally unavailable to you. Gratuitous love is similar in that you expect nothing in return for your gift of love but you don't tolerate abusive behavior. The word *gratuitous* comes from the same root word as *gratitude* and *grace* and means something given freely, without expectation of compensation.

Practicing gratuitous love means (1) increasing your ability to love another person while (2) letting go of the need to change him or her and (3) establishing and maintaining your personal boundaries. You have a right to be treated with honesty and respect. This often develops in close friendships where these qualities are fostered. You may also experience gratuitous love developing for your parents after you have worked through your anger and forgiven their behavior.

When you love someone with a reality-based love, you can be there for him as he struggles through recovery or other personal problems. Gratuitous love is based on compassion, understanding, gratitude, honesty, and trust in your higher power.

Consider your capacity for gratuitous love as you contemplate the questions below:

GRATUITOUS LOVE

1. From whom have you experienced gratuitous love in your life?

_____

_____

_____

_____

_____

2. For whom do you feel gratuitous love?

_____

_____

_____

_____

_____

3. Are there any individuals in your life whom you cannot love gratuitously? What stands in the way?

_____

_____

_____

_____

_____

Your capacity for gratuitous love grows out of your emerging sense of solidity in yourself and the strength you derive from knowing how to take care of yourself.

Your Living Program for Selfhood

Even though you may now be experiencing wonderful changes in your life, this is only the beginning. The spiritual dimension is infinitely deep and mysterious, and maintaining your recovery program is essential to plumbing the depths.

Steps 11 and 12 of the Twelve Steps provide a living program for selfhood, a prescription of ongoing steps you can take to maintain your health and deepen your contact with your higher power.

Step 11. We sought through prayer and meditation to improve our conscious contact with God *as we understood Him,* praying only for knowledge of His will for us and the power to carry that out.

This step stresses the importance of maintaining your spiritual practices. They are your link with your inner self and your higher power. What practices will you use to improve and deepen your conscious contact with your higher power?

At times you will have a strong sense of your higher power's will in your life. Sometimes it will take courage to walk the path of your higher power's will, but doing so will bring you power. Other times you may have no clear sense of what to do. That's the time to check in with yourself honestly and surrender control, trusting that the path will eventually reveal itself to you.

Step 12.   Having had a spiritual awakening as the result of these steps, we tried to carry this message to alcoholics and to practice these principles in all our affairs.

Step 12 asks you to share your experience and hope with others who suffer from the anguish of codependence and addiction. In addition, you commit yourself to the lifelong task of expressing the truth of your inner self one day at a time.

In his book *Shambhala: The Sacred Path of the Warrior*, Chogyam Trungpa says that the good warrior must have a sad and tender heart. Recovery will expand your heart and your ability to feel love, compassion, and empathy. Knowing your own pain and the defenses you used to hide it, you will look at other people and life differently.

You are likely to sense an inner call to service. This might be expressed in any number of ways, including church work, volunteering, or active involvement in a Twelve-Step group. You will want to share what you have learned in recovery. And you will find that giving of yourself does not diminish you but in fact increases your depth of feeling, love, and compassion. Now, as you experience the fruits of your recovery, you truly have a sense of self to share and give to others. You have the power of presence to walk your own walk and also walk beside others without tripping over their issues.

REACHING OUT

1. How do I feel drawn to serve others and share the gifts of my recovery?

_____

_____

_____

_____

_____

2. How will my desire to be of service take form?

_____

_____

_____

_____

_____

Maintaining your own recovery program is the greatest service you can offer to the world. When you are expressing the light of your inner self, in co-creation with your higher power, your light shines for everyone.

SUMMARY

Use the following suggestions to help deepen and maintain your contact with your inner self and your higher power during Stage Four:
1. Affirm your dignity using the questions on page 314 to pinpoint areas of concern.
2. Make a list of the things you would like to do and the aspects of yourself that would emerge as a result, using the exercise on pages 315–16.
3. Review the values you expressed through your past decisions as suggested on pages 317–18.
4. Consider those things that come easily to you and to which you are naturally attracted as signs of your inner self as described on pages 319–20.
5. Make a list of the inner resources you developed in response to difficulties and hardships as described on pages 320–21.
6. Affirm yourself by writing a statement about your talents and resources (page 323).
7. Reflect on your capacity for gratuitous love using the questions on pages 324–25.
8. Work Steps 11 and 12 of the Twelve Steps.

• • • • • • •

The Wheel Keeps Turning

The long days of summer diminish as the cycle of the seasons turns toward the decay and disintegration of autumn. The crops have been harvested; the fields are bare. Nights get longer. A chill creeps into the air. The leaves begin to turn colors, and one day they start to fall from the trees.

Like the cycle of the seasons, recovery is a process that doesn't end. You have come through the cycle of growth and change, and basked in the warm light of a new sense of solidity and selfhood. As a result of your recovery program, you know you have the inner strength and skills to grow and change. You will find yourself facing the stage of disintegration again. You will be challenged to let go and let your higher power work through you. You will have many opportunities to become more of the loving, self-directed person you were created to be. With the resources you have developed in recovery, life will become the joyous adventure it was intended to be.

PART FOUR

· · · · · · ·

Experiencing the
Inner Self

13

. . . .

The Emergence of
Your Inner Self

THE TERM RECOVERY IMPLIES
getting back to normal, healing after sickness. But recovery is actually much more
profound. Recovery also means reclaiming. Reclaiming the power, love, and joy
deep within. Reclaiming your own (w)holiness. Reclaiming who you truly are at the
core of your being—your inner self.

By healing the physical and mental dimensions you become able to experience
and thus reclaim your inner self. You create the space for the inner self to flourish.
As one of my clients said: "It feels like an indestructible part of me. I know it was
always there, but I was out of touch with it."

I believe that each of you has experienced that "indestructible part." Perhaps you
felt it during times of great struggle and hardship or while pursuing the fulfillment
of a deep desire such as learning a new skill. I've felt it while writing this book.

The inner self is the essence of all that you are and all that you are capable of
becoming. As this self gradually emerges into your awareness during the healing
process, you will feel more solidly yourself. You will experience this not mentally
but as a felt sensation.

Have you ever known something without a shadow of doubt? Recall that
experience. Did you feel that certainty in your mind or through your body? Mental
comprehension is quite different from the absolute certainty of a felt sense. You
might call this bodily knowing "gut sense." Your gut sense gives you signals about
plans you make and situations and relationships in which you are involved. In

codependence you ignore this inner guidance, thus cutting yourself off from your own inner wisdom about what is right for you.

When you heed the wisdom of your gut sense, you are as solid as Gibraltar. You stand firm in your truth. You acquire the ability to say yes or no in any situation that confronts you without equivocation. I can still remember the countless times I tried to decide yes or no by looking outside myself, taking cues from other people. I cherish the freedom that comes from having a source of truth within.

One of my clients, Susanna, described her experience of her inner self during our last counseling session. She had worked through some deep pain in recovery and healed some of the wounds of the past. She forgave herself for the damage she had done to herself while trying to live her life through other people's eyes. It had been a long and arduous odyssey that she was committed to continue.

"I have the strength to live in integrity now," she told me with a bright smile and a light in her eyes. "I feel a lot of joy and freedom knowing that when I'm honest and risk being myself, I am truly loving other people. I feel the difference."

I asked her more about this difference, and she responded: "I just feel that I have a source of love in me. I don't know how else to say it."

I knew what she meant. As I wrote this last chapter, I am feeling the same source of love and a little sadness that I am not able to describe it adequately. So I will rely on the wonderful gifts my clients have provided to me by describing their experiences of the inner self.

The Centering Process

As you heal yourself, your inner self emerges into awareness. This emergence is a centering process. One of my clients described this sensation by putting his hand over his solar plexus and saying "It feels like there's a little something, right here. It's small, but it feels very real."

You move from the self-centeredness of codependence into the stance of a centered self. As you become more centered, you will experience changes in three areas of your life:

1. *Relational Maturity*—your relationships with others and things
2. *Harmony of Being*—your relationship with yourself
3. *Spiritual Integrity*—your relationship with a higher power.

The changes in these three areas of life draw you closer to your center; at the same time, your inner self emerges more and more as the true reality of your life.

Relational Maturity

When you are living life as a codependent, your relationships to others are based on your need to get them to do things for you. You try to control other people to satisfy your needs and avoid your feelings. This need drives many of your relationships and distorts your ability to truly love and accept others.

One of my clients who was involved in a codependent and needy relationship spent his first several sessions complaining about his girlfriend's behavior. He wanted her to do what was right, which, according to him, meant marrying him. I pointed out that he was trying to control her. And while he was waiting for her to change, he was forgoing the fulfillment of his own unmet needs. Gradually he was able to focus on his reactions to her behavior rather than her behavior. Then he started facing the feelings of fear and abandonment that he had been avoiding by staying in this unhappy relationship.

As you heal the emotional wounds of your past and develop your ability to love, you become more secure in yourself. As you become more secure in yourself, you are able to accept others for who they are and let go of the need to change them. By making choices and communicating those choices clearly, you free yourself from the enmeshment of codependent relationships. Aware of your needs and your ability to get those needs met in healthy ways, you develop new dimensions in relationships with others.

As a result of the insights you gain from your own recovery, you will develop an awareness and appreciation for the importance of the struggles each person experiences. In my own life I am grateful for my growing ability to be a loving witness to the recovery process as well as the codependence process. At times when I see people struggling and in pain, I want to jump in and change them, but I recognize this impulse and am able to let go of this compulsion most of the time. I can provide feedback about my experiences and make choices about my responses. I truly cherish the honesty that becomes possible when I accept that I can love myself and other people and not have to change them.

I also find that I am more open to information from other people about my impact on them. Healing my "hot buttons" has made me less vulnerable to comments that I previously experienced as threatening. One of my clients, Dawn, who has been working on her recovery for more than two years, was surprised by her developing capacity to be authentic with her mother, especially during interactions that formerly ended in an argument or withdrawal. She had this to say about one incident:

"I was surprised, but I just wasn't hooked by her statements about me. When she told me she thought I was still holding a grudge against her, I felt myself coil up inside. Before, I would have ignored her or tried to change her mind. But this time I just asked her how she knew that and told her that I was upset and confused by her statement. I didn't have to defend myself. As a matter of fact, I really wanted to know more about what was happening. It felt so good not to be overwhelmed and controlled by my fear."

Feeling Harmony of Being

As you heal your body and mind, you will feel, and you will feel better and different. I experienced feelings of strength that were like an inner resolve. It was as if I were shifting inside my body, like settling into myself. My clients describe similar experiences. As one client put it, "I feel less flighty and scattered. My body feels like it's changed even though I don't think it has. I don't know quite how to say it, but I feel like there's more of me inside me."

As you heal your inner feeling space and change dysfunctional thinking patterns, an inner alignment takes place. When you surrender control, the spiritual dimension of your being becomes important. Your body and mind are gradually restored to their true functions: experiencing and expressing your natural essence, your inner self. Your personal autonomy, sense of freedom, and a healthy interdependence emerge. Autonomy is knowing that you are responsible for your life. Freedom is the ability to exercise that responsibility. Interdependence is exercising that responsibility in relation to others.

One of the benefits of this harmony is that you will become less judgmental and critical of yourself. Your ability to sense deviations from your inner truth will increase, as will your courage to respond to these deviations.

You may find your emerging sense of your inner self is uncomfortable at first. I know that for me feeling more like myself has been a wonderful surprise. It's like an inner grin that radiates inside of me. If you are used to feeling bad or not feeling at all, you might not be prepared for feeling alive and good. But I bet you will get used to it.

Living in Spiritual Integrity

Codependence fosters a form of spirituality that I call "assumed spirituality." This kind of spirituality is more concerned with rules and the reactions of others than living the truth of your life. It means being nice to people instead of being honest, hiding your feelings because you think they are bad or wrong, and not speaking up when your values are being violated. It's more concerned with adherence to rules and laws than with truth. Some religions prize rigid adherence to rules of behavior that replicate the dynamics of a dysfunctional family. For instance, denial of feelings and control are valued in some New Age and Christian religious groups. Assumed spirituality is based on playing roles like being a caretaker or rescuer or a good Christian martyr. It does not respect the individual human spirit.

As I became more aware of my inner reality, I realized that formal religion was the vehicle for expressing my spiritual awareness, not the source of it. Timmen Cermak, writing in A *Time to Heal*, describes the role of spiritual awareness in recovery:

> Spirituality refers to the relationship we *feel* to the universe as a whole, while philosophy refers to the relationship we *think* we have to the universe. Spirituality goes well beyond the intellect by involving our emotions as well. As healing proceeds, your relationship to the world about you undergoes radical shifts. These shifts are particularly profound as your true self emerges, strengthens, and begins to eclipse the false self. You experience these shifts as changes in your identity. The subjective experience of coming into a radically different relationship with the world around you is deeply moving. "Spiritual experience" is probably the best label we have for such feelings.

True spirituality is a felt experience. When you live with spiritual integrity, you live in truth to this felt experience.

Living from the Center

Centering, like healing, is a lifelong experience. As you let go of control and allow life to flow naturally, you will experience the emergence of the inner self as the center of your being.

For some this is an experience of being grounded. Others describe feeling solid or experiencing inner strength. This is how Arlene described it: "I've spent most of my life apologizing for and avoiding being powerful." She paused, then went on: "Now I realize," she said, pointing at her chest, "that God lives here."

When I asked how she knew that, she said with emphasis, "I feel it like a solid core that is within me but is more than me." She took a deep breath and went on. "I'm tired of having to apologize for being myself. I want to maintain this centeredness that I feel. I feel connected to myself and connected to people."

Living at the center means living in paradox—the place where opposites meet. A paradox is based on a polarity—two things that seem to be incompatible but are not. Living at the center means going from either-or thinking to both-and thinking, feeling the power generated by the union of opposites.

For example, many of the men I work with believe there are only two ways to deal with anger: passive withdrawal or destructive expression. I encourage them to find another mode of being that unites these two poles. Both of the extremes are codependent strategies for controlling others. When you are living from the center, anger can be an act of love.

Living from the center, you have the opportunity to co-create the world you experience with your higher power. This means living responsibly, and that can be an awesome challenge. Like balancing on a razor's edge, you will experience this paradox of life—you will understand how significant and important you are and, at the same time, how insignificant and unimportant.

The selfish/selfless paradox is also resolved at the center. Most of us have spent our lives avoiding being "selfish." But centered selfishness is really selfless. At the center you will experience self-acceptance, self-love, self-determination, self-esteem, self-respect, and many other self-oriented qualities. It is only when you accept yourself that you no longer need to control others.

As you become less and less externally oriented, you will move from thinking in terms of "them" to thinking of "us." This is a great mystery to me—that only when you are living from an internal, centered orientation do you realize your participation in and responsibility for "us," for all of us.

You Are Sacred Ground: Within You Is a Burning Bush

The Old Testament contains a story about Moses and his encounter with a burning bush. As Moses was tending sheep and goats on the slopes of Mount Sinai, he saw a bush that was in flames but was not being consumed. A voice spoke to him from the bush, telling him to come closer but to take off his sandals since he was walking on holy ground. He did so and became engaged in a dialogue with the voice of God. In the end he promised to lead his people out of captivity in Egypt. In return God promised to guide him and support him in this endeavor.

Moses could have ignored the voice or refused to participate in the dialogue. In fact he tried to persuade God to send someone more capable than he thought he was. But God insisted.

In our codependence we live in captivity. We are slaves to our dysfunctional behavior patterns and beliefs, to our habits and our roles. But each of us also has within us the spark of a higher power's love and fire, our own inner burning bush. Our bodies are sacred ground for the experience of the divine within.

The healing process is heroic and revolutionary. As you grow in awareness of your inner self, you will know the burning bush within you. Your light and radiance will shine in the world, and you will stand strong, knowing your blessedness and true essence. And your higher power will be there to support and guide you.

The Sacredness in Your Woundedness

As you near the end of this book, I hope you have acquired some sense of what the journey is like, the journey on which you heal yourself and recover your inner self.

I have often wondered whether or not I would have the opportunity to know and experience myself as I am today if I had not been born in a dysfunctional family. Obviously I will never know. I do know that without that experience I could not have written this book. My pain has been a gift.

William James wrote in *The Varieties of Religious Experience* that "man's extremity is God's opportunity." A Sufi story, recorded by Idries Shah in *Tales of the Dervishes*, makes this point particularly well. It is the story of Fatima, the daughter of a prosperous spinner, who is shipwrecked while traveling with her father. She is washed up on shore and rescued by a poor family of cloth makers who take her in and teach her their trade. But two years later, while she's walking along the beach, she's captured and carried off by slave traders, who sell her in the market at Istanbul. The man who buys her intends to make her a serving maid for his wife, but when he arrives home he learns that he has lost all of his money. So he puts Fatima to work, teaching her his trade, making masts for ships. Eventually she becomes his trusted assistant, so much so that one day he sends her with a cargo of masts to Java as his agent. But, alas, the ship on which she is traveling is wrecked by a typhoon and Fatima is washed ashore in China. She bitterly laments her fate: "Why is it that whenever I try to do something it comes to grief? Why should so many unfortunate things happen to me?"

It so happens, though, that in China everyone is waiting for a foreign woman who will make a tent for the emperor. When Fatima wanders into a town, she's promptly dispatched to the court, where the emperor asks her if she can make a tent. She asks for rope but is told there is none. Then she remembers what she learned of spinning as a child and makes her own rope. She asks for stout cloth, but there is none heavy enough in China, so, using the craft she learned with the family of cloth makers, she weaves her own tent cloth. Then she looks about for tent poles, but of course there are none. Luckily she's experienced at making masts, so she uses this skill to produce tent poles. And, lo and behold, a tent. The emperor is so pleased that he offers her whatever she wants. Fatima chooses to marry a handsome prince and live in China in happiness for the rest of her days.

This tale has much to teach us. It was precisely because of her misfortunes that Fatima acquired the skills that brought about the fulfillment of all her dreams.

The pain caused by codependence affects all the dimensions of your being. Some people choose to numb the pain with addictions, bury it and live a life of quiet desperation, or end it with suicide. Other people hide the pain by creating a life that is apparently blameless and meets all the criteria for a good life.

Some people choose to feel the pain as a way of knowing their true and inner self. I hope that you are one of these. Your pain can be the impetus for an inner quest that will take you to the depths of your being. You will know the truth and joy of your experience of life. By a strange paradox the pain of codependence can bring you to the place where you learn to live in accordance with your deepest truths, the truths that are found at the core of your being.

Peace be with you on your journey to selfhood.

Appendix

The Twelve Steps
of Alcoholics Anonymous

1. We admitted we were powerless over alcohol—that our lives had become unmanageable.

2. Came to believe that a Power greater than ourselves could restore us to sanity.

3. Made a decision to turn our will and our lives over to the care of God *as we understood Him.*

4. Made a searching and fearless moral inventory of ourselves.

5. Admitted to God, ourselves, and to another human being the exact nature of our wrongs.

6. Were entirely ready to have God remove all these defects of character.

7. Humbly asked Him to remove our shortcomings.

8. Made a list of all persons we had harmed, and became willing to make amends to them all.

9. Made direct amends to such people wherever possible, except when to do so would injure them or others.

10. Continued to take personal inventory and when we were wrong promptly admitted it.

11. Sought through prayer and meditation to improve our conscious contact with God *as we understood Him,* praying only for knowledge of His will for us and the power to carry that out.

12. Having had a spiritual awakening as the result of these steps, we tried to carry this message to alcoholics and to practice these principles in all our affairs.

The Twelve Steps reprinted with permission of A.A. World Services Inc.

Bibliography

Alexander, Franz. *Psychosomatic Medicine*. New York: W. W. Norton and Company, 1987.

Assagioli, Roberto. *The Act of Will*. Baltimore: Penguin Books, 1974.

Barnard, Christiaan, ed. *The Body Machine*. New York: Crown Publishers, 1981.

Beattie, Melody. *Codependent No More*. New York: Harper & Row, 1987.

Bettelheim, Bruno. *The Uses of Enchantment*. New York: Vintage Books, 1977.

Black, Claudia. *It Will Never Happen to Me*. New York: Ballantine Books, 1987.

Borysenko, Joan. *Minding the Body, Mending the Mind*. New York: Bantam Books, 1988.

Bradshaw, John. *Bradshaw on the Family*. Deerfield Beach, FL: Health Communications, 1988.

Campbell, Joseph. *The Power of Myth*. New York: Doubleday, 1988.

Campbell, Peter A., and Edwin M. McMahon. *Bio-Spirituality: Focusing as a Way to Grow*. Chicago: Loyola University Press, 1985.

Cermak, Timmen L. *Diagnosing and Treating Co-Dependence*. Minneapolis: Johnson Institute Books, 1986.

Cermak, Timmin L. *Time to Heal: The Road to Recovery for Adult Children of Alcoholics*. Los Angeles: Jeremy P. Tarcher, Inc., 1988.

Co-Dependency: An Emerging Issue. Pompano Beach, FL: Health Communications, 1984.

Cooper, Cary L., Rachel D. Cooper, and Lynn H. Eaker. *Living with Stress*. New York: Penguin Books, 1988.

Couch, Jean. *Yoga Book*. Mountain View, CA: World Publications, Inc., 1979.

Creation. Friends of Creation Spirituality, PO Box 19216, Oakland, CA 94619.

Crum, Jessie K. *The Art of Inner Listening*. Wheaton, IL: Theosophical Publishing House, 1975.

Curran, Dolores. *Stress and the Healthy Family*. Minneapolis: Winston Press, 1985.

de Mello, Anthony. *One Minute Wisdom*. Garden City, NY: Doubleday, 1986.

de Mello, Anthony. *Sadhana: A Way to God*. Garden City, NY: Image Books—Doubleday and Company, Inc., 1984.

de Mello, Anthony. *Wellsprings*. Garden City, NY: Doubleday and Company, Inc., 1985.

Dychtwald, Ken. *Bodymind*. Los Angeles: Jeremy P. Tarcher, Inc., 1986.

Fensterheim, Herbert, and Jean Baer. *Don't Say Yes When You Want To Say No*. New York: Dell, 1975.

Ferder, Fran. *Words Made Flesh*. Notre Dame, IN: Ave Maria Press, 1986.

Fossum, Merle A., and Marilyn J. Mason. *Facing Shame: Families in Recovery.* New York: W. W. Norton and Company, 1986.

Fox, Matthew. *Meditations with Master Eckhart.* Santa Fe: Bear and Company, 1983.

Fox, Matthew. *Original Blessing.* Santa Fe: Bear and Company, 1983.

Frankl, Victor. *Man's Search for Meaning.* New York: Washington Square Press, 1963.

Fried, Edrita. *The Courage to Change.* New York: Grove Press, 1981.

Friedman, Edwin H. *Generation to Generation.* New York: Guilford Press, 1985.

Fritz, Neil. *Journey into Me: The Twelve Step Workbook for Everyday Problems.* Irvine, CA: Journey Company, 1986.

Gendlin, Eugene T. *Focusing.* New York: Bantam Books, Inc., 1978.

Hall, Calvin S., and Gardner Lindzey. *Introduction to Theories of Personality.* New York: John Wiley and Sons, 1985.

Hammarskjöld, Dag. *Markings.* London: Faber and Faber, Ltd., 1964.

Hays, Edward. *The Ethiopian Tattoo Shop.* Easton, KS: Forest of Peace Books, 1986.

Heaney, John J., ed. *Psyche and Spirit.* New York: Paulist Press, 1984.

Horney, Karen. *Neurosis and Human Growth.* New York: W. W. Norton and Company, 1950.

Houston, Jean. *The Search for the Beloved.* Los Angeles: Jeremy P. Tarcher, Inc., 1987.

Huxley, Laura Archera. *You Are Not the Target.* North Hollywood, CA: Wilshire Book Company, 1977.

Jaffe, Dennis T. *Healing from Within.* New York: A Fireside Book—Simon and Schuster, 1986.

James, Muriel. *Breaking Free.* Reading, MA: Addison-Wesley, 1985.

James, William. *The Varieties of Religious Experience.* New York: New American Library, 1958.

Jerome, John. *Staying Supple.* New York: Bantam Books, Inc., 1987.

Johnson, Robert A. *Ecstasy: Understanding the Psychology of Joy.* San Francisco: Harper & Row, 1987.

Johnston, William. *The Inner Eye of Love.* San Francisco: Harper & Row, 1982.

Johnston, William. *The Mirror Mind.* San Francisco: Harper & Row, 1981.

Jourard, Sidney M. *The Transparent Self.* New York: Van Nostrand Reinhold Company, 1971.

Jung, C. G. *Modern Man in Search of a Soul.* New York: Harv./HBJ Books, 1955.

Keller, John. *Let Go Let God.* Minneapolis: Augsburg Publishing House, 1985.

Kerr, Michael E., and Murray Bowen. *Family Evaluation.* New York: W. W. Norton and Company, 1988.

Kritsberg, Wayne. *The Adult Children of Alcoholics Syndrome.* Pompano Beach, FL: Health Communications, 1985.

Appendix

Kritsberg, Wayne. *Gifts of Personal Growth and Recovery*. Pompano Beach, FL: Health Communications, 1988.

Larsen, Earnie. *Stage II Recovery*. New York: Harper & Row, 1985.

Levine, Stephen. *A Gradual Awakening*. Garden City, NY: Anchor Press, Doubleday, 1979.

Levine, Stephen. *Healing into Life and Death*. Garden City, NY: Anchor Press/Doubleday, 1987.

Lewis, Howard R., and Martha E. Lewis. *Psychosomatics*. New York: Viking Press, 1972.

Linn, Matthew, and Dennis Linn. *Healing Life's Hurts*. New York: Paulist Press, 1978.

Locke, Steven, and Douglas Cooligan. *The Healer Within*. New York: New American Library, 1986.

Lowen, Alexander. *The Betrayal of the Body*. New York: Collier Books, Macmillan Publishing Company, 1969.

Lowen, Alexander. *Bioenergetics*. New York: Penguin Books, 1975.

Maslow, Abraham. *Religions, Values and Peak Experiences*. New York: Penguin Books, 1970.

May, Gerald. *Addiction and Grace*. New York: Harper & Row, 1988.

May, Robert M. *Physicians of the Soul*. Warwick, NY: Amity House, Inc., 1988.

May, Rollo. *The Discovery of Being*. New York: W. W. Norton and Company, 1983.

Merton, Thomas. *The Hidden Ground of Love: Letters on Religious Experience and Social Concerns*. Shannon, William H., ed., Scranton, PA: Farrar, Straus & Giroux, Inc., 1986.

Metzner, Ralph. *Opening to Inner Light: The Transformation of Human Nature and Consciousness*. Los Angeles: Jeremy P. Tarcher, Inc., 1986.

Middleton-Moz, Jane, and Lorie Dwinell. *After the Tears*. Pompano Beach, FL: Health Communications, Inc., 1986.

Milkman, Harvey, and Stanley Sunderwirth. *Craving for Ecstasy*. Lexington, MA: D. C. Heath and Company, 1987.

Miller, Alice. *The Drama of the Gifted Child*. New York: Basic Books, 1980.

Miller, Sherod, Daniel Wackman, Elan Nunnally, and Carol Saline. *Straight Talk*. New York: Signet, New American Library, 1982.

Mindell, Arnold. *The Dreambody in Relationships*. London: Routledge & Kegan Paul, 1987.

Mindell, Arnold. *Working with the Dreaming Body*. London: Routledge & Kegan Paul, 1987.

Monte, Christopher F. *Beneath the Mask*. New York: Holt, Rinehart and Winston, Inc., 1987.

Norwood, Robin. *Women Who Love Too Much*. New York: Pocket Books, 1985.

Padus, Emrika. *The Complete Guide to Your Emotions and Your Health*. Emmaus, PA: Rodale Press, Inc., 1985.

Paul, Jordan, and Margaret Paul. *Do I Have to Give Up Me to Be Loved by You?* Minneapolis: CompCare Publications, 1983.

Peck, M. Scott. *The Road Less Travelled.* New York: Touchstone Book, 1978.

Peele, Stanton. *Love and Addiction.* New York: New American Library, NAL Penguin, Inc., 1976.

Phillips, Dorothy Berkley, Elizabeth Boyden Howes, and Lucille M. Nixon. *The Choice Is Always Ours.* Wheaton, IL: Re-Quest Books, The Theosophical Publishing House, 1977.

Progoff, Ira, ed. *The Cloud of Unknowing.* New York: Dell, 1983.

Progoff, Ira. *At a Journal Workshop.* New York: Dialogue House Library, 1975.

Rainer, Tristine. *The New Diary.* Los Angeles: Jeremy P. Tarcher, Inc., 1978.

Rama, Swami, Rudolph Ballantine, and Alan Hughes. *Science of Breath.* Honesdale, PA: Himalayan Institute of Yoga Science and Philosophy, 1979.

Reber, Arthur S. *Dictionary of Psychology.* New York: Penguin Books, 1985.

Richardson, Ronald W. *Family Ties That Bind.* Vancouver, BC: International Self-Counsel Press, Ltd., 1987.

Rosenberg, Jack Lee. *Body, Self and Soul: Sustaining Integration.* Atlanta: Humanics, Inc., 1985.

Rossi, Ernest L. *The Psychobiology of Mind-Body Healing.* New York: W. W. Norton and Company, 1986.

Satir, Virginia. *Peoplemaking.* Palo Alto: Science and Behavior Books, 1972.

Schaef, Anne Wilson. *Co-dependence: Misunderstood—Mistreated.* Minneapolis: Winston Press, Inc., 1986.

Schaef, Anne Wilson. *When Society Becomes an Addict.* San Francisco: Harper & Row, 1988.

Schuon, F. *Light on the Ancient Worlds.* Trans. Lord Northbourne. London: Perennial Books, 1965.

Seligman, Martin. *Helplessness: On Depression, Development and Death.* New York: W. H. Freeman and Company, 1975.

Selye, Hans. *Stress Without Distress.* New York: Signet Books, 1975.

Shah, Idries. *Tales of the Dervishes.* New York: E. P. Dutton and Company, 1970.

Simon, Sidney B., Leland W. Howe, and Howard Kirschenbaum. *Values Clarification.* New York: Hart Publishing Co., 1972.

Singer, June. *Boundaries of the Soul.* Garden City, NY: Anchor Press/Doubleday, 1973.

Stroebel, Charles F. *QR: The Quieting Reflex.* New York: Putnam and Sons, 1982.

Taub-Bynum, E. Bruce. *The Family Unconscious.* Wheaton, IL: Theosophical Publishing House, 1984.

Tavris, Carol. *Anger.* New York: Touchstone Books/Simon and Schuster, 1984.

Tennov, Dorothy. *Love and Limerence*. New York: Stein and Day, 1980.

Tillich, Paul. *The Courage to Be*. New Haven: Yale University Press, 1969.

Trungpa, Chogyam. *Shambhala: The Sacred Path of the Warrior*. New York: Bantam Books, 1986.

Von Durckheim, Karlfried Graf. *The Way of Transformation*. London: Unwin Paperbacks, Mandala Books, 1980.

Wegscheider, Don. *If Only My Family Understood Me*. Minneapolis: CompCare Publications, 1979.

Wegscheider-Cruse, Sharon. *Another Chance*. Palo Alto: Science and Behavior Books, Inc., 1981.

Wegscheider-Cruse, Sharon. *Choice-Making*. Pompano Beach, FL: Health Communications, Inc., 1985.

Wells, Joel. *Coping in the 80's*. Chicago: Thomas More Press, 1986.

Whitfield, Charles L. *Healing the Child Within*. Deerfield Beach, FL: Health Communications, Inc., 1987.

Woititz, Janet. *Adult Children of Alcoholics*. Pompano Beach, FL: Health Communications, Inc., 1983.

Ze, Nancy. *The Art of Breathing*. New York: Bantam Books, Inc., 1986.

Resources

Adult Children of Alcoholics
Central Service Board
P O Box 3216
Torrance, CA 90505
(213) 534-1815

Al-Anon/Alateen
Family Group Headquarters, Inc.
Madison Square Station
New York, NY 10010
(212) 683-1771

Alcoholics Anonymous
World Services, Inc.
468 Park Avenue
New York, NY 10016
(212) 686-1100

Co-Dependents Anonymous
P O Box 33577
Phoenix, AZ 85067
(602) 277-7991

Debtors Anonymous
General Service Board
P.O. Box 20322
New York, NY 10025-9992

Emotions Anonymous
P O Box 4525
St. Paul, MN 55104

Gamblers Anonymous
P O Box 17173
Los Angeles, CA 90017

Narcotics Anonymous
World Service Office
16155 Wyandotte Street
Van Nuys, CA 91406
(818) 780-3951

National Association for Children
    of Alcoholics
31706 Coast Highway
Suite 201
South Laguna, CA 92677
(714) 499-3889

Overeaters Anonymous
World Service Office
P.O. Box 92870
Los Angeles, CA 90009
(213) 542-8363

Sexaholics Anonymous
P O Box 300
Simi Valley, CA 93062
(805) 581-3343

Or call your local chapter of Alcoholics Anonymous or Al-Anon (both should be listed in the phone book or available from an information referral service) to find out about local meetings that will be appropriate for you.

Permissions

I want to gratefully acknowledge the following individuals and publishers for permission to use this information:

The Twelve Steps of Alcoholics Anonymous reprinted with permission of A.A. World Services Inc. The suggestions regarding the use of the Twelve Steps in recovery are those of the author only and not of AA.

Excerpts from *Physicians of the Soul* by Robert May © 1988 Robert May used by permission of and published by Amity House, Inc., 16 High Street, Warwick, NY 10990.

Excerpt from *If Only My Family Understood Me* by Don Wegscheider © 1979 Don Wegscheider used with permission from CompCare Publications.

The lyric from "It's My Turn" © 1980 used with permission from Unichappell Music, Inc. All rights reserved.

The cartoon of "Maxine" © 1989 Marian Henley used with permission from Marian Henley.

Excerpt from *Wellsprings* by Anthony de Mello © 1984 Anthony de Mello, S.J., reprinted by permission of Doubleday, a division of Bantam Doubleday Dell Publishing Group, Inc.

Excerpt from *Focusing* by Eugene Gendlin © 1981 Eugene Gendlin used by permission of Eugene Gendlin. Reprinted from *Focusing*, Bantam Books, 1981.

Excerpts from *Healing from Within* by Dennis Jaffe © 1986 Dennis Jaffe reprinted by permission of Alfred A. Knopf, Inc.

Permission for the revision of the "Prayer for Healing Life's Hurts" by the Linn Brothers granted by Matthew Linn, S.J.

Excerpt from *The Ethiopian Tattoo Shop* by Edward Hays © 1986 Edward Hays reprinted by permission of Forest of Peace Books, Route One, Box 427, Easton, KS 66020.

Excerpt from *Craving for Ecstasy* by Harvey Milkman and Stanley Sunderwirth © 1987 D.C. Heath and Company reprinted by permission of the publisher, Lexington Books, D.C. Heath and Company, Lexington, MA.